Britain and Commonwealth Africa

To the memory of my father
Alimamy Momoh Bangura

Yusuf Bangura

Britain and Commonwealth Africa

The politics of economic relations 1951—75

Manchester University Press

Published by
Manchester University Press
Oxford Road, Manchester, M13 9PL
51 Washington Street, Dover, N.H. 03820

British Library cataloguing in publication data

Bangura, Yusuf
    Britain and Commonwealth Africa.
    1. Economic assistance, British — Africa
    2. Africa — Foreign economic relations — Great Britain.
    I. Title
    361.6'09171'24   HC515

Library of Congress cataloging in publication data

Bangura, Yusuf, 1950–
    Britain and Commonwealth Africa; the politics of economic relations,
1951–75.
    Revision of thesis (Ph. D.) — University of London.
    Bibliography: p.
    Includes index.
    1. Great Britain — Foreign economic relations — Africa, Sub-Saharan.
2. Africa, Sub-Saharan — Foregin economic relations — Great Britain.
3. Africa, Sub-Saharan — Dependency on Great Britain — History. 4.
Decolonization — Africa, Sub-Saharan — History. 5. Sterling area —
History. I. Title.
HF1534.5.A4B36   1983   337.41067   82-62265

ISBN 0-7190-0854-9

Printed in Great Britain by
Butler & Tanner Ltd, Frome and London

Contents

Tables

Figures

Abbreviations

ACP	African, Caribbean and Pacific
BACS	British Aided Conditions of Service Scheme
BESS	British Expatriates Supplementation Scheme
BLS	Botswana, Lesotho, Swaziland
CAL	Commonwealth Assistance Loans
CBI	Confederation of British Industry
CDC	Colonial Development Corporation; later Commonwealth Development Corporation
CD and WA	Colonial Development and Welfare Act
CFTC	Commonwealth Fund for Technical Co-operation
Cmnd	Command Paper
COI	Central Office of Information
CPC	Conservative Political Centre
CPP	Convention People's Party
EAC	East AFrican Community
EACB	East African Currency Board
ECA	Economic Commission for Africa
ECGD	Export Credits Guarantee Department
EEC	European Economic Community
EFTA	European Free Trade Area
GTA	General Technical Assistance
H.C.	House of Commons
H/R	House of Representatives
IBRD	International Bank for Reconstruction and Development
IMF	International Monetary Fund
MOD	Ministry for Overseas Development
NIEO	New International Economic Order
OAU	Organisation of African Unity
OECD	Organisation for Economic Co-operation and Development
OSAS	Overseas Service Aid Scheme
SCAAP	Special Commonwealth African Assistance Plan
TANU	Tanzania African National Union
UGCC	United Gold Coast Convention
UNCTAD	United Nations Conference on Trade and Development
WACB	West African Currency Board

Preface

This study is an attempt to explore the relationship between a former colonial power and its dependencies by concentrating on four major economic variables: trade, investment, aid and monetary relations. As my research advanced, it became obvious to me that no serious understanding of centre—periphery relations, particularly Anglo-African relations in the post-war period, is possible without a firm grasp of the monetary relationship, as the monetary variable exercises an all-pervading influence over the other three. Susan Strange's *Sterling and British Policy*, Richard Gardner's *Sterling—Dollar Diplomacy* and the vast literature on the international monetary system and on sterling as an international currency helped to shape my ideas in the early period of my research. The book is not an account, however, of international monetary negotiations but a study of the changed place of sterling as an international currency, with particular reference to Commonwealth Africa.

During the period of decolonisation Anglo-African economic relations were conducted within the Commonwealth—sterling area system, whose primary object was to protect the international role of the pound sterling. Although the British government accepted the principle of decolonisation, it insisted also on Africa's continued participation in the sterling area. The implicit contradiction between the politics of decolonisation and the economics of the sterling area was partially concealed by the absence of revolutionary politics in Africa, the creation of a nationalist—colonialist alliance, and the injection of British capital into the African colonies.

African independence, from 1957 on, the establishment of sterling convertibility in 1958 and the end of dollar discrimination in 1959 changed the pattern of Anglo-African economic relations and affected the cohesion of the Commonwealth—

sterling area system itself. Starting with Ghana's independence, Commonwealth African States projected an independent image and introduced measures which clashed with the sterling area's goals: they diversified their trade, aid and investment links, ran down their sterling reserves and introduced the issue of development as the central consideration in their foreign economic policies. Development was also adopted as the central preoccupation of the Commonwealth when the Secretariat was established in 1965, a process which was extended with the formation of the Commonwealth Fund for Technical Co-operation in 1971.

Special thanks are due to my graduate supervisor at the London School of Economics, James Mayall, for his kindness, inspiration and advice in presenting an earlier version of this work for the PhD to the University of London. His interest in Africa and in the politics of international economic relations helped to provide valuable insights. I am also grateful to Dennis Austin of the University of Manchester for his comments on the politics of decolonisation.

My one-year teaching appointment (1979–80) with the Department of Political Science, Dalhousie University, helped in revising the earlier version and testing some of my new ideas in the seminars at the Center for African Studies. I am grateful to the graduate students and professors at the Center for their comments on the political economy of decolonisation. Needless to say, I alone am responsible for the ideas presented herein.

I was able to make extensive use of the library facilities of the following institutions and would like to extend my thanks and gratitude to their various staff: the British Library of Economic and Political Science, the library of the School of Oriental and African Studies, the Press Library of the Royal Institute of International Affairs and the library of the Royal Commonwealth Society.

I should acknowledge too the assistance offered to me by the staff of the Commonwealth Fund for Technical Co-operation. I am indebted to them for discussions on the development programme of the Secretariat and for providing me with useful statistics on the activities of the CFTC.

Finally, I would like to thank Virginia E. Innis of T & T Services, Halifax, and Doris Boyle of the Center for Foreign Policy Studies, Dalhousie University, for turning my manuscript into a finished product quickly and efficiently.

This study was made possible by a Sierra Leone government scholarship award.

Introduction

This book is a political study of the economic relations between Britain and Commonwealth Africa from 1951 to 1975. Two broad themes form the background: in the early period, the politics of decolonisation were deliberately orchestrated to fit into the Commonwealth—sterling area system, whose major objective was to defend sterling's international status. The second theme is the mirror image of the first: with the granting of independence and the establishment of sterling convertibility, Anglo-Commonwealth African economic relations loosened, thus gradually undermining the cohesion of the Commonwealth—sterling area system itself.

The book concentrates on the interplay between politics and economics. It considers, for instance, how political questions such as the transfer of power affected (or were affected by) the policy of dollar discrimination, monetary co-operation and aid and investment policies; and on the other side, how African policies of nationalism, independence and separate development clashed with the need to promote rapid economic development in the context of scarce capital resources and dependence on the Western economic system.

Most of what is now called Commonwealth Africa came under British rule in the nineteenth century,[1] a period that witnessed the reckless dismemberment and partitioning of Africa by the major European powers and the accelerated co-option of that continent into the world capitalist system. Both processes of political and economic conquest ran parallel in the politics of colonisation; indeed, colonial conquest enabled the European powers to impose a specific economic order upon their respective territories. This economic order was the colonial system of production and exchange which led to the peripheralisation of Africa in the international economy.

Africa's systems of administration and government were irreparably destroyed and its political leaders ruthlessly coerced into accepting alien European rule; its political economies lost their self-reliant character and became instead appendages of the European capitalist economies. Colonialism indeed stultified the progressive development of Africa's social and economic systems. This is not altogether surprising, because Africa's point of entry into the Western economy was the export-producing areas which provided no backward or forward linkages within the domestic economy; instead there were strong links between the export-producing enclaves and the overseas markets.

Britain dominated this crucial period in Africa's history as the world's leading trading nation, the greatest capital-exporting country and banker to the international economy, with sterling as the recognised currency of international payments.[2] This pre-eminence enabled her to pursue an 'open door' colonial economic policy. She supported free trade and allowed the colonies to trade with other imperial powers and to receive private capital investment from them.[3] She also allowed open monetary relations to prevail in the colonies, and for the whole of the nineteenth century and the first decade of the twentieth most African colonies used non-British currencies in their transactions. Indeed, during the nineteenth century, although Britain's political authority had been firmly established in her African colonies, systematic control of their main external economic variables remained incomplete.

The twentieth century saw an erosion of this open-door policy as the international financial and trading system came under sustained pressure from economic forms of nationalism and as the United States emerged as the undisputed leader of the Western economic system. The first world war largely destroyed the nineteenth-century economic order of open multilateral trade, with stable currencies based on the gold standard. Europe's productive power was depleted, and persistent inflation resulted in heavy debts to America, a slump in foreign investment and tremendous difficulties in payments transfer. The European colonial powers found it necessary to retreat into their empires by forming trade and currency blocs. Gradually, but emphatically, Britain started to regulate and strengthen her relations with colonial Africa in a defensive move aimed at checking the American onslaught and helping the domestic economy to recover from persistent economic problems.

Firstly, in 1912 the British government appointed a committee

which examined the practicability of regulating colonial monetary relations in Africa.[4] This committee devised the exchange
standard which gave sterling, through the Bank of England, an
undisputed predominance over colonial monetary relations.
During the period of dollar discrimination this colonial sterling
exchange standard effectively acted as an insurance protecting
sterling against the reserve mobilisation demands of the African
nationalists.

Secondly, a system of formal control was introduced over
trade and aid relations. During the late 1920s the world economic
crisis deepened as economic activity across national frontiers
came almost to a halt. The major industrial countries put up
barriers to trade and payments arrangements; the prices of raw
materials collapsed, and in most colonies the agricultural and
mining industries suspended production. Britain was forced to
take defensive measures. The first came with the institutional-
isation of an aid programme in 1929.[5] Previously Britain had
expected the colonies to raise most of the resources necessary
for their administration and development through domestic
taxation. Except for occasional grants-in-aid for emergencies,
real and sustained development was possible only through the
Colonial Stocks Acts, the first of which was passed in 1877.
These Acts enabled the colonies to raise capital on the London
market on a trustee basis. However, in 1929 Britain extended
her responsibilities in the colonies by creating the Colonial
Development Fund, with the dual objective of assisting colonial
development and helping to regenerate British industry.

This aid programme was followed three years later, in 1932,
by the historic economic conference of Commonwealth
countries in Ottawa which led to the establishment of imperial
preference.[6] It marked a great turning point in Anglo-imperial
relations by emphasising the importance of the empire in trade
relations and by demonstrating that in moments of international
economic crisis Britain would — and, as important, was in a
position to — turn to its vast empire.

Thirdly, during the second world war Britain established control over colonial production and exports through the bulk purchase system,[7] as part of the Anglo-American condominium for
chanelling Allied resources to the war effort.[8] Control was also
exercised over the payments system when in 1940 the sterling
area was legally created, making payments to non-sterling
countries require exchange control permission.[9] By legally cir-
cumscribing the sterling area in this way Britain's investment

policy was also *formally* biased towards the Commonwealth—
sterling area for the first time.

By 1945, therefore, the pattern of Anglo-African economic
relations had already been established: monetary relations had
been standardised by the colonial sterling exchange standard
and reinforced by the creation of the sterling area itself. Trade
preferences had been established in 1932, and trade relations
generally had been controlled by the system of bulk purchase
during the war. Aid had been established in 1929 and investment policy had been oriented towards the Commonwealth—
sterling system.

However, two circumstances — Britain's post-war problems
of economic and monetary reconstruction and African demands
for independence — were first to complicate and eventually to
undermine this pattern. Although the extent of the damage
took some time to reveal itself, Britain emerged from the war
enfeebled both politically and economically. In the face of a
persistent and chronic weakness in the balance of payments and
a real threat from the dollar as the new 'top currency',[10] the
government had little choice but to continue the wartime system
of trade and payments control, and in particular to institute a
wide-ranging system of discrimination against dollar products.
But Britain was in fact doubly constrained, for besides her
economic difficulties she also had to face the demands of
African nationalists for independence, demands moreover which
were supported by a United States opposed to her defensive
imperial policies and by the Soviet Union, which had a long-
standing ideological mission to aid national liberation struggles.

One major problem in any study of this nature is to determine
what analytical framework to adopt in explaining the complex
economic diplomacy, the conflict of interests between the
colonial power and its colonies, the strategies used by both
parties in pursuing their divergent interests, and the changing
structural relationships from colonialism to independence.

Three models of economic decolonisation can be identified in
most colonial relationships, each resting on different historical
boundaries and analytical methods. The first is what can be
called *domestic economic decolonisation*. It corresponds to the
rate of progress in self-government; economic power is devolved
in porportion to the amount of political power transferred,
which is often expressed in terms of the different stages of constitutional development. Nationalists are given broad powers to
manage some aspects of the domestic economy — to determine

fiscal policies, prepare development plans and implement policies aimed at persuading foreign entrepreneurs to train and employ indigenous people in business and industry. Domestic economic decolonisation is often set against a specific external context, determined by the colonial authority. Decolonisation is encouraged only in so far as it does not affect the external economic balance. In other words, the colony is not free to determine its external economic relations. It may, however, enjoy a measure of 'freedom' when the colonial power is of first-rank status, has no adjustment problems and has considerable advantages over its trading competitors. Such a colonial power may pursue an 'open door' strategy by espousing free trade and liberal monetary and investment policies.[11] Correspondingly, its colonies may be allowed to establish economic contacts with other countries. It is important to recognise that this 'freedom' does not mean complete economic sovereignty, as the colonial power may introduce restrictions if faced with persistent economic problems.

The historical boundaries of this model correspond with the boundaries of political decolonisation. It rejects the problems usually associated with the colonial system of production and exchange by maintaining that colonialism has nothing to do with the relative underdevelopment of the colonies.[12] What is important (so the argument goes) is that the colony should achieve autonomy in running its own domestic economy and, at independence, all external controls will disappear as the new State will be free to determine the kind of external economic policy that will be appropriate to its mode of development.

The second type of economic decolonisation, often espoused by the dependency school, is what can be referred to as *global economic decolonisation*. This model plays down the significance of the first type (though in fact it incorporates it) by maintaining that the 'gains' made in domestic decolonisation make sense only when seen from the perspective of the wider structure of economic relations between the metropolitcan country and the colonies. This model often takes a multilateral approach and concentrates less on the bilateral relationship between one colonial power and its colonies and more on the capitalist mode of production, the structures and processes of the international economy, the unequal system of exchange and the general dependence of the developing countries on the industrialised ones. Economic decolonisation is the extent to which the poor countries have succeeded in eliminating this dependence.[13] Because of the practical difficulties in achieving such an objective, the model tends to rest on long-term goals with infinite historical boundaries.

The third falls midway between the first two and may be styled *regional economic decolonisation.* It deals with the attempts of nationalists to break free of the external regional economic system constructed by the colonial powers to prevent a radical deterioration of their universal economic power. This type of colonialism is usually associated with colonial authorities facing adjustment problems in the international economy. The creation of the franc zone by France and of the Commonwealth–sterling area by Britain are classic examples. Regional economic decolonisation posed awkward problems for the evolving new States: apart from assuming domestic economic power, nationalists discovered that they also had to reduce or eliminate the influence of the external regional systems if economic independence was to be meaningful. This form of decolonialisation often spans both the decolonisation and the independence periods. Unlike the second model, however, it could be achieved without a fundamental restructuring of the world economy.

Undoubtedly the most comprehensive of the three models is the dependency model. Concentrating on the mode of production and the development of social classes between and within States affords a deeper perspective on the imperialist or asymmetrical economic relations between rich and poor countries. The dependency model also exposes the limitations on the elites of poor countries as they attempt to grapple with the problems of underdevelopment; it further challenges the persistent claims of those elites that their foreign and domestic policies represent the interests of (and benefit) the mass of their people. Indeed, the sterile debate about the creation of a new international economic order in which the elites of the poor countries have failed to persuade the metropolitan governments to change the rules of power politics or the rates of exchange between commodities, coupled with their stubborn refusal to introduce the necessary social and economic changes in their own societies, clearly underlines the fragile position of Third World elites. But despite its comprehensiveness and ability to explain many of the problems of north–south relations, the dependency model suffers from certain basic defects. The most serious (especially for its variant, underdevelopment theory) is the tendency for analysts to assume that development is impossible without complete disengagement from the present international economic system[14] and to dismiss as meaningless any changes which do not lead to a fundamental restructuring of that system. This tends to give the model a static outlook; for we are still left with the problem of how to explain some of the important changes that have actually taken place in the relations between rich and poor countries.

Another serious omission in dependency literature (though it is not a fault of the model) is the part played by monetary factors in consolidating dependency and imperialism.[15] There has been too much emphasis on trade, investment, military and cultural factors. What is often overlooked is that most of these indicators of dependence are underpinned by the monetary situation. Indeed no serious study of Britain's, or any other traditional imperial power's relations, with its ex-colonies will be complete without a discussion of monetary relationships. Any close study of the relationship between an imperialist State and its investors in this epoch of recurrent monetary crises will readily demonstrate the level of co-operation and conflict between State authorities (who have to defend the rate of accumulation by providing a healthy monetary order) and the investors, who are mainly motivated by profit. Rather than collapsing State interests with those of the individual investors, as some mechanistic dependency writers have done, this study will bring out much more clearly the organic relationship between the State and the various dominant interests it serves in maintaining a capitalist world economy. Not surprisingly, British policy-makers were often at loggerheads with British investors during sterling's problems as the government tried either to impose restrictions on the outward flow of British capital or attempted to channel it to areas which were supportive of British policy — the sterling area.

This study will focus mainly on the third area of decolonisation: the decolonisation of the sterling area system as it affected the African countries. I attempt to unravel, on an empirical basis and using some of the analytical insights of the dependency model, the complex relationships between the actors paying close attention to their policies and modes of interaction. The key actors in this study are the British governments and the African nationalists in the decolonisation era and the British governments and the African governments after independence; others involved are third-party States, British companies, parastatal organisations and international or regional institutions.

One dominant theme which runs through the study is the problem of sterling, and British policy in defending its international roles. Perhaps a brief theoretical explanation of the roles of international currencies would be useful at this point. International money, like domestic money, performs three different functions — as a medium of exchange, as a unit of account and as a store of value. These three functions operate at two different levels, international private transactions and official transactions. International currencies perform three different roles at each of these two levels: transaction, quotation and asset roles at the private level; and intervention, unit of account and reserve roles at the official level.

Intervention currencies are those used by central banks to defend the exchange value of their currencies; under the Bretton Woods system of fixed rates the value of currencies would fluctuate within a band of ± 1 per cent, later revised to ± 2¼ per cent in the Smithsonian agreements of 1971.[16] Private entrepreneurs do not intervene in the foreign exchange market to protect currencies; they use international currencies mainly to pay for goods and services, hence the distinction between intervention and transaction currencies. Reserve, as distinct from intervention, currencies are used mainly to correct balance of payments deficits or protracted deficiencies in the currency value and to pay off debts. They are to be distinguished from asset currencies, although both perform store-of-value roles: asset currencies operate at the private level. Currencies are also necessary to measure, value or price goods and services but a distinction should also be drawn between unit of account currencies at the official level and quotation currencies at the private level.[17]

Not all currencies qualify as international, and certainly not all international currencies perform all six roles at both the private and the official level. Before the war the only fully developed international currency was sterling. After it the dollar alone could lay claim to global status. Sterling and the French franc were fully developed currencies in the sterling area and franc zone respectively. Some European currencies, the Swiss franc and the German mark, were of minor importance at the private international level.

In her preceptive study of the politics of international currencies Susan Strange attempted to break new ground by distinguishing four different types of international currencies:[18] master currencies, top currencies, passive or neutral currencies, and political or negotiated currencies. Instead of the functional classification used by economists, she offered a political framework which combined economic motives with the power status and objectives of the States whose currencies have been used for international payments. Master currency status is based largely on political power and control, whereas the other three types are purely economic. A top currency is usually that of the leading economic power in the international system. Passive or neutral currencies are those of States that perform minor but useful services to businessmen at the private level. A negotiated currency is that of a former master-currency State in decline which has to offer inducements to other States to keep the currency operating as an international one.

The most important contribution of Strange's study is the political dimension she offers to explain the complex relationships between currencies and State policies. However, her master and top currencies still have to satisfy the six functional conditions of a complete international currency, although the distinction she draws between master and top currencies is helpful and important because of the different experiences of sterling and the dollar as international currencies; the latter had no large political empire comparable to that of Britain. Negotiated currencies are currencies in decline and do not satisfy all the six functional rules of an international currency.

British policy-makers were mainly concerned about sterling's official roles (intervention, unit of account and reserve) and generally believed that an alteration in any one of them was bound to affect the others. So far as relations with Africa were concerned, sterling was a complete master currency. The colonies used it for unit of account, reserve, transaction, store of value and quotation purposes. Because of Africa's colonial status and the mechanical operation of the currency boards, which required 110 per cent sterling backing, the intervention role of sterling became redundant. It became important only in the post-independence period with the proliferation of central banks. It was British policy to preserve the five roles of sterling in Africa and to persuade the African nationalists to help in defending sterling's roles at the global level.

The most important parties to these arrangements were the sterling area and Commonwealth countries. Not all Commonwealth countries were part of the sterling area (e.g. Canada) and not all sterling area countries were members of the Commonwealth (Portugal, Sweden, Denmark, Norway, Egypt, Iraq, Iran and Thailand). Throughout I have perforce used the rather clumsy term 'Commonwealth–sterling area' to refer mainly to those countries which were an integral part of the arrangements: the Commonwealth minus Canada, except where the latter was part of the policy process, as sterling area goals were often shaped and discussed in Commonwealth meetings. The Commonwealth itself evolved out of the British empire, with the Indian subcontinent setting the pace, for the African colonies, as independent members between 1947 and 1948.

Sterling convertibility was established in 1958 and dollar discrimination ended in 1959. Coming immediately after the independence of the first African country, these two policies changed the pattern both of the Commonwealth–sterling system and of Anglo-African economic relations. Slowly but surely, Commonwealth African countries gained confidence and started to project an independent image. In pursuit of development they all adopted policies of economic nationalism and diversification. Indeed, the issue of development came to dominate their economic policies towards Britain, and with the co-operation of Asian and Caribbean States they succeeded in converting the Commonwealth into an organisation preoccupied with economic development.

This, then, in summary outline is what this study will be concerned with. The twelve Commonwealth African countries it deals with are Ghana, Nigeria, Sierra Leone, Gambia, Tanzania, Uganda, Kenya, Malawi, Zambia, Botswana, Lesotho and Swaziland. Rhodesia and South Africa are referred to only when any of the Commonwealth African countries' relations with Britain are affected by their relations with Rhodesia or South Africa. For instance, Botswana, Lesotho and Swaziland (BLS) are part of the Southern African Customs Union and the rand currency area.[19] Discussion of Britain's relations with the BLS countries deals, therefore, with their relations with South Africa. And since Malawi and Zambia were members of the Federation of Rhodesia and Nyasaland between 1953 and 1963, the Federation is referred to in the sections which deal with monetary and trade relations in that period.

In the analysis of the earlier period of decolonisation which deals mainly with monetary, aid and investment relations, special attention has been given to Ghana and Nigeria. Apart from the fact that they set the pace of decolonisation, these two countries were also the most important African members of the sterling area. Both provide useful insights into the nature of conflict and co-operation between Britain and colonial Africa in the sterling area.

After decolonisation clear differences emerged in the economic policies of the Commonwealth African countries, and while the special cases of Ghana and Nigeria still provide a general model, attention has been paid to the differences in approach between the different countries. The aim throughout has been to offer a country-by-country and region-by-region analysis as appropriate.

Notes

1 Tanzania came under British rule as a mandated territory after the first world war.
2 Alan Day, *The Future of Sterling*, 1956.
3 Because of this open-door policy Germany, France and the United States were able to make inroads into Britain's commanding trading position in Africa during the second half of the nineteenth century. See, for instance, C. W. Newbury, 'Trade and Authority in West Africa, 1850–1880', in L. H. Gann and P. Duignan (eds.), *Colonialism in Africa, 1870–1960*, Vol. 1.
4 Cmnd 6426 (1912).
5 The Colonial Development Act, H. C. Bill 9, 1929.
6 The Ottawa Agreements Act, 1932 (Bill 127, 1932), Cmnd 4174.
7 'Some notes on Bulk Purchase of Colonial Commodities', Memo No. 3 (Colonial Office), 12 March 1948.
8 K. Hancock and M. M. Gowing, *Britain's War Economy*, 1959.
9 The Defence (Finance) (Definition of Sterling Area) (No. 5) Order, October 1941, 28 November 1941, No. 1890. The origins of the sterling area could be traced back to 1925, when Britain left the gold standard and several countries decided to peg their currencies to sterling.
10 Susan Strange, *Sterling and British Policy*, 1971.
11 British policy in the nineteenth and early twentieth centuries.
12 The Conservative Party in Britain held this view. See, for instance, G.P.C. No. 141, March 1955, p. 5, and David Goldsworthy, *Colonial Issues in British Politics, 1945–1961*, 1971. Even the Fabian Labour Party Colonial Secretary, Arthur Creech Jones, argued along similar lines. (*New Fabian Essays*, 1959, p. 23.)
13 J. Galtung, 'A Structural Theory of Imperialism', *Journal of Peace Research*, Vol. 8, 1971; Colin Leys, *Underdevelopment in Kenya*, 1975; A. G. Frank, *Latin America: Underdevelopment or Revolution*, 1969; Paul Baran, *The Political Economy of Growth*, 1957; S. Amin, *Accumulation on a World Scale*, Vol. 1, 1974.
14 C. Leys, *Underdevelopment in Kenya, op. cit.*, pp. 18–20.

15   Some studies have now started to appear on this theme. See F. Dixon Fyle, 'Monetary Dependence in Africa: the case of Sierra Leone', *Journal of Modern African Studies*, Vol. 16, No. 2, 1978.

16   Under the present floating rates, fluctuations are within wider bands.

17   See B. Cohen, *The Future of Sterling as an International Currency*, 1971; chapters 1 and 2; and W. M. Scammell, *International Monetary Policy*, 1975.

18   Susan Strange, 'The Politics of International Currencies', *World Politics*, Vol. XXIII, No. 2, January 1971, and *Sterling and British Policy*, 1971, chapter 1.

19   Botswana withdrew from the rand currency area in 1974.

Part one

Decolonisation

1

Post-war economic problems

In the immediate aftermath of the second world war, Anglo-African economic relations were conducted in a specific context. On the one hand, Britain's monetary problems and West European reconstruction in a dollar-dominated world gave monetary affairs an unprecedented significance in Britain's foreign economic policy. On the other, the rapidly unfolding force of African nationalism and the quest for immediate self-government led to an emphasis on development as Britain insisted that political advancement should be matched in the social and economic spheres. The acceptance of decolonisation as a necessary phase in the transfer of power enabled her policy-makers to link social and economic development in the colonies to the wider monetary and political objectives of post-war reconstruction.

Britain accepted American guarantees in the Western security system and American financial aid to assist West European recovery, but the policy-makers still regarded Britain, with her Commonwealth and empire connections, as a power of the first rank.[1] They refused to yield to American pressures to join the European integration movement.[2] At the economic level, the superstructural trappings of world power status — a highly developed, open economy and an international currency — proved difficult to abandon or reappraise.[3] The British wanted to maintain an open economy, with the pound sterling as an international currency, in the face of persistent balance of payments problems, growing American dollar power and an uncertain political atmosphere in which the foundations of British power — the empire — were in the process of disintegration, under the sustained attack of the two super-powers and the force of nationalism within the colonies themselves.

From the Anglo-African perspective, one of the most difficult problems was how to decolonise the African territories which were an integral part of the British policy of maintaining sterling's international role and a stable balance of payments. Britain attempted to resolve the conflict by committing herself to the principle of self-government while stressing the prior need for a reasonable measure of social and economic development, and for the decolonisation process itself to be pursued within the Commonwealth—sterling area.

This chapter traces the development of British attitudes towards Africa in the post-war period and the response of the leading African nationalists, the development of the nationalist—colonialist alliances in Africa to implement the dual policies of economic development and monetary co-operation, and the structure and evolution of the Commonwealth—sterling system.

Britain's post-war attitudes towards Africa

Colonisation and centuries of European technological, military and political dominance created a syndrome of European racial superiority as those concerned with formulating State policies, including the intelligentsia, businessmen and explorers, arrogantly asserted the superiority of European values and justified European expansionism in terms of a civilising mission. This belief in European dominance was not completely abandoned even after the ascendancy of revolutionary politics, although it was to be re-examined and recast in the light of post-war realities. British attitudes to the African colonies after the war were greatly influenced by this backlog of European self-assertiveness, which over the years became translated into competing traditions of thought between and within the various political parties.

The Conservative Party has been traditionally associated with the empire; indeed, the party itself believed it was the quintessence of the empire and always felt a profound sense of involvement with imperial problems. To most Conservatives colonialism mirrored the high-water mark of British supremacy; it was something to be proud of in the best traditions of Disraeli and Chamberlain. It was the Conservatives who developed the racial typology in the empire which placed Africa in the 'Third Estate' of least developed territories, with India occupying the middle position, and the dominions the top category. According to this typology, the African colonies needed the help and guidance of the developed members of the family to fulfil themselves within the framework of the empire.[4] The party held to this paternalistic attitude for most part of the decolonisation period.[5]

Although Labour never subscribed to the Conservative Party's sentimental attachment to the empire, the implicit assumption of British leadership permeated the various factions within the movement. The belief was held that Africa could not develop separately from and independently of Europe without European assistance and co-operation. Attitudes differed, however, as to the right type of policy to be adopted: whether there should be immediate independence as demanded by the revolutionary Marxists, or whether the empire should be transformed into a Socialist Commonwealth as advocated by the left wing of the Labour Party, or whether, as the Fabians stressed, independence should follow a transitional period.

Marxist views on colonialism could be traced back to Marx's essays on British rule in India, in which he accorded colonialism a historic role in the development of universal capitalism: 'England has to fulfil a double mission in India: one destructive, the other regenerative — the annihilation of old Asiatic society, and the laying of the material foundations of Western society in Asia.'[6] This view is in accord with the progressive character of capitalism in developing the productive forces of the world economy, albeit in an uneven manner. About three decades later, in 1882, Frederick Engels restated the Marxist position on the colonies by maintaining that, with the inevitable outbreak of socialist revolutions in Europe, the colonial people 'must be taken over for the time being by the proletariat and led as rapidly as possible towards independence'.[7] This condescending role given to the European proletariat in the liberation of the colonies should not be altogether surprising, because the Marxist theory of historical materialism accords substantial weight to the forces of production and the class struggle. The European proletariat was assumed to be objective, non-racial and cosmopolitan. Indeed, because Africa belonged to the pre-capitalist stage of development, it was assumed that the European proletariat, being the most advanced and revolutionary class, should take the lead in African decolonisation.

In their analytical approach to the colonies Marxists stressed the dominance of class interests and the exploitation of the colonies as a source of raw materials for industries and an outlet for profits. Towards the end of the nineteenth century and in the early twentieth they began to take a much keener look at the structure of imperialism, which led them to formulate the most sophisticated and radical programme against imperialism. The authoritative exposition of the theory was provided by Lenin, who described imperialism as the highest stage of capitalism — the stage of monopoly capitalism.[8] He believed that the weakest link in capitalist development was to be found in the colonies, as colonial profits temporarily postponed the outbreak of revolution in Europe; European rivalry for colonies to maintain the rate of profit and the resultant partitioning of the world would lead inevitably to world war; he believed that this would intensify the revolutionary process in both the capitalist countries and the colonial territories. Marxists had a duty, therefore, to 'free the enslaved nations and establish relations with them on the basis of a free union'.[9]

The Marxists in the British Labour movement, who were very thin on the ground, embraced these ideas after the second world war and demanded the immediate recognition of the right of self-determination for the colonies and a policy of financial collaboration with them at independence.[10] The Marxist contention that the underdevelopment of the colonies was a direct result of imperialism profoundly influenced the left wing of the Labour Party. During the early stages of decolonisation Labour left-wingers articulated these views in such organisations as the Centre against Imperialism and the Congress of Peoples against Imperialism. For instance, the Congress's charter rejected the traditional theories about the cultural and political unfitness of the colonies for immediate independence and emphasised the alliance between the native bourgeoisies and the imperialist class, which it saw as a 'joint exploitation of the colonial peoples' and the 'dominance of finance capital' in the colonies. It demanded that Britain should 'appoint a time limit after which British rule will cease'.[11]

Labour left-wingers differed from the Marxists in their attachment to the Commonwealth idea; they demanded that the empire should be transformed into a Socialist Commonwealh. One of the leading advocates of this view, Harold Laski, tried unsuccessfully to make it party policy when he was chairman of the 1946 and 1947 party conferences.[12] It was the Fabians, however, with their numerical strength, who exercised the strongest influence over Labour party and government policy. While rejecting colonialism, they did not believe in immediate independence, but argued that, without a transitional period to bring about the necessary socio-economic development and the 'appropriate' political framework, African independence would be fraught with political instability.[13] The Fabians were at one with the Conservatives in advocating a continued British presence in the colonies and in seeing colonialism not in terms of the class analysis of exploitation but in terms of the underdevelopment of the territories themselves. This approach was staunchly defended by Labour's post-war Colonial Secretary, Arthur Creech Jones:

Much of what is wrong in underdeveloped societies comes because of the poverty of nature and the backwardness of people who have been insulated for centuries and tied by tradition and tribalism and oppressed by ignorance and superstition. It is not due to rapacious capitalism or modern exploiting 'colonialism', tragic and appalling as have been many instances of cruelty and exploitation and interventions from outside. Colonial problems are more fundamental than the regulation of alien exploitation.[14]

It was the conviction that immediate independence would not cure the problems of underdevelopment, and the condescending belief that the imperial power had a duty to provide the conditions for 'responsible' self-government, that shaped British policy in the post-war period. This policy had earlier been embodied in the Labour Party's celebrated document on colonial policy in 1943, which called for continued British presence in Africa through a system of trusteeship.[15] Labour did not find it difficult, therefore, to support Oliver Stanley's policy statement on the colonies in the Conservative-led coalition, in August 1943, in which he pledged 'to guide the colonial peoples along the road to self-government within the framework of the British empire.'[16]

When Labour came into office in 1945 it was concerned primarily with the domestic problem of economic reconstruction and the building of 'socialism' for the British people. Its policy towards Africa — in contradistinction to Asia — was still coloured by the racial typology of the Conservative Party and the Colonial Office.[17] The development of the Welfare State in Britain, the promotion of full employment and the reconstruction of the war-ravaged economy depended, however, upon external foundations, the balance of payments and the complex economic relations with the empire. Labour's specialists on colonial and international affairs, Arthur Creech Jones, Ernest Bevin and Clement Attlee, stressed the dangers of implementing radical policies in the colonies, rejected a complete break with colonialism and insisted on a gradualist-reformist approach.

The scene was set at the pre-election party conference in 1945 when Attlee and Bevin hinted that the pace of decolonisation would be slow and that foreign policy would have to reflect Britain's position as an imperial power. Attlee maintained that although Labour would support 'a steady increase in self-government in the colonial territories' decolonisation must be determined by economic progress.[18] And Bevin underlined the geo-political necessity of maintaining strong links with the empire and Commonwealth.[19] The government's policy on decolonisation was stated, in July 1946, in terms of guiding the colonies towards independence.[20] Particular stress was laid on the need to develop social services, health, eduction, transport and communication and to improve agricultural development. Many research bodies for welfare and economic development were created as part of the enlarged colonial development and welfare schemes, which the government believed would provide the necessary socio-economic development for ultimate self-government.

What would have been a simple process of decolonisation was complicated, however, by a more serious problem of more universal character: the problem of financial instability which manifested itself in acute balance of payments deficits, a general collapse of the West European economies and a steep decline in Britain's position as a world power. In its attempt to solve these problems the government came close to denying an independent role for the colonies by attempting to create a third centre of power in the international system.

British policy was specifically aimed at using the full resources of the empire to support this third centre of power.[21] The desire became more compelling as differences with America over the vital issues of trade and monetary arrangements sharpened.[22] With American insistence on immediate multilateralism in trade and the full convertibility of all trading currencies, Britain was increasingly forced to look to the Commonwealth and the colonies for allies. Ernest Bevin was emphatic — 'the United Kingdom must keep in step with the Commonwealth' — and he regarded the decision to hold two meetings a year of Commonwealth Ministers as a step in the right direction.[23]

He pursued this line of thought with Hugh Dalton at a Foreign Office meeting on 15 October 1948, when he spoke of the 'middle planet' and the grand design of marshalling Africa's potential resources in sustaining the third force of Europe, Britain and the empire:

To organise the middle of the planet — Western Europe, the mediterranean, the Middle East, the Commonwealth ... If we pushed on and developed Africa, we could have the United States dependent on us, and eating out of our hand in four or five years. Two great mountains of manganese ore in Sierra Leone etc. U.S. is very barren of essential minerals, and in Africa we have them all.[24]

British policy-makers were greatly worried about the fate of the pound and the payments situation not only of the sterling area but of Western Europe as a whole. In Bevin's view, only a concerted programme linking the colonies with the production plans of Europe would enable Western Europe to withstand the might of the two super-powers in general, and the economic challenge of America in particular. There was an implicit conflict, however, between this universal monetary policy and the policy of creating the socio-economic conditions in the colonies necessary for self-government. Should Britain put the brakes on decolonisation and concentrate on the production drive to save sterling and cure the payments problems of Western Europe? Or should the promise of self-government be honoured by channelling British resources to the social and economic development of the colonies?

Creech Jones believed that it would be difficult to keep a fair and just balance between the conflicting claims of both Britain and the colonies over the limited resources of the empire.[25] The conflict was partially resolved, at least from the British perspective, by the decision to link the policy of socio-economic development for self-government with that of developing Africa's vital resources to assist European recovery, and by emphasising the principle of interdependence and complementarity. Bevin was very clear on this:

The overseas territories are large primary producers, and their standard of life is evolving and is capable of great development. They have raw materials, food and resources which can be turned to very great common advantage, both to the people of the territories themselves, to Europe and to the world as a whole. The other great powers, the United States and Soviet Russia have tremendous resources. There is no need of conflict with them in this matter at all. If Western Europe is to achieve its balance of payments and to get a world equilibrium, it is essential that these resources should be developed and made available, and the exchange between them carried out in a correct and proper manner. There is no conflict between the social and economic development of their people and their development as a source of supplies for Western Europe, as a contributor, as I have said, so vital to the balance of payments.[26]

krumah, like the moderate nationalists, was forced to adopt a
estern liberal approach which saw the political process as
ndamentally different from the economic process. As the
litical struggles intensified in the Gold Coast, Nkrumah was
ced to revise his revolutionary strategy. With the decision to
d elections in 1951, on the recommendations of the Coussey
mmittee for a mainly African executive responsible to an
cted legislature, he entered the contest and, in winning,
ched from a strategy of positive action to one of tactical
on. Largely because of this compromise by the radicals,
r differences with the moderates petered out. All African
onalists were prepared to co-operate with Britain in estab-
ng nationalist-colonialist governments as a transitional move
rds full African political independence.

nationalist—colonialist alliance

use of the separation of politics from economics in Africa's
nse to the colonial problem, the politics of decolonisation
ed a purely nationalist and reformist-oriented guise.
n was able to maintain control over the colonies' external
mic relations. Although somehow committed to the
le of self-government, it insisted that decolonisation
take place within the Commonwealth—sterling system.
policy-makers racognised the problems that a hasty de-
sation would create for the sterling area, which was
ingly dependent upon the colonies for its success. Britain
oured therefore to direct the nationalist movements
onstitutional lines by co-opting the leading figures into
hal programme of responsibility sharing, and thus per-
the nationalists to accept orthodox financial and
ic policies.
roblem of the transfer of power had been with the
Office since the outbreak of the second world war.
st Indian crisis, Lord Haley's *African Survey* (which
the deficiencies of British rule) and the appointment
Donald to the office of Colonial Secretary in 1938
a fitting background and the requisite guidelines for
raisal of colonial policy.[40] But throughout the war
ial Office was still confident that it could control the
ecolonisation, no doubt because the nationalist input
insignificant. The focus then was on reform of the
l system of indirect rule, which would prevent the

Throughout the decolonisation period these two attitidues
dominated British policy towards Africa. The universal monetary objective dictated that the political-economic system of the
colonies should be linked to the British programme of West
European reconstruction, but the success of this policy within
the constraints of the politics of decolonisation also demanded
a firmer commitment to support economic development and
political advancement in Africa. Against this background there
was no question of surrendering British power to the African
nationalists without the necessary arrangements for continued
monetary and economic co-operation. Bipartisanship became
the official policy of both parties and continued stress was placed
on the need to guide the colonies towards self-government
within the Commonwealth. It was assumed that an understanding could be reached with moderate nationalists in pursuing
these objectives.

African nationalist attitudes on international economic relations

In turning to the attitudes of the African nationalists, several
questions arise. How did they react to Britain's policy of guided
decolonisation? What was the level of African political consciousness in their quest for self-government, and what type of
economic system did they want to substitute for colonialism?

Unlike Britain, which had a clearly defined policy on decolonisation, the nationalists developed no solid alternative
strategy, either with reference to Britain's objectives or with
regard to the type of economic relations they wanted to establish
with her at independence.

To most of them the overriding concern was how to achieve
political power. In so far as any attention was paid to the
structure of their economic relationship with Britain, they
believed it could be turned to Africa's advantage after political
power had passed into African hands. Kwame Nkrumah coined
the catch phrase which successive nationalists were later to
repeat: 'Seek ye first the political kingdom ... and all that you
want will be added on to it.' This is not altogether surprising,
since the ideological Cold War between capitalism and com-
munism had less impact in Africa than in Asia. In Africa the
struggle against colonialism took on a purely nationalist form
without the ideological commitment to destroy both capitalism
and colonialism. Although some nationalists often referred to

the twin problems of both systems, they generally preferred to express their disapproval of Britain's imperial economic policies in a piecemeal and reformist-oriented fashion. African attitudes were therefore, in the main, reactive and dependent; reacting, that is, to Britain's policies within the imperial—sterling area framework.

To be sure, African nationalists were 'anti-imperialist' and outspoken in their denunciation of colonialism. For example, the veteran African nationalist Nnamdi Azikiwe, in his address to the second annual conference of the Congress of Peoples against Imperialism and War, in 1949, maintained that 'factors of capitalism and imperialism have stultified the normal growth in Nigeria in the community of nations'.[27] However, there was hardly any co-ordinated or systematic policy regarding the type of Anglo-African economic relationship that would succeed colonialism. On this question the spectrum of attitudes ranged from the moderates who were prepared to collaborate with Britain in building a new relationship leading to independence, to the radicals who rejected colonialism in all its form and showed an initial reluctance to accept the policy of guided decolonisation.[28] Chief among the former were Azikiwe, Awolowo and Danquah. Awolowo, more than any other, developed the British policy of 'trusteeship' for the African colonies as a means of gradual development towards political independence. In line with British policy, he assumed a kind of trusteeship status for Britain, which would enable Africa to acquire the necessary training in administration and provide the social and economic development for the long-term ideal of economic and political self-government.[29]

All moderate African nationalists accepted the need for a transitional period leading to independence and, with the formation of the alliance governments in the 1950s, radical nationalists were forced also to adapt their policies to the trusteeship framework. There was the lingering problem, however, of how such a system of trusteeship would promote African interests in view of the conflict between colonialism and sustained indigenous development. Recognising this,[30] Azikiwe advocated the idealist aspirations of a Socialist Commonwealth; he hoped that it would transform the old-type colonial economic relationship to one which would enable Africa to 'evolve into a fully democratic and Socialist Commonwealth in order to own and control the essential means of production and distribution ...'[31]

As we have seen, this concept was embraced wing of the Labour Party, which was unable to influence on the government's colonial policy Jones even stated that it was not the duty of th ment to impose socialism on the colonies.[32] nationalists were forced, therefore, to acce trusteeship or British presence in the form o Africa's development. Given this situation, alists tried to force the British hand in spee economic development for ultimate self-gove centrated on domestic issues, such as educ administrative facilities, with a fair mea development in agriculture and industry; t rapid Africanisation.[33]

The radical nationalists, headed by Nkr tematic theory of imperialism which empha relationship between Britain and Africa only this approach could provide the righ colonialism and the policy of trusteeshi isation. Most of Nkrumah's views during were expressed in his book *Towards Colo* a sharp critique of British colonialism, 'the inherent contradictions between th countries ... and the nationalist aspir people'.[35]

Relying on these contradictions, N decolonisation and demanded compl Convention People's Party developed Action', aimed achieving power ou trusteeship and partnership.[37] Nkru controlling the exports of the coloni sterling balances should be handed earned them. He maintained that th to protect trade and profits, since facture their own goods, and he cer welfare programmes which, he sai effective aid.[38]

Although his ideas touched o post-war monetary policy, greater theory of imperialism as a quest f manufactured goods and fields f capital.[39] In resolving the prac political independence and eco

N
W
fu
po
fo
ho
Co
ele
swi
acti
the
nati
lishi
tow

The

Beca
respo
assum
Britai
econo
princi
should
The
coloni
increas
endeav
along
a diarc
suaded
econom
The
Colonia
The We
exposed
of Macl
provided
the reap
the Colo
pace of
was still
traditiona

educated nationalists from any effective participation in the mainstream of decolonisation, by making the native administration system the linchpin of the decolonisation process.

The Atlantic Charter, and the debate which it generated in Westminster, clearly exposed the inconsistencies in British colonial policy. The government categorically ruled out immediate self-government and slammed the door on the educated nationalists who were demanding independence along the lines of the Atlantic Charter.[41] However, on 3 May 1943 the government came up with a policy which emphasised a pragmatic approach to decolonisation. Independence was to be considered for large territories; there should be no time table for independence; social and economic development should precede self-government.

During the same period, summer 1943, the Colonial Office had prepared a key memorandum on 'Constitutional development in West Africa' which tried to marry native administration with modern representative government in five separate stages, but which saw self-government as occurring in 'a good many generations'.[42] This memorandum was followed by the Colonial Secretary's statement on colonial policy in the House of Commons, in August, when Oliver Stanley pledged to 'guide the colonial peoples along the road to self-government within the framework of the British empire'.

With pressures mainly from the governors of the Gold Coast and Nigeria, the Colonial Office reluctantly accepted the decision to include Africans in the executive council in September 1942. This decision did not, however, transform the power of the executive council; it certainly did not lead to immediate control by the nationalists.[43] Another major development occurred during 1946–1947: the theory of indirect rule and the system of native administration were rejected in favour of more modern forms of representative government. This change of policy marked a new development in the politics of decolonisation in which the educated nationalists came to occupy the central stage.

On 29 July 1947 Creech Jones announced that Britain would hold a conference in London of the governors of the African territories, and another conference of the members of the legislative councils, to discuss economic, administrative, social and political questions.[44] The governors' conference took place in November 1947 and the legislators' from 29 September to 8 October 1948.[45]

The principal topic at the governors' conference was the devolution of financial and political authority to the African colonies against the background of Britain's monetary problems. The Chancellor of the Exchequer spelled out the significance of the sterling area's objectives in dollar earning and saving, Britain's payments difficulties and the need to cultivate colonial interest in the sterling area programme by pursuing social and economic development.[46]

The problem of devolving financial authority, and defining the roles and boundaries of the new institutions within Britain's wider financial framework, was also resolved.[47] There was no doubt about the need to allow some financial authority to the colonies as part of the decolonisation process, but it was equally apparent that Britain would maintain overall control in the co-ordinated plan for monetary and economic stability.[48]

At the conference of legislators the African delegates discussed with British Ministers and officials of the Colonial Office a wide range of problems. The Africans voiced wholehearted support for the British policy of constitutional and local government development as steps towards independence within the Commonwealth. The two conferences were symbolic of the constitutional changes that were taking place in Africa against the backdrop of the post-war difficulties of economic reconstruction.

Between 1947 and 1951 colonial Africa was set on a course of constitutional developments. These developments represented limited advances towards self-government in a participatory frame of reference rather than a root-and-branch rejection of colonialism. The great turning point was the Watson Report on the riots in Accra and Kumasi in January and February 1948.[49] The report made startling recommendations for a measure of self-government, after a thorough analysis of the causes of African discontent.[50] Its recommendation for substantial African representation in the executive administration prompted the British government to appoint an all-African committee under Justice Coussey to advise on a new constitution. The committee's proposals for an African executive responsible to an elected legislature were partially accepted, and a new constitution, based on power-sharing, came into effect in 1951.

The landmark in West African constitutional development was indeed 1951, when real participation in decision-making started in Ghana, with the introduction of a parliamentary and Cabinet system of government. The control exercised by the governor and expatriates in the executive was transferred to an African majority. The executive council which had hitherto been a mainly advisory body to the governor became the principal instrument of policy. On 26 February 1951 Nkrumah was made leader of government business. In an executive council of eleven the nationalists had a majority of eight. But the strategic portfolios of finance, defence and justice were reserved for the colonial wing of the alliance; the veto and reserve powers of the governor were also retained.

Similar developments took place in Nigeria in 1951 with the introduction of the Macpherson constitution, which created representative assemblies in the three main regions and a central legislature to which the assemblies sent delegates; this constitution established an African-dominated ministerial system. The ministerial system was established in Sierra Leone in 1953 and in the Gambia in 1960.

Decolonisation was much slower in East and Central Africa because of the racial problem and the need to protect European interests in any future African-dominated political system. In Kenya the situation was complicated by the Mau Mau, which led to the banning of political parties. Whilst the ban lasted the British government was unable to establish a working relationship with the most effective nationalists. Several steps were taken in the 1950s to speed up African representation in both the legislative and the executive councils, but throughout this period the powerful hand of the European settlers prevented any meaningful changes from being introduced. In 1954 the British government established a Council of Ministers of six official members of the legislative council and six unofficial members (three European, two Asian and one African), with two extra Ministers nominated by the governor; in 1957 it held elections to the legislative council in which Africans voted for the first time. In 1958 it increased the number of African members of the council. These developments still fell far short of African demands and could not be compared to what the West Africans had achieved in 1951. It was not until the London conference of 1962 that the system of African responsible government was firmly established in Kenya.

The delay in establishing an African ministerial system in Uganda had more to do with domestic ethnic conflicts than with the presence of Europeans, although as in Kenya the government spent much time and thought trying to protect European and Asian interests in the pre-independence constitutions. The major problem in Uganda was the powerful position of the Kabaka and the demand of the Baganda for a confederate system which would guarantee their supremacy. An African-dominated ministerial system was not established until after the elections of March 1961 which gave the Africans a majority in both the legislative and executive councils.

Tanganyika did not have the intense raciàl problems of Kenya, or the acute ethnic problems of Uganda, but the ministerial system was delayed by the slow development of nationalist parties. A partial ministerial system was established in March 1955, but it did not give the Africans a majority in the executive; the council, in any case, was still a purely advisory body whose advice the governor could ignore. It was not until after the 1961 election, which gave the Tanganyikan African National Union an overwhelming majority, that the full ministerial system was introduced.

Decolonisation followed a slightly different pattern in Central Africa. There, both Northern Rhodesia and Nyasaland were forced to federate with European-dominated Southern Rhodesia as the European settlers sought to extend their control over all of Central Africa. The development of the copper industry in Northern Rhodesia and the advent to power in South Africa of the Afrikaner-dominated South African Nationalist Party, which was less enthusiastic about maintaining strong links with Britain, persuaded the settlers in Central Africa that federation was the only alternative to Afrikaner domination in the south and African control of the copper mines of Northern Rhodesia.[51] Despite African protests, the Conservative government agreed to join the three territories in August 1953. However, the African nationalists in Northern Rhodesia and Nyasaland continued to challenge the federation and eventually forced a reversal of British policy.[52] The Federation finally collapsed in 1963, paving the way to independence for Northern Rhodesia and Nyasaland as Zambia and Malawi.

Although the politics of decolonisation varied from region to region and according to category, the same principle of collaboration underlay British policy. The primary objective was to prevent or contain the development of revolutionary politics which would challenge the programme of 'consensual decolonisation'; the attempt everywhere was to create what can only be described as a nationalist—colonialist alliance. This diarchy was much more clearly defined in West Africa, where nationalists first began to agitate seriously for self-government and independence.

It was the nationalist—colonialist alliance governments that were entrusted with the power to implement the two main post-war policies: the sterling area policy of dollar earning and saving, under which the pace of monetary decolonisation had to be controlled in the interests of strict financial discipline, and the African-oriented policy of accelerated economic development and Africanisation. Often the nationalist—colonialist alliances found it difficult to implement both policies at the same time, given the demands of the nationalists for a greater stress on African interests, and the conditions imposed by Whitehall.[53]

In drawing up plans for general economic development the alliance governments 'had to work within the limits of the responsibilities conferred upon' them. The nationalists accepted the broad principles of the sterling area and the colonial economy. One of the most important instruments of economic change was the budget, usually drawn up with an eye on the sterling area payments situation. The nationalists were forced to accept orthodox budgetary policies.

When Sir Arden Clark, Governor General of the Gold Coast, made his first major speech to the new assembly on 29 March 1951 he stressed that the new government had decided to 'use the budget prepared before they took office as a working basis'.[54] This was confirmed by Nkrumah when he said that the budget had been prepared nine months before he joined the government, and although they disagreed with some aspects of it the nationalists would take it as a working basis 'because if we want to go out and start turning things down there is going to be a lot of trouble ...'.[55] This was also the situation in Nigeria when, in 1952, the nationalists were allowed to participate in the government. The nationalist Ministers 'after earnest consideration decided that the wisest and practical course was to accept the proposals of the former government as a working basis'.[56]

Despite provisions for slight modifications and amendments, the pattern of post-1951 African decolonisation budgets did not depart much from the form and substance of previous years. The central tenets were fiscal discipline and moderate economic development; great stress was laid on growth and export promotion,[57] and the virtues of a budgetary surplus to keep a tight hold on the economy. The alliance governments were faced, however, with the pressing problem of stimulating social and economic development, which demanded a greater injection of money into the economy through public expenditure and higher wages and salaries. It soon became clear that strict ad-herence to a policy of budgetary surplus would hamper develop-ment programmes if alternative methods of long-term finance were not introduced. Hence the establishment of Development Funds in the colonies, with the aim of pooling resources without radically altering the internal balance.[58]

These cautious budgetary policies supplemented the monetary and commercial policies of financial restraint at the international level. The wider aspect of this international economic diplomacy was conducted in the Commonwealth—sterling area system itself.

The sterling area—Commonwealth economic system

In turning to the Commonwealth system, two major points should be stressed. Firstly, the sterling area policy was bequethed to the African nationalists when the alliance governments were formed. Secondly, the nationalists could not influence the decisions of the system, as only independent members were allowed full participation in its policy-deliberating conferences. The Commonwealth's decisions were applied equally, however, to independent Commonwealth countries and the colonies.

Although not all Commonwealth countries were members of the sterling area,[59] the Commonwealth system of the 1940s and 1950s was concerned mainly with the pursuit of sterling area goals, which were to promote stronger and more amicable re-lations between Britain and the rest of the Commonwealth. Emphasis was placed on functional co-operation rather than the creation of an autarkic system. Britain, the centre of the system, was committed to the principle of multilateralism, but recog-nised the short-term necessity of developing the special relation-ship with the Commonwealth.

Commonwealth—sterling area members had a common com-mercial policy in discriminating against dollar products and in defending the system of imperial preference established in Ottawa in 1932. They collaborated closely in monetary affairs by pooling dollars, gold and other foreign exchange reserves. Those who had an export surplus with the dollar area sold the dollars in London for sterling and left the sterling balances there, and restrictions were placed on members' use of the dollars; this was limited to essential needs. For the independent members the restrictions were made through 'informal gentlemen's agreements'.[60] All Commonwealth—sterling area members except South Africa were full participants in the dollar pooling scheme. South Africa, a major gold producer, kept its own gold and dealt direct with non-sterling area countries demanding dollars. Agreements were drawn up between Britain and several members of the sterling area unlikely to honour the 'gentlemen's agreements'. Iraq and Egypt were regulated in their dollar drawings from January 1945. The financial arrangements on blocked balances limited Indian and Pakistani drawings between 1 January 1948 and 30 June 1949. And an agreement was signed with South Africa under which she reimbursed Britain in gold for all non-sterling area currencies purchased by her in Britain.[61]

For most members of the Commonwealth—sterling area, drawings from the dollar pool were left to informal consultation and agreement. For instance, members agreed at the Commonwealth Finance Ministers' Conference of 1949 to reduce dollar expenditure by 25 per cent in the financial year 1949—50. In the case of the colonies the question of 'gentlemen's agreements' did not arise, as Britain drew very little distinction between the metropole and the colonies in financial matters. Thus the 25 per cent cut in dollar expenditure was made known to them by limitations on the system of import licences on dollar imports. Even the alliance governments found it difficult to depart from this policy. When the Commonwealth Economic Conference of 1952 decided on a 15 per cent reduction in dollar imports, despite nationalist protests, they had very little option but to implement it.[62]

Members accepted the pound sterling as the ultimate means of payment in their transactions with each other and third countries; they pegged their currencies to sterling and used sterling for intervention purposes, that is, to maintain the IMF-declared par values of their individual currencies. They maintained free convertibility with the pound and relatively free movement of capital among themselves. Members pursued domestic economic policies which did not affect the payments situation of the sterling area. There was also an unwritten, though explicit, understanding that Britain was the main source of development capital and private investment, and had an obligation to provide such capital.

For colonial Africa, using a colonial sterling exchange standard, which provided extra security for sterling's position in Africa, there were three other rules of co-operation: the automatic exchange of local currencies with the pound sterling on demand; the full backing of the local currencies with the pound; and the compulsory investment of sterling funds in Britain.

For the entire period 1945–58 the Commonwealth economic system addressed itself mainly to the monetary problem. The Commonwealth was clearly evolving as an extension of Britain's economic diplomacy as she came to rely on the collective strength of the Commonwealth to defend sterling's position. There was more concern in Britain to strengthen sterling area unity because of her unique position as banker to the sterling area and centre of the Commonwealth. Pressures in her domestic economy were often related to the misfortunes of the pound and the balance of payments. In December 1951, for instance, the Conservative government's policy of gradual convertibility of sterling, with the reopening of the international market for foreign exchange dealings, coincided with the stormy period of balance of payments deficits after the slight improvement in 1950. This led to calls for a greater intensification of Commonwealth co-operation and sterling area co-ordination. It manifested itself in two important debates in Parliament in February and November 1952 and in the convening of the special Commonwealth Economic Conference in December the same year.

On 22 February 1952 a private member's motion in the Commons called for urgent and closer sterling area co-operation and for resistance to any attempts to weaken imperial preferences and Commonwealth ties.[63] The significance of this debate was the platform it created for a bipartisan approach to Commonwealth economic policy. There was general consensus on the need to defend sterling's international status and to develop the Commonwealth as a centre of world finance, which would include Western Europe.[64] Most MPs advocated the strengthening of imperial preferences, discrimination against dollar goods, more regular meetings of Finance Ministers, and the abrogation of GATT, which, they maintained, hindered stronger commercial co-operation among Commonwealth countries. Some also called for the elevation of Commonwealth relations to the level of a customs union, and for Commonwealth representation on the staff of the Bank of England; failing that, the creation of a separate sterling area central bank.[65] Similar arguments were deployed in the second debate, on 27 November 1952, in which MPs called for the consolidation of Commonwealth and colonial bonds.[66]

The idea of a Commonwealth federation involving one customs union, one currency and one external balance of payments did not appeal to the British government, under Churchill, which preferred co-operation through the Commonwealth's functional institutions.[67] However, continued pressure for closer co-ordination in Commonwealth and sterling area relations led to the first post-war Commonwealth economic conference on 11 December 1952. By this time alliance governments had been formed in Ghana and Nigeria. The question of colonial representation was therefore raised in Britain because of their contribution to the dollar pool.[68] Although the British government invited them, the traditional policy of awarding full participation to independent members only was emphasised.[69] The African delegates tried to defend their interests by demanding a reform of the dollar discrimination policy.[70] The nationalists' political status did not allow them, however, to influence the general course of the conference or its results.

The conference was important in Anglo-African relations as it underlined Britain's general external economic policy in the 1950s. The overriding factor was the monetary balance. Emphasis was laid on internal economic policies designed to curb inflation. It was agreed that inflation frustrated sound development by increasing costs and destroying the savings necessary to finance it. More significantly, inflation could damage the external balance by stimulating excessive imports and by diverting exportable commodities to domestic use.[71] Thus 'an adequate and stable balance must be a first objective for all governments. Failure to achieve this means repeated crisis ...'[72]

On trade relations, there was still the need to discriminate against dollar products, and on Britain's initiative a discussion took place on the need for all Commonwealth countries to join in seeking release from the 'no new preference' rule under GATT. Although some supported the proposal, the majority of Commonwealth countries opposed it on the grounds that it would hamper the return to full multilateralism in trade. All agreed to co-operate with Britain, however, in approaching the other GATT members to meet the difficulties arising on the UK tariff. The primary objective was to enable Britain to continue the duty-free entry of Commonwealth goods.

Commonwealth members agreed to work together in achieving certain broad objectives. There was no intention of seeking to create a permanent discriminatory economic bloc; rather the objective was to strengthen themselves for future multilateralism. Britain's development policy was also spelled out. The United Kingdom was regarded and accepted as 'the traditional source of external capital for Commonwealth investment and has special responsibilities in the colonial territories'. Britain promised that 'the flow of capital from London for sound development throughout the Commonwealth shall be maintained and increased'.[73] This Commonwealth-oriented policy depended, however, on the domestic economy and the balance of payments situation.[74] Aid and investment relations were to be determined by the monetary objective, and Britain was to guard against any policy which threatened the external payments position.[75]

Notes

1   F. S. Northedge, 'Britain's Place in the Changing World', in M. Leifer (ed.), *Constraints and Adjustments in British Foreign Policy*, 1972, p. 193.
2   R. B. Manderson-Jones, *The Special Relationship: Anglo-American Relations and Western European Unity, 1947–1956*, 1972.
3   Susan Strange, *Sterling and British Policy*, 1971.
4   David Goldsworthy, *Colonial Issues in British Politics, 1945–1961*, 1971, p. 166.
5   C.P.C. No. 141, Conservative Political Centre, March 1955.
6   Shelmo Avineri, *Karl Marx on Colonialism and Modernisation*, 1969, pp. 132–3.
7   In D. Boersner, *The Bolsheviks and the National and Colonial Questions*, Geneva, 1957, p. 25.
8   V. I. Lenin, *Imperialism; the Highest Stage of Capitalism* (Peking), 1970.
9   *Id., On the National and Colonial Questions* (Peking), 1970, p. 2.
10 *Commonwealth Information Bulletin* No. 5 (September 1944), pp. 18–19, 'The Policies of the Left'.
11 *Charter of the Congress of Peoples against Imperialism* (mimeographed), 1948, p. 1.
12 *Report of the 46th Annual Conference of the Labour Party*, 1947, pp. 110–11.
13 See, for instance, Arthur Creech Jones (ed.), *New Fabian Colonial Essays*, 1959.
14 *Ibid.*, p. 23.
15 *The Colonies: the Labour Party's Post-war Policy*, 1943, p. 2.
16 H.C. Debates, 13 August 1943, Vol. 391, col. 48.
17 G. A. Gupta, *Imperialism and the British Labour Movement, 1914–1964*, 1975, p. 275.
18 *44th Annual Conference of the Labour Party*, 1945, p. 109.
19 *Ibid.*, p. 109.
20 H.C. Debates, 9 July 1946, Vol. 425, col. 238–9.

21 R. B. Manderson-Jones, *op. cit.*, chapter 1.
22 Richard Gardner, *Sterling–Dollar Diplomacy, op. cit.*, Parts I and III.
23 *The Diaries of Hugh Dalton* (London School of Economics), 17 October 1948.
24 *Ibid.*, 15 October 1948.
25 A. C. Jones, *The Labour Party and Colonial Policy, op. cit.*, p. 25.
26 H.C. Debates, 22 January 1948, col. 388–9.
27 Nnamdi Azikiwe, *Selected Speeches*, 1961, p. 159.
28 The Youth Movement in Ghana and the CPP and the Nigerian Youth Movement in the 1940s and 1950s.
29 Obafemi Awolowo, *Path to Nigerian Freedom*, 1947, p. 37.
30 Zik, *Selected Speeches, op. cit.*, p. 159. For Nigeria read Africa.
31 *Ibid.*, p. 159.
32 A. C. Jones, *The Future of the African Colonies, op. cit.*, p. 21.
33 Zik, *Selected Speeches, op. cit.*, pp. 212–13.
34 Kwame Nkrumah, *Towards Colonial Freedom*, 1962.
35 *Ibid.*, pp. xiii–xiv.
36 *Ibid.*, p. xvi.
37 Denis Austin, *Politics in Ghana, 1946–1960*, 1964, provides a good background to Nkrumah's political strategy.
38 Kwame Nkrumah, *Towards Colonial Freedom, op. cit.*, pp. 15, 16 and 19.
39 *Ibid.*, chapter 2.
40 Curtis Nordman, 'Prelude to Decolonisation in West Africa: the Development of British Colonial Policy, 1938–1947' (Oxford University, unpublished D.Phil. thesis), 1979.
41 *Ibid.*, chapter 2.
42 *Ibid.*, p. 93.
43 *Ibid.*, p. 143.
44 H.C. Debates, 29 July 1947, Vol. 441, No. 152, col. 270.
45 *Ibid.*
46 Full speech in Rita Hinden's *Common Sense and Colonial Development*, 1947, p. 10.
47 *Financial Devolution the Gold Coast* (Accra), 1948, No. IV.
48 *Ibid.*, p. 7.
49 *Report of the Commission of Enquiry into Disturbances in the Gold Coast*, 1948, Colonial No. 231.
50 *Ibid.*, p. 8.
51 Andrew Roberts, *A History of Zambia*, 1976, pp. 206–8.
52 *Ibid.*, p. 208.
53 Kwame Nkrumah described this conflict within the Ghana government vividly in his *Autobiography, op. cit.*, p. 122.
54 G/C Debates, 29 March 1951, p. 8.
55 G/C Debates, 30 March 1951, p. 173.
56 Nigeria H/R Debates, 11 March 1952, p. 8.
57 G/C Debates, 29 March 1951, 11 March 1952, p. 9.

58 G/C Debates, 30 March 1951, p. 43; also Nigeria H/R Debates, 12 March 1952.
59 Canada, though an important member of the Commonwealth, belonged to the dollar area.
60 Philip W. Bell, *The Sterling Area in the Post-war Period, 1946—1952*, 1956, p. 54.
61 *Ibid.*, pp. 59—60.
62 See chapter two.
63 H.C. Debates, 22 February 1952, Vol. 496, col. 657.
64 H.C. Debates, 22 February 1952, Vol. 496, col. 644.
65 *Ibid.*
66 H.C. Debates, 27 November 1952, col. 952.
67 H.C. Debates, 8 July 1952, col. 1092.
68 H.C. Debates, 7 November 1952, col. 532.
69 H.C. Debates, 7 November 1952, col. 532.
70 Nigeria H/R Debates, 31 March 1955, pp. 982—3.
71 Commonwealth Economic Conference, Final Communiqué (London, 1952), para. 5.
72 *Ibid.*, para. 6.
73 *Ibid.*, para. 11.
74 *Ibid.*, para. 11.
75 *Ibid.*, para. 12. Special concessions were made to the colonies, as development plans were being implemented in their territories which would provide the infrastructure for further economic development. (*Ibid.*, para. 9.)

2

The politics of monetary relations, 1945—57

As we have seen, the monetary problem exercised an all-pervading influence over Britain's economic relations with colonial Africa. After 1945 trade became functionally related to the payments situation and formed the central pillar of British economic policy towards Africa. Under this framework, aid and investment were used to facilitate the decolonisation process and to enable the colonies to participate in the sterling area programme. With the formation of the alliance governments Britain was able to get the co-operation of the leading nationalists in implementing its monetary programme. There was resistance, however, from some nationalists who insisted that decolonisation should include moves towards nationalist control of economic policy: there were pressures for a more liberal trade policy, to link the colonial sterling reserves to economic development, and to dismantle the colonial monetary system.

This chapter concentrates on monetary relations. The first two sections trace the history of colonial monetary relations and sterling's post-war problems; the latter two examine the conflict and co-operation between Britain and colonial Africa in the sterling area.

Anglo-African monetary relations

Successive British governments never seriously questioned sterling's role as an international currency.[1] Its success depended, however, on co-operation between Britain and the empire within the sterling area. Britain's monetary relations with Africa were facilitated by the colonial sterling exchange standard, whose origins had nothing to do with the sterling area. The colonial exchange standard was first established in West Africa in 1912. Although active British colonialism started in

Africa in the nineteenth century, controlled monetary relations lagged far behind administrative developments. It was not until 1825 that Britain started to develop an interest in the monetary affairs of the colonies.[2] Before 1825 she had been content to allow them to use the currencies of their preference.[3]

The development of British maritime, commercial, financial and political power on a world scale saw the emergence of the pound as an international currency,[4] and the increasing involvement of Britain in the trade, administration and finance of the colonies necessitated a more orderly and controlled relationship between the pound and their currencies.

It was the report of the departmental committee appointed to enquire into matters affecting the currencies of British West Africa that fully established the colonial sterling exchange standard.[5] The report stressed that sterling backing for the local African currencies was necessary 'if at any time the silver currency in West Africa should prove to be temporarily redundant, and if in consequence a considerable portion of it should be sent back to the United Kingdom'.[6] It was the report also that led in 1912 to the establishment of the West African Currency Board to issue and redeem currency in the West African colonies. This scheme was duplicated in East Africa in 1919 and in Central Africa in 1938. It was never extended to Botswana, Swaziland and Lesotho, where, in 1933, the South African currency was made legal tender.

The currency board's main function was to issue local currency fully backed by and exchangeable for sterling. Backing for the local currencies was 100 per cent–110 per cent.[7] The expansion of domestic money supply for economic development depended upon the export performance of the colonies, as every local pound had to be fully supported by sterling.[8] Thus a favourable trade balance meant more sterling and more local cash, and an adverse trade balance meant a contraction of local cash as sterling holdings would be withdrawn from London to correct the adverse trade balance. The currency boards had no control over the expatriate banks, they could not pursue monetary policies, and their surplus funds were invested mainly in Britain. They were legally prohibited from investing in the colonies.[9]

The currency boards created an efficient and stable framework for Britain's monetary relations with Africa. It was in fact the pound sterling that was in effective operation, the local currencies merely acting as symbols of sterling. Sterling was a

complete 'master currency'. This colonial monetary system
came to be linked to the wider sterling area arrangements during
the second world war. Closer economic relations between Britain
and the colonies were strengthened by the Anglo-American
condominium for total economic planning in the raw materials
board, the combined food board and the combined production
and resources board.[10] Britain formalised these wartime arrangements through the system of bulk purchase of colonial commodities. In the field of finance, Britain attempted to strengthen
the movement of capital and payments within the empire—
sterling area, and between the area and the rest of the world, by
imposing rigid exchange controls against non-sterling countries
in July 1940.

Worsening commercial and monetary relations with America
prompted Britain to extend these wartime arrangements into
the post-war period. The different attitudes towards Lend—
Lease[11] and its termination in 1945 clearly aggravated the
already unstable British economy and demonstrated its dependence on America. Thus after the war Britain, having lost a
quarter of its pre-war national wealth,[12] with external disinvestment accounting for more than half of this, and with an adverse
balance of payments, needed American co-operation[13] and
Commonwealth support to sustain the pre-war international
position of sterling. Co-operation with America on a multilateral basis was the long-term goal but, as British politicians
saw it during this critical period, the emphasis was on closer
co-operation with the Commonwealth in a limited payments
system. This was stressed by the Chancellor of the Exchequer:

While we are with the help of our friends finding a long-term solution to
our problem which will we hope give stability to world trade, we must
maintain the strength of our own great multilateral area of trade, the
Sterling area.[14]

The dollar problem became the greatest post-war financial
problem as it was realised that Britain's reserves of gold and
dollars had fallen far short of her overall liabilities. From then
on her balance of payments made sense only when seen from
the wider perspective of the sterling area.[15]

For commercial transactions Britain introduced a dual policy
of Open General Licences and Specific General Licences.[16] The
former were applicable mainly to sterling area countries which
enjoyed relatively free trade and capital movements and payments. The latter were for non-sterling, mainly dollar, countries,

which were given only limited access to sterling markets. The Colonial Primary Products Committee was established in May 1947 to review colonial commodity production and to increase the sterling area's foreign exchange earnings.[17] Preference was to be given to the needs of Britain, particularly for commodities in short supply.[18] The committee's report recommended a three-pronged approach to the problem of commercial relations. The colonies were to be encouraged to sell more to the dollar area and buy less from it; Britain was to buy less from the dollar area and buy more from the colonies; and Britain was to sell more of the goods which the colonies would otherwise have bought from America.[19]

The sterling area's trading arrangements departed substantially from the requirements of the post-war US-dominated economic order, the Bretton Woods system. The latter stressed the need for all countries to conduct their international trade in an open and non-discriminatory manner. The two trading systems can be contrasted diagramatically (Fig. 1).

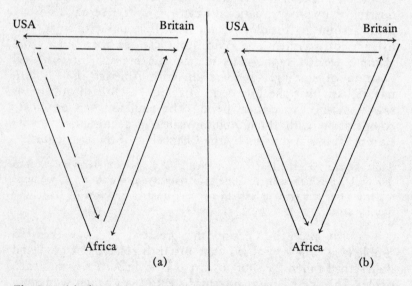

Fig. 2.1   (a) The Commonwealth—sterling area system and (b) the Bretton Woods system. Continuous lines represent free trade, broken ones, controls. Diagram (a) shows the controls imposed by the British government on US exports to Britain and colonial Africa. The only free trade was between Britain and the sterling area. Continuous lines between Britain and the USA and colonial Africa and the USA show US acquiescence in accepting British and colonial African exports.

Grain, food products, tobacco, cotton, wood, iron and steel, non-ferrous metals, machinery, petroleum, chemicals and coal made up more then 90 per cent of Britain's imports from the United States from 1948 to 1957.[20] Colonial Africa was instrumental in reducing her dependence on America for five of these: tobacco, cotton, wood, iron and non-ferrous metals. This was more clearly illustrated in the case of tobacco, which formed the main British import from the US. Because of the production drive in the empire, particularly in Northern and Southern Rhodesia, Britain's dependence on America was drastically reduced. In 1957 the United States supplied hardly more than 50 per cent of total UK imports, as against 70 per cent in 1945.[21] A similar picture emerged in copper imports, which were the chief constituent of the trade in non-ferrous metals. There was a marked reduction in the volume of imports from the US as refinery capacity in the empire expanded. Until after 1952 there were usually some 100–150 million lb per annum, while the annual average for the four years 1953–56 was only 50 million lb.[22]

This system of discrimination was facilitated by the programme of bulk purchase which was introduced during the war. Producer Control Boards were established in the colonies, and most of the boards' products were sold direct to the Ministry of Food. Apart from enabling Britain to get imports at reasonable prices and save precious dollars, bulk purchase created a guaranteed market in Britain for the products of the colonies. The Conservative government of 1951 gradually phased out this system of long-term contracts and reopened the pre-war commodity markets which operated on free-market principles. However, with the establishment of the post-war marketing boards colonial Africa continued to sell most of its products to Britain and reduced her dependence on dollar markets.

The policy of dollar discrimination also aimed at reducing colonial dependence on US exports by improving Britain's export performance in the colonies. The chief products which Africa imported from the US were tobacco and manufactures, iron and steel, machinery and parts, vehicles and parts, petroleum and petroleum products, chemicals and wheat flour.[23] By policies of direct import controls, Britain, acting through the alliance governments, was able to limit the general purchase of some of these products from the US.

Imports of vehicles were the most tightly controlled. In East Africa US sales slumped from $2.4 million to $1.0 million from

1948 to 1957. In Nigeria they fluctuated between $1.0 million and $1.3 million. The situation was similar in the Federation of Rhodesia and Nyasaland, where imports of American vehicles were $1.5 million in 1948 and $1.3 million in 1957. In Ghana purchases of American vehicles were more tightly controlled than in the other colonies, despite local pressure.[24] In 1948 and 1949 $0.8 million worth of vehicles were imported from America; imports declined the following year to $0.4 million and stayed level until 1957, when they fell to $0.2 million.

Britain also controlled imports of American machinery. In Ghana purchases were between $0.7 million and $1.9 million. In Nigeria imports fluctuated between $0.7 million and $4.8 million. In East Africa fluctuations were greater, between $3.9 million and $5.9 million. The same was true of the Federation, with fluctuations ranging between $4.1 million and $10.5 million.[25]

The core of the dollar discrimination policy was the establishment of the dollar pool. The colonies were encouraged to earn hard currency to make up for the large dollar deficit of the sterling area. Britain and the independent members were the heaviest dollar users. Africa supplied about half of some twenty products imported by America: cocoa, coffee, tea, iron ore, non-ferrous metals, diamonds, wood, rubber, hides and skins. In addition Africa exported significant quantities of manganese ore, chrome ore, asbestos, beryllium, columbium, sisal, pyrethrum and whattle extract.

The contribution of colonial Africa towards the dollar pool was remarkable. Of all the Commonwealth and colonial territories only Africa, Malaya and Ceylon showed a positive balance of trade with America for the period between 1948 and 1957. The United Kingdom showed a massive deficit throughout. Ghana, Nigeria and Northern Rhodesia (Zambia) accounted for most of the surplus, in cocoa, copper, manganese ore, wood and natural rubber.

Africa's contribution to the dollar pool was acknowledged by both major political parties in Britain. To the Conservative Party:

great efforts have gone to the stimulation of UK dollar exports, but if the Sterling Area has succeeded in balancing its books it is thanks rather to the primary products of British overseas dependencies — the cocoa of West Africa and the rubber and tin in Malaya. Much will depend on the future relationship with the Sterling Area of Malaya, Nigeria and the Gold Coast ...[26]

Labour also stressed the important contribution of the colonies — 'the palm oil producer of Nigeria', 'the cocoa grower of the Gold Coast' and 'the raw cotton imports from East and West Africa' — as dollar savers and earners.[27] Both these views echoed the tribute by the Secretary of State for the Colonies, James Griffiths, on 12 July 1950 when he acknowledged the colonial contribution to the dollar pool and insisted that British policy should aim at maintaining those benefits.[28]

Monetary decolonisation was very slow, therefore, in the African colonies, as it was conducted within the constraints of the sterling area. This manifested itself in three broad areas: (a) Britain's attempt to persuade the African colonies to hold sterling and invest their sterling balances in Britain; (b) Britain's policy of impressing upon the African nationalists that dollar discrimination was vital not only for the sterling area but for Africa, as their economies were inextricably linked with Britain's and with sterling; (c) Britain's attempt to slow down the re-structuring of the colonial sterling exchange standard whose mechanical operation and close association with sterling led to colonial financial stability and the investment of surplus sterling funds in Britain. These three areas of Anglo-African relations will now be examined.

The policy of sterling investment

One of the conditions for maintaining a successful international currency under a regime of fixed exchange rates was that countries trading with the currency should have confidence in it. For sterling, this meant holding substantial reserves and restrictions on converting them to hard currencies. It was British policy to ensure that maximum sterling reserves were maintained by the Commonwealth—sterling area members. Countries that had an export surplus with non-sterling countries sold their earned foreign currencies in London for sterling. These reserves, and the export earnings of Commonwealth—sterling area members, which were denominated in sterling, were invested in British securities. These export earnings and the investments of the public corporations, expatriate banks and currency boards made up the sterling balances of the African colonies.

By 1955 the colonies had contributed about £1,281 million towards the pool out of a total of £3,000 million for the entire sterling area. In 1952 colonial Africa held £621 million out of £1,222 million[29] for all the colonies, with Ghana and Nigeria accounting for about £400 million. It was characteristic of this period that, whereas the independent Commonwealth countries ran their sterling balances down, the colonies rapidly increased theirs.

Between 1950 and 1955 the sterling balances of Australia, New Zealand and South Africa declined from £640 million to £313 million; those of India, Pakistan and Ceylon from £787 million to £704 million; whereas those of the African colonies rose from £336 million to £720 million.[30] At the end of the war India, Pakistan and Ceylon held more sterling reserves than any other territory: about £1,352 million. The African territories could boast of only £204 million. The problems which might have been created for the sterling area as the independent subcontinent started to mobilise its huge sterling reserves for rapid economic development were greatly mitigated by the massive accumulation of sterling reserves by colonial Africa and the Far East.[31]

Colonial Africa was able to maintain these large sterling reserves because of the heavy earnings of the marketing boards during the Korean war boom, and because of the legal requirement prohibiting the investment of the currency boards' surplus funds in the colonies.

The only way this sterling-oriented policy could have been prevented would have been the granting of monetary autonomy to the African territories through independent central banks which would have centralised all the reserves, or the creation of local money and capital markets in the colonies for the investment of the sterling reserves. But for most of the decolonisation period Bank of England officials opposed the development of autonomous monetary systems for the colonies, defending the traditional qualities of the currency board system and the efficiency of London as a financial market place for colonial investments. These views were articulated in three separate reports on banking decolonisation in the West African colonies.[32]

The Fisher Report on Nigeria stressed the importance of holding 'sterling assets not presently needed in Nigeria'.[33] J. B. Loynes emphasised in his report on central banking in Nigeria the need to maintain large sterling reserves and use the services of the London market 'until money market facilities could be created locally'.[34] He dismissed the idea of concentrating official sterling assets in any future African central banks, still less the sterling assets of the expatriate banks.[35]

There were pressures, however, from sympathetic British

politicians,[36] and African nationalists with large sterling investments, for a review of this policy, which, as they saw it, deprived
the colonies of valuable capital for economic development.
Kwame Nkrumah had advocated handing the sterling balances
over to the farmers who earned them.[37] This demand was included in both the UGCC and CPP manifestoes for the 1951
elections.[38]

Faced with these pressures, the Colonial Secretary, Lennox
Boyd, announced in Parliament on 15 December 1954 that he
was prepared to allow for the local investment of a small part
of the cover for colonial currencies.[39] This moderate revision
was limited, however, to the currency board investments, which
did not include the investments of the marketing boards, the
public corporations or the expatriate banks. Thus, although the
East African colonies welcomed the proposal,[40] and the British
government entered into consultations with them on the
amounts that might be invested in locally issued securities, the
greater part of colonial Africa's investments were still held in
British securities. About two-thirds of these reserves were held
in short and medium-term securities.[41]

Conflict and co-operation in the policy of dollar discrimination

The second policy was that of impressing upon the African
nationalists that discrimination against dollar products was vital
for the survival of the sterling area and the economic development of the colonies. This policy was related to the three-
pronged commercial programme of dollar earning and saving.
Nationalists in the alliance governments did not reject dollar
discrimination entirely. They accepted it as a framework for
continued negotiation and bargaining. There was a groundswell
of opposition, however, from nationalist quarters against the
policy of import controls and dollar rationing.

When the alliance government was established in Ghana in
1951 a small but articulate opposition group was formed,
headed by J. B. Danquah, Kofi Busia and Ofori Atta. Often
they addressed themselves to the dollar discrimination problem.
On one of these occasions Ofori Atta challenged the very
foundations of the colonial economic relationship by emphasising the need to link trade policy with the economic development of the colonies.[42]

In advocating this strategy Busia spelled out the specific
problems created for Ghana by the policy of import controls

and dollar rationing and demanded that the government should release more dollars for the country's development.[43] The Gold Coast was the largest dollar earner among the African colonies and the second largest among all the colonies, after Malaya. In 1951 it earned £30,047,000 from the dollar area; in 1952 £25,539,000, and in 1953 and 1954 £25,407,000 and £20,009,000 respectively. But during those four years it was allowed to spend an average of only 18 per cent of those dollars.[44]

Many nationalists opposed dollar discrimination on the grounds that American co-operation in finance and commerce was indispensable to the colonies' development objectives. J. B. Danquah was convinced that Ghana could not develop 'without American aid and assistance'.[45] He questioned the rationale of too great a financial dependence on Britain.

Between 1951 and 1956 there was periodic debate in Ghana and Nigeria on the question of import controls and the need for some form of relaxation backed by a fairer allocation of dollars to the main producers. The nationalists argued that Britain could not supply all their essential imports, that restrictions affected development adversely, that inflation in the colonies was due to the limitations on imports, and that badly needed foreign investment was being denied to the colonies.[46]

Such criticisms came mainly from members of the opposition parties who were supported by a substantial number of ordinary members of the ruling nationalist parties. In Nigeria Anthony Enahoro actually advocated withdrawal from the sterling area, believing this would be advantageous in terms of capital investment and economic development.[47] In Ghana nationalist opposition was expressed on four different levels. Firstly nationalists tried to persuade the alliance governments to release more dollars and issue more import licences. This was a request for a sort of stand-by reserve fund for the more immediate purpose of importing American cars.[48] Secondly nationalists tried to persuade the government to remove all import restrictions.[49] Thirdly they tried to follow this up by exposing the irrelevance of the programme and its harmful effect on the Gold Coast's economy.[50] The failure of these three attempts led to a fourth approach, viz., to work within the rules of the sterling area by remaining in the dollar pool but using the dollars allocated to the Gold Coast to import freely without restrictions.[51]

The ruling nationalists were in the difficult and embarrassing position of trying to reconcile pressure for trade liberalisation from the opposition parties and their own rank and file with the fact that they were members of governments that had pledged themselves to the sterling area programme. The policy they adopted in the face of this dilemma was to demonstrate the usefulness of belonging to the sterling area to their sceptical followers while simultaneously making representations to Britain, either direct or through Commonwealth conferences, that trade liberalisation would be in the colonies' best interests.[52]

The Ghanaian Minister of Commerce and Industry, K. A. Gbedemah, achieved limited success with this approach in 1953, although he was assisted by a slight improvement in Britain's balance of payments. In response to a British demand in 1952 for a 15 per cent cut in dollar expenditure, he was able to announce a partial relaxation of controls on imports from non-sterling countries after discussions in London in September.[53]

This was also the situation in Nigeria, where the nationalist Minister of Mines and Power expressed the view that much could be done to strengthen the interests of the colonies in negotiations with the British government. He advanced the argument on industrialisation to show that restrictions should not be rigidly applied to Nigeria.[54]

However, throughout the period of dollar discrimination, the ruling nationalists were forced to support the sterling area programme of import controls. Gradual relaxation took place only when there was an improvement in the balance of payments of Britain and the sterling area.[55]

Nationalist demands for central banks

The other major preoccupation was in the area of banking and monetary relations. The replacement of the currency board system with independent central banks could have adverse effects on sterling's international position and role in Africa; it could lead to independent monetary policies, separate national currencies, the centralisation of colonial sterling reserves and the use of the central banks to provide long-term development capital. This, it was believed, would undermine confidence in sterling and affect the sterling reserves of the colonies. Bank of England officials attempted, therefore, to preserve some of the salient structures of the currency board system in their recommendations on colonial monetary reform.

In the changes introduced on 15 December 1954 the Colonial Secretary, Lennox Boyd, was prepared to allow only limited local investment and a small fiduciary issue. He maintained that the currencies of the colonies should still be fully backed and automatically redeemable for sterling.[56]

The timing of this policy was appropriate only for the East African territories. Although it was meant to apply to all colonies, with the formation of the Federation of Rhodesia and Nyasaland a Federal Reserve Bank was established for the three Central African territories in 1956; while in West Africa, particularly in Ghana and Nigeria, the demands of the nationalists for the establishment of central banks were already too strong to be checked by such cosmetic reforms.

It was only in East Africa that the reformist policy was operationalised. There, in 1955, the East African Currency Board (EACB) was able to depart from its traditional role as a purely automatic money changer. The Secretary of State for the Colonies issued specific regulations for this to the EACB in December 1955, allowing the board to hold local securities not exceeding £10 million.[57]

In Ghana and Nigeria the nationalists advocated the setting up of central banks, which, they believed, were necessary for any meaningful development. However, through the influence of three Bank of England officials, Fisher, Trevor and Loynes, the nationalists were persuaded to accept some of the salient structures of the colonial exchange standard in the form of central banks.

The central tenets of the reports of these three officials were to prevent the application of radical policies in the colonies' monetary affairs and to preserve the sterling system in Africa. The three experts were, in principle, opposed to the setting up of central banks because, in their view, the imperial banking and monetary system already offered adequate facilities. When this idea failed to impress the nationalists, the Bank officials came round to accept the idea of central banks with limited functions and powers.

The Trevor[58] and Fisher[59] reports were careful to draw a distinction between development and central bank functions. Both officials and Loynes were convinced that it was not the function of a central bank to promote development. They argued that development could be promoted by domestic taxation[60] and by floating loans on the London market. These views conflicted with those of the nationalists, who believed that development must take precedence over orthodox central bank functions.

J. L. Fisher seized on the problem that if the central banks were used for development purposes they would end up becoming an arm of the government. This he warned, could lead to inflation and could defeat one of the cardinal objectives of the post-war economic system, which was internal financial discipline to prevent the ravages of inflation on sterling reserves:

One of the surest ways to destroy the value of and impair confidence in a currency is the inflation of the money income of a country beyond the resources available and in sight. One of the readiest ways in which inflation is achieved is by undue government spending even if it is for politically desirable development.[61]

Fisher maintained that governments might want to borrow to finance a budget deficit or provide funds for development purposes, and find themselves 'under constant pressure to turn to central banks for funds for long-term purposes ...'.[62] This could lead to inflation, which could impair confidence in the currency in turn affecting the reserves and the external balance.[63]

The strategy of the Bank of England, therefore, was to demonstrate to the nationalists that a central bank was not essential in their present level of development. According to Fisher, 'the financial environment hardly exists at present for a central bank to function in Nigeria other than semi-automatically as a bank of issue'.[64] All three officials maintained that the prerequisites for the successful operation of central banks — securities markets, bill market, a stock market and banking and insurance systems — did not exist in Africa.[65] They were convinced that the link with sterling was sufficient for monetary and economic development. For instance, the Trevor Report stated that 'through sterling the Gold Coast has free access not only to the whole Sterling Area but also to the foreign exchange pool where exchange into other currencies is available'.[66] And when Fisher submitted his report in 1953 he used a large section of it to extol the virtues of sterling and the colonial sterling exchange standard.[67] He stressed the stability afforded to 'merchants, banks and private corporations' who could 'carry on their business and plan their investment in the confident knowledge of the rate of exchange'.[68]

These financial and banking edicts met with strong resistance from the nationalists, particularly on the central question of whether or not to establish central banks. To the nationalists the issue was at bottom a political one. They associated central banks with political maturity and independence. On the other hand, they shared the concern of the Bank officials about establishing sound and stable currencies, which meant closer collaboration with Britain and sterling. The result was that central banks were established which failed to alter the fundamental structures of the colonial sterling exchange standard.

Ghana was the first country to demand the setting up of a central bank. In 1948 J. B. Danquah suggested that there should be a national bank financed by the Cocoa Marketing Board. In the same year an experienced banker was invited to the Gold Coast to report on how banking could be satisfactorily organised. He ruled out the idea of a central bank but recommended a modest beginning in the form of a State-aided commercial bank.

Paton's recommendations did not satisfy the nationalists. In 1949 J. B. Danquah moved in the legislative council that a select committee be appointed to investigate the establishment of a central bank. The motion was carried, and in 1950 the committee started to collect information from other parts of the Commonwealth. It later decided to invite Sir Cecil Trevor to investigate the banking conditions of the Gold Coast and the desirability of establishing a national bank.

By the time Trevor submitted his report in 1952 the alliance government had been formed. Danquah's party was now in opposition, and the ruling nationalists (the CPP) were pledged to work within the Commonwealth—sterling area system. Under these conditions the ruling nationalists scaled down the importance of a central bank immediately.

Trevor recommended that a bank of issue would not be desirable, as the Gold Coast was adequately catered for by the West African Currency Board. He stressed that a central bank should be established only when all the instruments necessary for an advanced economy were available. With the need to maintain the confidence of Whitehall, as defined by the Colonial Finance Minister, Trevor's recommendations became the cornerstone of the new government's policy.[69]

Opposition to the Anglo-Gold Coast banking alliance was conducted mainly from the perspective of the political struggle against colonialism. The most articulate was Danquah, who was quite prepared to see a break with Britain on financial matters. He accused the ruling nationalists of letting the people down 'at the very moment when power is coming into our hands, when we want to seize the throat of imperialism'.[70] He was supported by Ofori Atta, who maintained that 'the cry for a national bank follows the tempo of the cry of national liberation'.[71] At this stage, however, the ruling nationalists were prepared to go along with the Trevor Report and the views of the expatriate Ministers who wanted a bank, short of a central bank.

Ghana achieved internal autonomy in 1954, and between this period and independence in March 1957 the attitudes of the ruling nationalists hardened partly in an effort to take the wind out of the sails of the UGCC, already emerging, in the eyes of the electorate, as the radical party for fundamental monetary reforms. They also realised that progress towards self-government required some elements of financial power. This change was more political, however, than financial, as the nationalists came to see the establishment of a central bank as a mark of independence, even if it failed to perform the functions of one.[72]

The prominence given to the political aspect led to a compromise solution which enabled the Gold Coast to disengage from the West African Currency Board without fundamentally altering the stable structure of the colonial sterling exchange standard. This compromise was reflected in the Bank of Ghana Ordinance (1957): the exchange rate of the Ghana pound would be one Ghana pound to £1 sterling; the Bank of Ghana must at all times redeem its notes and coins on demand against an equivalent amount of sterling; the Act prescribed the proportion of the assets of the expatriate banks that should be kept liquid; but it was deliberately silent on the question of whether or not to concentrate their sterling reserves in the newly created central bank; only a limited fiduciary issue was permitted; up to £12 million of the backing for the Ghana currency could be held in local treasury bills or in other securities of the government provided that not more than £6 million was held in securities with a maturity exceeding two years; the bank should not be a source of long-term development capital.[73]

Thus there was not much difference between the new Ghana Central Bank and the WACB which it replaced; it remained firmly within the sterling system. Many Ghanaian nationalists resented this situation, as they wanted a more dynamic central bank with a measure of independence from sterling.[74] They were worried about the political and economic consequences of an automatic and rigidly close relationship with sterling. For instance, in expressing the political fears, Victor Owusu said that the Ghana pound should approximate to the pound sterling rather than being tied to it, lest it create an impression that

Ghana's financial matters were being managed by outsiders.[75] His fellow nationalist, Apaloo, emphasised the economic consequences of the relationship. He was worried about the harmful effects of any devaluation of sterling on the Ghanaian economy.[76]

The Finance Minister, Gbedemah, was under no illusions, however, about the limitations of the new Central Bank of Ghana.[77] He was more concerned about the success of the new currency and the importance of giving it confidence and stability.[78]

In Nigeria the demand for a central bank was first expressed in 1952, when K. O. Mbadiwe put down a motion in the House of Representatives for the creation of one.[79] His greatest concern[80] was that Nigeria's resources were 'not within its territorial waters but ... scattered all over the world'.[81]

In the debate that followed, the alliance government, acting through the strong influence of the expatriate Finance Minister, rejected the motion, leaning heavily on the traditional arguments against central banks in the emergent African nations. The Finance Minister maintained that the WACB was efficient in meeting Nigeria's needs because of its one hundred per cent sterling backing of the currency, and accepted Cecil Trevor's arguments in Ghana by pointing out that 'the central bank has no great merits to offer to the country'.[82] He stressed that, apart from the dangers of inflation, a central bank in Nigeria would be hamstrung in the absence of an established money and capital market.[83]

Because of the strong demand in the House for a central bank, the government agreed to commission an independent study, and in November 1952 J. L. Fisher was invited to conduct it. Fisher recommended, however, against setting up a central bank.[84] This was a temporary setback, for, as in Ghana, the ruling nationalists later came round to settle firmly for a central bank on political grounds. It was seen as an institution that would enhance the independence of the country.[85]

When J. B. Loynes was asked to report on the establishment of a central bank in Nigeria, he was therefore more constrained than Fisher had been, in that the Nigerian government had already made the decision. However, he did not conceal his preference for the continued sterling connection and his respect for the cardinal rules of the WACB.[86] He recommended that the value of the Nigerian pound should be fixed by law at par with sterling and that the currency should be redeemable or issuable against sterling at any time.[87] His recommendations were accepted.[88] The Bill maintained that for five years the new bank must hold external reserves of not less than 60 per cent of its notes and coins in circulation. After five years the reserves could drop to not less than 40 per cent.[89]

Unlike Ghana, in Nigeria there was a general atmosphere of caution and a willingness to co-operate with, and learn from, Britain. Only one prominent nationalist, Jaja Wachuku, spoke defiantly against close monetary relations with Britain. He argued that the Bank of England should not be a model for Nigeria's central bank because it had grown up under different conditions.[90] He attacked the lack of provision for the new bank to mobilise indigenous resources. The bank should contribute to mobilisation because 'the United Kingdom is not in a position to lend any of the Commonwealth countries sufficient funds that will be adequate to their needs'.[91]

This radical but singular opposition was not enough to prevent the establishment of the central bank on the lines of the Loynes Report. Thus although Ghana and Nigeria established central banks, in 1957 and 1958 respectively, the colonial sterling exchange standard still operated in all the African territories. The fixed relationship with the pound sterling was still unaltered; there was still free convertibility into sterling and vice versa; there was a high percentage of sterling backing for the local currencies; there was no centralisation of reserves and no curtailment of the expatriate banks' freedom of operation; the holding of reserves was only in sterling; and, finally, controls were imposed on the central banks on long-term loans to their governments.

Notes

1 Susan Strange, *Sterling and British Policy*, 1971, pp. 303–4.
2 Ida Greaves, *Colonial Monetary Conditions*, 1953, p. 5.
3 Cmnd 6426, 1912, p. 2.
4 Judd Polk, *Sterling: its Meaning in World Finance*, 1956, chapter 2; Alan Day, *The Future of Sterling*, 1954, chapter 2.
5 Cmnd 6426, 1912, p. i. See also J. B. Loynes. *The West African Currency Board, 1912–1962*, for an exposition of the committee's report.
6 Cmnd 6426, *op. cit.*, p. 7.
7 Some specialists in International Finance have maintained that the 100 per cent backing was unnecessary because not all the country's currency would be presented for conversion. To them, this policy was deflationary. See R. A. Sowelem, *Towards Financial Independence in*

a Developing Country, 1967, p. 27; *The Banker*, 1950, 'The Monetary Systems of the Colonies'; O. Olankapo, 'The Loynes Report and Banking in Sierra Leone', *Bankers Magazine*, No. 1420, July 1962, p. 20.

8   This has been seen as a transfer of real resources from the colonies to Britain. Polk, *Sterling: its Meaning in World Finance, op. cit.*, examines this argument.

9   Ida Greaves, spokesman for the Colonial Office, maintained that the colonies lacked the financial institutions for the investment of surplus funds: 'The Colonial Sterling Balances', *Essays in International Finance*, No. 20, September 1954, and *Colonial Monetary Conditions, op. cit.*; A. R. Conan, *The Rationale of the Sterling Area*, 1961, and W. F. Crick, *Commonwealth Banking Systems*, 1965, p. 12, put forward similar arguments. However, C. V. Brown, *The Nigerian Banking System*, 1966, Judd Polk, *op. cit.*, p. 185, and Shannon, *IMF Staff Papers*, April 1951, differed from this argument. They stressed that the currency boards prevented the development of local money markets.

10 W. K. Hancock and M. M. Gowing, *Britain's War Economy*, 1959, p. 403.

11 In the course of the war America supplied, without charge, some $30 billion of Lend-Lease materials to the Commonwealth, of which $27 billion went to Britain. R. Gardner, *Sterling—Dollar Diplomacy, op. cit.*, gives a good account of the financial diplomacy of these years.

12 Cmnd 6706, 1945.

13 Further American financial help was given in 1947, and under this Anglo-American Financial Agreement sterling became convertible on 16 July 1947. This led to further crisis and a tightening of controls.

14 H. C. Debates, 14 July 1949, Vol. 467, col. 673—91.

15 Day, *The Future of Sterling, op. cit.*, p. 46.

16 For details see *Nigeria: Handbook of Commerce and Industry* (Lagos), 1954, pp. 146—56.

17 Colonial Office, Colonial Primary Products Committee, *Interim Report*, January 1948, Colonial No. 214, p. 1.

18 *Ibid.*, p. 5.

19 *Ibid.*

20 *Commonwealth Trade with the United States, 1948—1957*, Commonwealth Economic Committee, 1959, Table 9.

21 *Ibid.*, p. 12.

22 *Ibid.*, p. 15.

23 *Commonwealth Trade with the United States, 1948—1957, op. cit.*

24 Ghana Debates, 27 March 1953, 11 December 1951, col. 707, 15 October 1952, p. 454, 3 April 1956, col. 436.

25 *Commonwealth Trade with the United States, 1948—1957, op. cit.*

26 Conservative Party, *The Expanding Commonwealth 1956. Conservative Policy on the Colonies* (Conservative Political Centre), pp. 19—20.

27 *Labour's Colonial Policy*, II, Economic Aid, 1957, chapters III and IV.
28 H.C. Debates, 12 July 1950, Vol. 477, col. 1369.
29 *Memorandum on the Sterling Assets of the British Colonies*, 1955, Colonial No. 298, p. 15.
30 See Table 4.1.
31 J. M. Livingstone, *Britain and the World Economy*, 1966, p. 63; Strange, *Sterling and British Policy, op. cit.*, p. 67.
32 Cecil Trevor, *On Banking Conditions in the Gold Coast and the desirability of setting up a National Bank* (Accra), 1951; J. L. Fisher, *Report on the Desirability and Practicability of a Central Bank in Nigeria* (Nigeria), 1953; J. B. Loynes, *Report on the Future of the Currencies of Sierra Leone and the Gambia* (Bathurst), 1961, and report *On the Establishment of a Nigerian Central Bank, the Introduction of a Nigerian Currency and other associated matters* (Lagos), 1957.
33 Fisher, *op. cit.*, p. 1.
34 Loynes, *Report on the Establishment of a Nigerian Central Bank, op. cit.*, p. 4.
35 *Ibid.*, p. 6.
36 H.C. Debates, 16 February 1955, Vol. 587, col. 59.
37 Nkrumah, *Towards Colonial Freedom, op. cit.*
38 Metclaffe, *Great Britain and Ghana: Documents of Ghana History, op. cit.*, p. 706.
39 H.C. Debates, 15 December 1954, Vol. 535, col. 143.
40 Lennox Boyd, H.C. Debates, 16 February 1955, Vol. 587, col. 59.
41 H.C. Debates, 16 February 1955, Vol. 587, col. 59.
42 G/C Debates, 2 April 1950, p. 60.
43 *Ibid.*, p. 70.
44 G/C Debates, 9 August 1955, col. 405.
45 G/C Debates, 3 April 1951.
46 G/C Debates, 11 December 1951; 15 October 1952; 23 March 1953; 3 April 1956; Nigeria H/R Debates, 7 March 1953.
47 H/R Debates, 7 March 1953, p. 335.
48 G/C Debates, 11 December 1951, col. 707.
49 G/C Debates, 15 October 1952, p. 454.
50 G/C Debates, 22 March 1953, p. 750.
51 G/C Debates, 3 April 1956, col. 436.
52 G/C Debates, 11 December 1951, col. 667; Nigeria, H/R Debates, 3 March 1953, p. 142.
53 G/C Debates, 13 February 1953, p. 121.
54 Nigeria, H/R Debates, 7 March 1953, pp. 373–4.
55 G/C Debates, 12 February 1953, p. 121.
56 H.C. Debates, 15 December 1954, Vol. 536, col. 143.
57 *East African Currency Board Annual Report*, 1955.
58 *Op. cit.*, para. 2.
59 *Op. cit.*, para. 7.
60 Trevor Report, *op. cit.*

61 Fisher Report, *op. cit.*, p. 5.
62 *Ibid.*, p. 7.
63 *Ibid.*, p. 7.
64 *Ibid.*, p. 18.
65 Trevor Report, *op. cit.*, para. 98; Fisher Report, *op. cit.*, p. 6; Loyne's report, *op. cit.*, p. 3.
66 Trevor Report, *op. cit.*, para. 98.
67 Fisher Report, *op. cit.*, section 1.
68 *Ibid.*, p. 1.
69 G/C Debates, 8 October 1952, pp. 214–15.
70 *Ibid.*, p. 237.
71 *Ibid.*, p. 225.
72 G/C Debates, 5 February 1957, p. 698.
73 G/C Debates, 5 February 1957.
74 *Ibid.*, col. 705.
75 *Ibid.*, col. 714.
76 *Ibid.*, col. 718.
77 *Ibid.*, col. 701.
78 *Ibid.*, col. 700.
79 Nigeria, H/R Debates, 21 March 1952, Vol. I, p. 377.
80 H/R Debates, 9 April 1952, Vol. II, col. 1176.
81 *Ibid.*, p. 1175.
82 *Ibid.*, p. 1180.
83 *Ibid.*, p. 1181.
84 Fisher Report, *op. cit.*
85 H/R Debates, 17 March 1958, Vol. II, col. 1681.
86 Loynes Report, *op. cit.*, p. 3.
87 *Ibid.*
88 Nigeria, H/R Debates, 17 March 1958, Vol. II, pp. 1676–7.
89 *Ibid.*
90 *Ibid.*, p. 1707.
91 *Ibid.*, p. 1709.

3

British development policy towards Africa

British development policy was governed by two major considerations: to enable the African colonies to participate in the sterling area and to facilitate decolonisation. Aid and investment constituted a leak in Britain's monetary programme, the primary objective of which was to check the outward flow of British capital. But Britain had a large empire and expected it to contribute to the defence of sterling. This could be done successfully only if the colonies were given alternative sources of capital as the mechanics of the sterling area stifled the economic development of the colonies; without this guaranteed flow of capital Britain would have found it difficult to construct a working relationship with the nationalists. Aid and investment thus became important elements in both the decolonisation of Africa and in Anglo-African monetary relations. This chapter will discuss British aid and investment policies towards Africa.

The development of British aid policy

British aid to Africa was shaped by two persistent themes: responsibility for the economic development of the colonies and the use of aid to promote Britain's own economic interests. Although the two were often difficult to separate, the second had always gained prominence in periods of economic crisis. A brief summary of the development of British aid policy since 1929 will bring this point into clearer focus.

An aid programme was established in 1929[1] mainly to counter the adverse effects of the depression as Britain attempted to stimulate economic development in the colonies and at the same time regenerate her own flagging economy.[2] The assistance provided by the Colonial Development Fund between 1929 and 1930 was £1,369,632 and the estimated expenditure to be incurred in Britain in connection with development projects (worth £5,629,499 for all colonies spread over a period of five years) was £2,288,187.[3]

During the 1930s the colonial development programme came under sustained criticism in Britain as the need to promote economic development unencumbered by considerations of the metropolitan economy was advocated by politicians concerned at the appalling poverty in the colonies. This situation was aggravated by riots in the West Indies, Mauritius and the Gold Coast which were precipitated by economic conditions. A Royal Commission was appointed to enquire into the causes, with special reference to those in the West Indies. The report sharply criticised British policy in the colonies and recommended the expansion of Britain's responsibility for development, especially in the social services.[4] The findings of the report led to the creation of the Colonial Development and Welfare Act (CD&WA) of 1940, which laid emphasis on development for the colonies, with a vote of £5 million a year for ten years.[5]

This programme was greatly affected, however, by the outbreak of the second world war.[6] Colonial governments were informed on 10 September 1940 that the Treasury would agree to make financial provision for any scheme only if three criteria were met: it could be carried out solely with local resources in men and materials and without detriment to the war effort; no expenditure outside the sterling area should be involved; finally, the scheme should be of such urgency and importance as to justify the expenditure of United Kingdom funds.[7]

These three criteria severely limited the operation of the 1940 CD&WA programme and made development extremely difficult. After the war a new Colonial Development and Welfare Act was passed as the basis of Britain's avowed policy of self-government within the empire. The 1945 Act increased financial help to the colonies to £120 million over a ten-year period and increased the ceiling on expenditure in any one year from £5 million to £17½ million.[8]

The Act called on the colonial governments to produce balanced social and economic projects which could be supported from the 1945 CD&WA funds. Like its predecessors, the 1945 CD&WA programme came to be related also to the economic problems of the period. Because of the colonies' significant contribution to the sterling area Britain attempted to channel its development capital to the areas most likely to earn dollars, and to win the nationalists' confidence greater emphasis came to be laid on improving the effectiveness of the CD&WA programme.

The first objective proved difficult because of the relative underdevelopment of the colonies and the concern everywhere for general social and economic development.[9] For the period 1946–58 the policy of providing aid to help dollar production was far from successful. True, the interdepartmental committee (the Colonial Primary Products Committee) which was formed in 1947 did actually invest in products which were suitable for large-scale export, like the ground-nut scheme in East Africa and the Gambia, lead in Tanganyika, rice in West Africa, tobacco in Northern and Southern Rhodesia and timber in Nigeria. Investment by the Overseas Food Corporation in some schemes, such as ground-nuts in East Africa and poultry in Gambia, was very unsuccessful. Most of them had to be abandoned. There was little scope for discriminating in favour of products which would earn dollars to promote real productive growth. For the period 1946–57 the CD&WA aid programme concentrated on the social services and communications (60 per cent). Aid for real productive enterprise was only 19.1 per cent.[10]

The second objective, greater commitment to general social and economic development as compensation for the colonies' contribution to the monetary programme, and as part of the decolonisation process, proved more successful than the first. Ernest Bevin underlined this policy in a foreign policy statement to the Commons in January 1948 in which he emphasised the need for economic planning in Africa if its resources were to be used to restore a surplus in Europe's balance of payments.[11] The CD&WA programme was severely constrained, however, by the amount of money voted for the fund. Competition among colonial governments for its limited resources was intense; many ambitious projects had to be streamlined, curtailed or rejected.

In 1948 the Labour government broke new ground by passing the Overseas Resources Development Act, which constituted two corporations designed to promote further economic development in the colonies, the Overseas Food Corporation and the Colonial Development Corporation (CDC). The CDC was a quasi-commercial corporation with the power to borrow from the government up to £100 million long-term and £10 million short-term. It was hoped that the CDC would add a new dimension to the provision of development capital to the colonies and that it would finance projects which would pay their way commercially.[12]

This was the situation of Britain's development policy towards Africa when the alliance governments were formed in the 1950s. Significantly, the nationalists were very much preoccupied with economic development. Modest development plans had already been forwarded to Britain by the pre-alliance governments. The nationalists, while accepting the framework of these plans, attempted to expand them by bringing in new projects and emphasising the need to industrialise.

For instance, on assuming office the nationalist Minister of Commerce and Industry, K. A. Gbedemah, commissioned Professor Arthur Lewis in November 1952 to prepare a report on industrialisation and economic policy in Ghana.[13] In his report Lewis calculated that Ghana would need, at a conservative estimate, an annual investment in manufacturing net of about £3 million a year.[14] He stressed that 'to industrialize the Gold Coast at the sort of rate which most people have in mind ... would require at least twice as much money as this estimate'.[15] The high cost of industrialisation was confirmed by the IBRD report Nigeria commissioned in 1954.[16] What it meant was that if the nationalists wanted rapid economic development and substantial industrialisation, then extra finance would have to be solicited.[17]

This demand for development capital posed critical problems for British policy, since it was feared that the nationalists would turn to the reserves to finance their programmes. The various British development programmes were clearly inadequate to meet the new African commitment to industrialisation. London, the traditional source of development capital, proved extremely problematic in the 1950s. Although the African colonies were allowed to raise loans on the capital market on a trustee status, it was in no position to meet the demands of the African and other colonial or Commonwealth countries. Each application was carefully scrutinised to ensure that the government concerned had made the maximum contribution from its own resources.[18] As the Nigerian Minister of Finance, Okotie Eboh, found out, many were turned down on this criterion.[19] Furthermore, conditions on the London market were not favourable to the raising of loans: investors were hesitant about the evolving countries' financial policies.[20] Funds also dried up because of competition from more attractive and lucrative British industrial offers.[21] Between 1950 and 1964 only thirty issues were launched on the capital market by African countries. The highest number in any one year was five, in 1951 and 1952.

The figure fell to two in 1953 and did not recover until 1964, when four issues each were launched by Zambia and Malawi. Between 1951 and 1957 there were only nineteen issues from the whole of Africa.[22]

The terms of the loans ranged from 2½ per cent to 6 per cent interest, maintaining an average of 5 per cent, and the length of repayment got stiffer as decolonisation advanced. Most loans in the 1950s were for periods between ten and twenty years; in the 1960s none was for more than ten.

The other source of British capital, the Colonial Development Corporation, was not yet in a sufficiently strong position to meet the demands of the African nationalists. From 1948, when it came into operation, to 31 December 1957 it recommended only £53,112,000 for all African countries and spent only £30,949,000 − an average of about £3 million annually.[23]

Nationalists were, indeed, wary about Britain's ability to finance their countries' development. This scepticism led some of them to demand that the policies of discrimination against America should be abandoned if the US was to become a source of capital for Africa.[24] They also argued that the sterling balances held by African countries should be mobilised for economic development.[25] The difficulties facing her economy, and the absence of any international approach to the development problem, meant that Britain had to continue to conduct her aid policy within the framework of the traditional programmes. Britain tried to influence the nationalists' development policies by advising them to refrain from radical and expansive programmes because of their limited administrative capacities. Despite protests from the rank and file and opposition parties, the leading nationalists were by and large prepared to accept moderation.

The British government was forced, however, to expand the CD&WA programme several times from 1945 to 1955. In 1949 the amount authorised to be spent in one year was increased, although the total amount for the ten-year period remained the same. In 1950 this total was increased from £120 million to £140 million for a ten-year period 1946−56. A new sum of £80 million was provided for expenditure in the five-year period 1955−60; and the annual amount to be spent was raised to £30 million. Between 1946 and 1958 the African territories received a total of £75,778,000 of CD&WA aid out of a total of £220 million for all the colonies; this represented about 34.4 per cent of the total.[26]

The development of Britain's investment policy

Britain's investment policy was closely related to its aid policy. As we have seen, one major characteristic of the sterling area was that members agreed to pool their earnings of foreign exchange for common use and to protect the pound. Most of the members were developing countries in need of massive capital flows for economic development. By contrast, Britain was a highly developed country and the centre of their payments arrangements. Britain agreed therefore to operate an open payments policy towards the sterling countries, to facilitate the flow of private investment. But it was the more advanced areas of the developing Commonwealth which benefited from this intra-sterling area investment policy. Because they had established financial institutions and market potential, private British investment was concentrated in Australia, South Africa and New Zealand rather than in the African and Asian countries.[27]

The flow of British capital to Africa varied according to region. In West Africa the Europeans failed to play a dominant role in domestic capital formation. Here the indigenous African people were mainly responsible for the important commercial developments which occurred, in for instance the cocoa industry in Ghana and Nigeria, unlike in East and Central Africa where the plantation system was introduced, giving the Europeans a crucial role in capital formation.

Apart from climatic conditions which precluded European settlement and the failure of earlier forms of experimental farms in Nigeria,[28] British capital was less concentrated in West Africa because the region did not appear at the time well endowed with commercially exploitable minerals. There was nothing like the great diamond discoveries of Kimberley in the 1870s, nor was there much in the way of gold compared to the Witwatersrand discoveries of 1885. In West Africa the only commercially exploitable deposits were diamonds and iron ore in Sierra Leone, gold in the Gold Coast and tin in Nigeria. This in fact led to a concentration of European investment in those areas.

In Kenya, Zambia and Rhodesia considerable progress was made in encouraging private investment. The discovery of gold in the Witwatersrand changed the whole political climate in southern Africa. The British government, acting through its surrogate Cecil Rhodes, gained control over the great diamond industry at Kimberley and sought to extend it over Africa's resources from the Cape to Cairo. Rhodes was able to secure a charter for his British South Africa Company which enabled him to sign 'treaties' with African leaders at the expense of other European powers. On failing to win control of the rich mining area of Katanga, Rhodes and his company consolidated their grip on the Rhodesias and Nyasaland.[29]

Northern Rhodesia was at first unimportant in terms of mineral wealth and was used mainly as a labour reserve for the mines of Katanga and South Africa. But the discovery of large copper deposits in the 1920s transformed the fortunes of the territory as capital was poured in by South Africa and the British South Africa Company to exploit the resources of the Copperbelt. Northern Rhodesia became an important source of copper for the Allies during the second world war, and by 1945 was firmly established as one of the world's leading producers and exporters.[30]

Apart from investments in plantation agriculture and mineral deposits, British capital was also involved in infrastructure enterprises such as harbours, railways and roads; they tended to concentrate in the mining and the plantation areas. It was a picture which reflected the classical structure of imperialism.

These developments helped to enhance foreign investment after 1945. In areas of large European settlement, Kenya and Zambia, considerable progress was made in stimulating private investment. In Kenya it was officially estimated that between 1949 and 1951 private investment was about £15 million a year. In 1950 and 1951 there were twenty-four and thirty-one foreign-registered companies respectively.[31] In Zambia the rapid investment was mainly in the copper mines.[32]

Private investment in Botswana, Swaziland and Lesotho came largely from South Africa. In Lesotho, for instance, there were no domestic-registered companies. All those operating in the country (three public and nine private) were registered in South Africa.[33] In Tanzania private investment between 1946 and 1954 amounted to only £18 million, nearly half of it in agriculture, and some 12 per cent in mining.[34] In Uganda there were only twelve foreign-registered companies.[35] The Gambia received no private investment of any significance except in the government's savings bank and small trading concerns.[36] In Ghana there were approximately 323 private companies, and of these 146 had registered offices overseas.[37] Nigeria had 208 registered private companies with a total nominal share capital of £5,564,899. As regards non-resident companies operating in

Nigeria, 135 were registered in Britain and twenty-one in other countries.[38] In Sierra Leone there were sixty registered companies in 1950, of which twenty-six were resident and thirty-four non-resident; of the thirty-four foreign companies, twenty-six were incorporated in Britain.[39]

After 1945 the flow of private investment to the colonies became a significant part of Britain's economic policy. The Labour government felt that a government-sponsored investment company would be able to provide extra capital by investing in areas where real economic development would take place. The Colonial Development Corporation (CDC)[40] was established in 1948, and attempted to strike a balance between profitability and 'real' economic development by investing in basic development projects such as power and water supply, transport, housing finance, agriculture, hotels and commercial/industrial enterprises.[41] By 31 December 1973 Commonwealth Africa had the highest number of CDC commitments.[42]

The early years of CDC activity were replete with abandoned projects and poor management. With rapid constitutional advances in the colonies and their need of capital, it was widely agreed that CDC's operations would have to be supplemented by private foreign capital. This meant that British private investment in Africa would have to be encouraged and protected, and the nationalists would also have to be persuaded to accept foreign private investment.

One of the more difficult areas in Anglo-African investment relations was the role of British companies in the decolonisation process. These companies had expanded their operations in Africa confident in the knowledge that they would continue to enjoy the protection of British law and administration. Decolonisation altered this sense of security and the companies were faced with the problem of developing new strategies for survival in the evolving independent States.

The major British companies in West Africa were Unilever, with its gigantic trading subsidiary the United Africa Company; the mining companies, Sierra Leone Selection Trust, Sierra Leone Development Company and the Amalgamated Tin Mines of Nigeria; and the shipping companies, chiefly Elder Dempster, which handled a substantial part of the West African trade.

British companies adopted several strategies aimed at protecting their interests in West Africa. Firstly, they attempted to shift their operations from general commerce to more specialised trades. The post-war period introduced not only a new political climate but an economic boom in West Africa.[43] The leading companies became more specialised, concentrating mainly on wholesale activities, leaving retail trading to the Africans, Indians, Levantines and a few department stores such as Kingsway.

Although the colonial system still favoured the expatriate companies,[44] many indigenous African businessmen took advantage of this diversification in expatriate trading interests and the shift in political power in favour of the Africans. Africans increased their share of the import/export trade. In Nigeria, for instance, the African share of the import trade increased from 5 per cent in 1949 to 20 per cent in 1963.[45]

A second strategy the British companies employed was to work closely with the nationalists in speeding up the Africanisation of management. African directors emerged in some of the subsidiaries, and finance companies were established to help African traders set up their own businesses. The UAC proved quite successful in this respect. For instance, whereas in 1939 Africans accounted for only 7 per cent of the company's total management staff, by 1957, in the year of Africa's first independent State, the proportion had increased to 21 per cent.[46] In Elder Dempster the process of Africanisation began even before the decolonisation period owing to the war time shortage of expatriate staff. Africanisation accelerated with decolonisation as Africans acquired managerial status. By 1965 the company employed only fifty expatriates in the whole of West Africa, compared with 110 in 1960 and 150 in the mid-1950s.[47]

Apart from the political rationale, Africanisation seemed to make economic sense. Salary differentials between Africans and Europeans were still weighted against the former, so that it was cheaper to employ Africans than Europeans; in addition Africans were far more useful in creating new markets and holding on to established ones because of their knowledge of the local scene.

In the case of the large shipping companies Elder Dempster and Palm Line the major problem was how to cope with the increasing demands by the new governments for a greater control over shipping. Ghana established the Black Star Line in 1957 with a government share of 60 per cent; Israel's Zim Line took the remaining 40 per cent.[48] The West African Lines Conference, which was dominated by the expatriate shipping companies, admitted the Black Star Line immediately, although it was at first limited to five vessels. The government increased the number of its ships to thirteen after 1959 by joining the

American West African Freight Conference. On the Zim Line's refusal to provide capital for this expanded programme, the Ghanaian government acquired complete control over Black Star Line.[49]

Nigeria also established its own shipping lines in 1959, with Elder Dempster and Palm Line controlling 33 per cent and 16 per cent of the shares respectively and the government 51 per cent. The two British companies agreed to help train Nigerians in navigation, engineering and management. The government assumed full control in 1961.[50]

Apart from helping the evolving African administrations set up their own shipping companies, Elder Dempster also attempted to introduce major changes in the structure and organisation of its shore-based operations. In 1954 the company decided to confine Elder Dempster Lines operations to purely ocean carriage. A new company was formed, West African Properties Ltd, to take care of shore-based activities, forestalling any nationalist criticism of Elder Dempster's coastal establishments.[51]

Thus the strategies adopted by British companies placated the emerging nationalists and helped to foster a favourable working relationship. This atmosphere of goodwill contributed to the alliance governments' policy of guaranteeing foreign private enterprise and the market economy in their evolving political economies.

African decolonisation occurred in an atmosphere where private investment was considered essential for development; Britain was committed to sustaining the flow of investment to Commonwealth Africa but insisted that it should also solicit American capital. All African nationalists accepted the need to develop their economies with foreign help, mainly because of the problems involved in trying to relate economic development specifically to internal resources. Kwame Nkrumah was emphatic on this point.[52] From 1951 onwards the Ghanaian government was committed to industrialisation, with the emphasis on local initiative, private enterprise and manufacturing industry. Through this process, Nkrumah maintained, 'foreign investors' would 'require assurances about the conditions which will apply to their investments'.[53] The only condition was that they should train Africans for the future administration of industry. Other than that the government was prepared to give them a free hand, 'encouraging as much as possible the entry and investment in industry of foreign capital'. They would be free to invest in any form of new industrial enterprise apart from public utilities; there would be no price controls except on monopolies, and membership of the sterling area would guarantee the free transfer of funds and convertibility into sterling. New industrial estates would be established and relief allowed from taxation for pioneer industries. Finally there would be no nationalisation, apart from public utilities, and even if it became necessary later there would be prompt, adequate and fair compensation. To demonstrate the government's anti-nationalisation stance, Nkrumah stressed that Ghana would request Britain to incorporate appropriate provisions in the independence constitution. It was infact made an entrenched clause of the constitution.[54]

Ghana's commitment to foreign private investment was reiterated by Nkrumah in an eve-of-independence-day speech.[55] Relations with Britain would 'of necessity be close because of the very many economic and historic ties' between the two countries,[56] but he recognised also the need to develop relations with the United States.[57]

During the decolonisation period, however, Ghana positively looked to Britain as the major investor and made several attempts to respond to British policies by bringing its own laws in line. Thus on 4 December 1957 the Mineral Profits Tax Bill was amended to take account of British double taxation relief for British companies overseas. Britain decided to grant relief on profits tax and not on production tax. Mining companies in Ghana were subject, however, to two types of taxation: income tax, which was a tax on profits, and minerals duty, which was a tax on production. Production tax was advantageous to Ghana from the revenue point of view, since at times sales were far below production and a profits tax would have brought in less revenue. The British government maintained that to qualify for relief a tax must be of a similar character to income tax, imposed on profits and not on production.[58] Ghana had to change its tax therefore in order to qualify for the double taxation relief provided by Britain.[59]

Nigeria was also well disposed towards foreign private enterprise, which had the support of all three political parties. In soliciting American capital in 1958, Awolowo denounced the principle of non-alignment and welcomed 'the drive and energy of American businessmen to start the wheels of industry turning in Nigeria'.[60] In 1954, in a speech to the Nigerian Eastern Assembly on the economic mission to Europe, Nnamdi Azikiwe affirmed his party's belief in the value of foreign private investment to Eastern Nigeria.[61] And in 1957 Tafewa Balewa asserted the federal government's concern to maintain and project a foreign policy that would 'perpetuate the high reputation' of Nigeria in the financial world.[62]

With this collective commitment, Nigeria implemented various policies aimed at attracting private investment from abroad.[63] The Aid to Pioneer Industries Bill, which stressed the need for private foreign investment and offered tax relief and protection to investment,[64] was passed in April 1952. In 1955 the federal government set up a committee to advise on how to stimulate industrial development by affording relief from import duties and taxes.[65] On the basis of its recommendations, the government passed a series of legislation aimed at protecting and developing private investment capital: the Industrial Development (Import Duty Tax) Act, 1957; the Industrial Development (Income Tax Relief) Act, 1958; the Customs Duties (Dumped and Subsidised Goods) Act, 1958; the Companies Income Tax (No. 22 of 1961) and industrial estates for investors.[66]

During the decolonisation period all African nationalists accepted the need to protect British capital and attract non-British investment, chiefly American, to speed up the development process; this orientation helped to strengthen the forces of private enterprise in the evolving political economies of Africa.

Notes

1   Colonial Development Act, H.C. Bill 9, 1929, p. 1.
2   Cmnd 3540, 1930, para. 39.
3   *Ibid.*
4   Cmnd 6174, 1940.
5   Cmnd 6175, 1940.
6   Cmnd 6422, 19??, p. 4.
7   *Ibid.*, p. 4.
8   *Colonial Development and Welfare Act*, 1945.
9   The Commonwealth Economic Conference, 1952, Final Communiqué, para. 9.
10 Cmnd 672, 1959, p. 4.
11 H.C. Debates, 22 February 1948, *op. cit.*
12 Sir William Rendell, *The Commonwealth Development Corporation, 1948–1972*, 1976, p. 7.
13 *Report on Industrialization and the Gold Coast* (Accra), 1953, p. vii.
14 *Ibid.*, p. 8, para. 96.
15 *Ibid.*

16 *The Economic Development of Nigeria*, 1955.
17 Lewis Report, *op. cit.*, chapter 3.
18 Nigeria. H/R Debates, 9 Feburary 1959, col. 75—6.
19 *Ibid.*, p. 76.
20 *Ibid.*
21 *Labour's Colonial Policy*, II, *Economic Aid, op. cit.*, p. 11.
22 See Y. Bangura, 'The Politics of Economic Relations between Britain and Commonwealth Africa, 1951—75', unpublished Ph.D. thesis, University of London, 1978, appendix 2(1), for detailed figures.
23 *The Colonial Development Corporation Annual Report and Statement of Accounts*, April 1958, Bill 64, p. 3.
24 See, for instance, Danquah's speech, H/C Debates, 3 April 1951, p. 127.
25 See, for instance, Jaja Wachuku's speech, Nigeria H/R Debates, 17 March 1958, p. 1710.
26 Cmnd 72, 1959, p. 11.
27 See Table 8.1.
28 A. E. Afigbo, 'The establishment of colonial rule, 1900—1918', in Ajai and Crowder (eds.), *History of West Africa*, Vol. II, 1974, p. 472.
29 Andrew Roberts, *A History of Zambia*, 1976, p. 177.
30 *Ibid.*, p. 185.
31 *An Economic Survey of the Colonial Territories*, 1951, Colonial No. 281 (2), 1954, p. 37.
32 *An Economic Survey of the Colonial Territories*, 1951, Vol. I, Colonial No. 281 (1), 1952, p. 27.
33 *Ibid.*, p. 72.
34 *An Economic Survey of the Colonial Territories*, Vol. II, *op. cit.*, p. 70.
35 *Ibid.*, p. 100.
36 *An Economic Survey of the Colonial Territories*, Vol. III, 1952, Colonial No. 281—3, p. 4.
37 *Ibid.*, p. 41.
38 *Ibid.*, p. 67.
39 *Ibid.*, p. 89.
40 The Colonial Development Corporation later became the Commonwealth Corporation.
41 See Bangura, *op. cit.*, appendix 7 (2).
42 *Ibid.*
43 A. G. Hopkins, *An Economic History of West Africa*, 1973, p. 277.
44 Zik, *Selected Speeches, op. cit.*, pp. 212—13.
45 Hopkins, *An Economic History of West Africa, op. cit.*, p. 273.
46 *Ibid.*, p. 277.
47 P. N. Davies, *The Trade Makers: Elder Dempster in West Africa, 1852—1972*, 1973, pp. 240—1.
48 Charlotte Leubuscher, *The West African Shipping Trade, 1909—1959* (Netherlands), 1963, pp. 66—7.
49 *West Africa* (London), 1959, p. 698.

50   Nigeria, H/R Debates, 19 February 1959, Vol. 787.

51   Davies, *The Trade Makers, op. cit.*, pp. 339—41.

52   *The Gold Coast: Handbook of Trade and Commerce* (Accra), May 1955, Fourth Issue, p. 20.

53   G/C Debates, 1 March 1954, col. 1080.

54   Colonial Office, *Proposed Constitution of Ghana*, February 1957, Cmnd 71, para. 45.

55   G/C Debates, 5 March 1957, col. 25.

56   Ghana Debates, 29 August 1957, Vol. 7, col. 309.

57   *Ibid.*, col. 309.

58   Ghana Debates, 4 December 1957, col. 346.

59   *Ibid.*, col. 346—7.

60   *Towards Independence: Speeches and Statements* by Obafemi Awolowo, 1958, p. 30—1.

61   Zik, *A Selection from the Speeches of Nnamdi Azikiwe*, 1961, p. 221.

62   *Mr. Prime Minister, op. cit.*, p. 14.

63   H/R Debates, Vol. II, 31 March 1953, p. 983.

64   H/R Debates, 7 April 1952, pp. 981—5.

65   *Report by the Committee to advise the Federal Government of the Stimulation of Industrial Development by affording Relief from Import Duties and Protection to Nigerian Industry* (Lagos), 1956, p. 1.

66   *Second National Development Plan, 1970—1974*, pp. 7—15.

Part two

Independence

4

Sterling convertibility

Two events — independence and the end of dollar discrimination — radically changed the pattern of controlled economic relations that characterised the decolonisation era. African independence introduced 'development' as the central issue in the relationship as the monetary priority of the 1950s collapsed after the relaxation of dollar discrimination and the establishment of sterling convertibility. The effect of the change was also felt in the Commonwealth—sterling area as British monetary dominance gave way to a more flexible and broadly based system of economic co-operation, with 'development' becoming an essential part of the new multi-dimensional Commonwealth. This chapter serves as an introduction to the remainder of the book, which deals with the independence period. It attempts to piece together the main points of difference between the decolonisation and independence periods by examining British and African relations within the evolving Commonwealth.

Britain's reappraisal of its attitudes towards Africa

British attitudes towards Africa underwent some radical changes as the policy-makers painfully tried to come to terms with the new African consciousness and the new international environment. Whereas in the 1940s and 1950s the policy-makers had a conception of a Greater Britain supported by the Empire/Commonwealth and in some ways linked to Western Europe, by 1957, the year of Ghana's independence, this conception of a third centre of power had been largely abandoned. European integration had become a reality, and the Six were willing to go ahead without Britain and her extended Afro-Asian identity. African independence had also brought with it a stronger commitment than earlier to nationalist political and economic policies. This commitment found expression in the development of pan-African forms of co-operation and participation in Third World politico-economic organisations.

British policy-makers were quick to recognise these changes and attempts were made to reappraise their attitudes towards Africa and re-examine their general political and economic policies. This change was underlined by MacMillan's 'Wind of change' speech in South Africa in 1960 in which he accepted African nonalignment, sovereignty and independence.[1] Although MacMillan did not refer to any specific economic issues, his policy statement represented a recognition of the changing structures of the Anglo-African relationship. At the economic level, the hard shell of monetary control had begun to disintegrate as there was no longer any talk about an automatic application of Britain's sterling policy in Africa or of using Africa's resources to sustain the sterling area's payments position. The end of discrimination had reduced the necessity for this; more important, the force of nationalism had introduced an African element concerned with development.

Britain still wanted to strengthen economic co-operation with Africa within the Commonwealth and sterling area, but this was now to be achieved through mutual self-interest and diplomatic negotiations. Although the Commonwealth—sterling area continued to be the main framework for conducting Anglo-African economic relations, as African and other independent States increasingly abandoned the collectivism of the 1950s, and sought to diversify their economic links, Britain was forced to introduce national policies which took into account her special position as banker and holder of an international currency in a period of full convertibility and multilateralism.

The new African objectives in the Commonwealth—sterling area

African nationalism grew stronger at independence. It centred on a commitment to rapid economic development. All African leaders realised the limitations of the economic policies of decolonisation and sought to pursue more African-oriented development policies.

This commitment was shaped by two ideological forces: Third World solidarity and pan-African co-operation. In their ideal forms they posed a challenge to Africa's relations with the Commonwealth and Britain.

The Third World system of co-operation was launched in the

Bandung conference of 1955 in which economic issues that affected the developing countries were articulated in a perspective that divided the world into the developed and the developing.[2] This created a major focal point for the African nationalists in reappraising their external economic relations as they began to interpret them in terms of shared LDC (less developed country) problems of structural economic imbalance, underdevelopment and worsening terms of trade.

This new sense of independence also found expreion in the concept and development of pan-Africanism. All African nationalists linked political independence with *ultimate* African unity, although some of the moderate leaders were merely reacting to Nkrumah's radicalism. The difference was mainly in the methods of achieving pan-Africanism — whether, as the radicals demanded, through immediate political independence, or, as was advocated by the moderates, through functional co-operation in economic and cultural matters.

To Kwame Nkrumah and the radical Casablanca group 'Colonialism, neo-colonialism and African underdevelopment' could only be ended by the total and immediate unification of the continent's political and economic systems.[3]

At the conference called to establish the Organisation of African Unity, Nkrumah put forward a far-reaching programme for a Union government of African States and recommended that a commission should work out a continent-wide plan for a unified or common economic and industrial programme. This included proposals to set up a Common Market for Africa, an African currency, an African monetary zone, and an African central bank.[4]

The moderates (the Monrovia group), with Nigeria as their natural leader, firmly believed that African unity should evolve through functional co-operation in economic, cultural and other technical areas. In their opinion, if differences at these levels were not sorted out first, on a gradual basis, the achievement of African unity would be seriously hindered.[5]

Nigeria and Sierra Leone were full participants in the Monrovia and Lagos conferences, and Tanganyika was an observer member. Ghana, alone among the Commonwealth African States, belonged to the radical Casablanca group. In East Africa there were optimistic plans for a political federation of Tanganyika, Uganda and Kenya, which convinced the nationalist leaders there that pan-Africanism should start at the regional level. According to Julius Nyerere, 'A federation of

East Africa must be well considered both for its own sake and because it must be a step towards African Unity.'[6]

In the immediate aftermath of independence, pan-Africanism, and the quest for its practical implementation, were a dominant issue in African diplomacy.[7] Positive steps were taken by the gradualists, through the charter of the African and Malagassy State Organisation, to effect functional economic and social co-operation, by the radicals through the formation of the Ghana-Guinea Union (with the later addition of Mali) and the proclamation of the Casablanca Charter in January 1961 which called for an African Common Market and an African High Command, and finally by the regional functionalists with their Kampala Declaration for a federation of East Africa. All these aspirations were later institutionalised in the Organisation of African Unity, which, although tailored along the lines of the gradualists' programme, held out the prospect of eventual political and economic unity.

On the economic level, this pan-African objective raised a theoretical problem for the Commonwealth—sterling area relationship, since if it was achieved a future African unity would include countries which had no Commonwealth connections.[8] Kenya's Minister of Justice and Constitutional Affairs, Tom Mboya, brought the conflict into clearer focus. He recognised the continued dependence of Commonwealth Africa on Britain in monetary relations, private investment and technical/financial aid,[9] and the problems this dependence posed for Commonwealth Africa's political independence and pan-African co-operation. He noted the flexibility of the Commonwealth system in trade, investment and monetary relations after independence and convertibility, which had enabled African States to remain in the Commonwealth, but emphasised that discussions in the Commonwealth about the possibility of permanent multilateral trade and technical arrangements and institutions 'were bound to run into conflict with pan-Africanism through the OAU'.[10]

Like Nyerere, Mboya concluded that if the conflict intensified he would support pan-Africanism. Both leaders belonged to the regional functionalist group which believed that pan-Africanism was not immediately feasible. It would coexist with the Commonwealth for a long time to come.[11] Thus, although pan-Africanism initially posed a theoretical challenge to Africa's relations with the Commonwealth, the refusal of most nationalists to accept the radical formulation meant that they would

still be free to construct, develop and maintain extra-continental
relations on a bilateral basis. Tafewa Balewa even regarded the
Commonwealth connection as promoting pan-Africanism in the
long run, through the Commonwealth's programme of aid and
private investment.[12]

Nkrumah's limited attempt to operationalise his version of
pan-Africanism by a political union with Guinea in 1958 also
took into account Ghana's Commonwealth commitments.
Nkrumah kept the British Prime Minister informed of developments during the negotiations,[13] and the Commonwealth connection was protected in the final declaration.[14]

Short of the total unification of Africa, the political and
economic value of the Commonwealth was acknowledged by
all Commonwealth African leaders, whether in terms of the
preference system, the flow of intra-Commonwealth aid or the
encouragement of foreign private investment, all of which were
considered necessary to economic development.[15]

The Commonwealth African States were determined, however, to change the traditional character and focus of the
Commonwealth by using their numerical strength to assert
African political and economic issues. Before the end of dollar
discrimination and the introduction of convertibility, African
countries were strongly influenced by the collective policies of
the Commonwealth—sterling system. Even at independence,
Ghana did not immediately suspend discrimination against
dollar products, but waited for Britain to take the lead. She also
continued to operate a limited sterling payments system until
universal convertibility was announced by Britain. Independence
was followed, however, by a slow but positive move towards
identifying African economic interests; this involved widening
the horizons of the Commonwealth system from its traditional
preoccupation with monetary affairs to include considerations
of African economic development.

At the Commonwealth Economic Conference of 1958, which
Ghana attended as a fully independent member — and with the
participation as observers by Nigeria, Sierra Leone, Tanganyika,
Uganda and Kenya — the African States welcomed the treatment of development as an autonomous issue on its own right
rather than as a subordinate aspect of monetary policy. This
was underlined in the preamble of the communiqué, which
called on the more developed members to contribute to the
rapid advancement of the less developed countries.[16]

It was against this background that the Commonwealth

system came to achieve its multi-purpose and multi-dimensional objectives in trade, monetary relations and development. Equal treatment was now accorded to these issues in the spirit of building a flexible Commonwealth which supported the economic interests of all members. The process was facilitated by the increasing movement towards multilateralism and convertibility, which the conference recommended, and which Britain promised it had already started to implement. Commonwealth preferences were to remain, and the significance of supporting the strength of sterling was reiterated, but these were now matched by the equal weight given to the trade problems of the developing members, particularly in commodities and the general flow of aid and investment.[17] Britain used the occasion to launch its new aid programme, the Commonwealth Assistance Loans, to replace the Colonial Development and Welfare aid programmes.[18]

This new Commonwealth image was remarked by *The Times* which pointed out that the new Commonwealth had shifted 'from its exclusiveness of imperial preference and the unspendable pound' to 'its new role as an international economic force',[19] a view which was shared by the African participants.

The Commonwealth–sterling area system, 1960–75

The political Commonwealth and its economic underpinnings, including its direct relationship with the sterling area, came under strain in the 1960s as different economic objectives and major political differences began to appear. The latter resulted in clear distinctions being drawn between membership of the political Commonwealth and participation in the economic programme, chiefly the preference arrangements and the sterling area. Whereas in the 1950s the Commonwealth was the political forum of the sterling area in which collective decisions were recorded, in the 1960s this role, although generally maintained, was subject to severe strain with the increased diversity of economic interests and the forced withdrawal of South Africa from the political but not from the economic Commonwealth and sterling area.

South Africa's continued participation in Commonwealth preference and the sterling area was fully supported by Britain.[20] Harold Macmillan stressed the distinction between the political Commonwealth and participation in the preference area and the sterling area. With regard to the former, he pointed out that the preferences had been established on a bilateral basis at the Ottawa Conference of 1932; as regards the sterling area he argued that there were non-Commonwealth States which were sterling area members.[21] He believed that South Africa's withdrawal should not prejudice her active participation in the preference system and the sterling area.[22]

Although in many ways not fully integrated into the sterling area, South Africa was a significant contributor to sterling's international position. She did not take part in the dollar pooling policy, but kept her own gold output and dealt direct with countries demanding dollars. She did enter into several arrangements with Britain, however, as a safeguard against draining the dollar pool. An agreement in 1946 obliged her to sell $280 million in gold to London each year and allowed her to draw freely on the dollar pool.[23] She also made a gold loan of $325 million to Britain in 1948. Throughout the 1950s South Africa continued to prop sterling. For instance, between 1950 and 1954 the dollar pool was strengthened by an agreement between South Africa and Britain under which South Africa paid for all major imports, regardless of their origin, in gold or dollars, and purchased all non-essential imports in the non-dollar area.[24]

South Africa was also an important trading partner of Britain in both imports and exports.[25] Thirty-nine per cent to 62 per cent of British exports to South Africa entered the Republic duty-free in 1961; and the average rate of duty on all United Kingdom exports to the Republic was between 8 and 14 per cent.[26]

It was not surprising, therefore, that Britain insisted on South Africa remaining a member of the sterling area and the preference area, especially as there was no pressure on her from the Commonwealth African States to choose between having the Republic in the sterling area and risking African withdrawal. South Africa was thus able to enjoy both Commonwealth preferences and membership of the sterling area, which had never been simultaneously open to any State without full membership of the Commonwealth. With the major Commonwealth African States' decision to terminate payments arrangements with South Africa and Britain's insistence on preserving her economic links, inroads were made into the cohesion and unity of the Commonwealth system.

The 1960s saw rapid changes in the Commonwealth–sterling arrangements. Britain continued to hold a substantial part of members' sterling reserves, but the nationalist desire was now strong to diversify reserves to match trade and sources of capital, as also to mobilise them for domestic development. After the devaluation of sterling in 1967 most members switched to the dollar or gold as unit of account. Sterling's unit of account role was gradually being phased out. Free convertibility between Britain and the Commonwealth—sterling area was observed only by Britain; in their efforts to conserve scarce foreign currency the Commonwealth African States introduced exchange control measures against sterling. Finally, the special monetary relations between Britain and Africa characterised by the colonial exchange standard was phased out and central banks proliferated.

However, the Commonwealth system still formed the major framework for Anglo-African economic relations. With regard to sterling it provided a forum, in its occasional meetings of Prime Ministers, Finance Ministers and Trade Ministers, to review the currency's international position. There were no more authoritative directives like those of the 1950s, members instead 'confidently look forward to a strengthening of sterling', as this would be 'to the mutual benefit of the Sterling Area as a whole'.[27] Sterling's international position was 'a consequence of certain measures taken by the United Kingdom ...'.[28] Commonwealth—sterling area members still supported sterling's position, but now it was British economic policies that mattered most, particularly as the new demands of the developing members began to be felt even at the monetary level. They manifested themselves on the question of liquidity, which, they insisted, should be expanded, as it was part-and-parcel of the development process.

Not surprisingly, after 1960 sterling's position was always discussed within the context of increased liquidity for developing countries. The 1966 and 1967 Commonwealth Finance Ministers' meetings underlined the twin problems of sterling's position and the trade and financial problems of the developing countries.[29]

When sterling was devalued in 1967 the economic conflict within the system was more clearly revealed, with the refusal of most members to devalue along with Britain. In Commonwealth Africa only Sierra Leone, the Gambia and Malawi followed suit. Sterling's role as a unit of account collapsed, and its reserve role proved difficult to sustain because of members' diversification policies and dwindling confidence in Britain's monetary policies and the pound's value. Britain had to enter into separate agreements with sterling area members when, in 1968, most of them withdrew substantial balances from London in anticipation of further devaluation.

The rapid decline in monetary co-operation partly reflected the decline in intra-Commonwealth trade during the 1960s. Whereas in the 1950s (1951–57) it was between 32 per cent and 43 per cent, in the 1960s (1961–70) it was running at between 32 and 23 per cent, and it fell to its lowest point of 19 per cent in 1973. Britain's imports from Commonwealth countries as a percentage of her world imports also declined rapidly. From 1951 to 1956 they were between 41 and 46 per cent; but they fell to between 31 and 23 per cent between 1961 and 1970, with a record low of 17 per cent in 1973. This was also the case with her exports. Her exports to the Commonwealth ranged between 41 and 46 per cent of total exports between 1951 and 1959, but from 1961 to 1970 they fell to something between 34 and 20 per cent, with a record low of 17 per cent in 1973.

This pattern was repeated for the other Commonwealth members. For Commonwealth Africa her percentage of imports from the Commonwealth was 49 and 54 per cent between 1951 and 1959; between 1961 and 1970 this fell to between 42 to 53 per cent, and reached 40 per cent in 1973. Her percentage exports to the Commonwealth also suffered the same rate of decline. From 1954 to 1959 they ranged between 60 to 44 per cent; from 1961 to 1970 they stagnated at about 46 per cent, declining to 38 per cent in 1973.

There were attempts in the 1960s by both Britain and Commonwealth Africa to improve Commonwealth trade, but for apparently different reasons. To the Labour government of 1964, after the rejection of Britain's application to join the EEC, the basis for a regeneration of British industry and solving the balance of payments lay in closer Commonwealth trade. The government put forward a plan which sought to persuade Commonwealth countries to give Britain special preferences in awarding contracts, as a consequence of which Britain would apply to take part in Commonwealth development. In Africa the Commonwealth was increasingly seen as an association which would help to reduce the harmful effects of the worsening terms of trade for primary products, and during the 1960s Ghana and Nigeria tried to commit the organisation to this objective, particularly for cocoa.

These two policies were discussed in the Commonwealth

Trade Ministers' meeting of June 1966 which was specially convened by the Commonwealth Prime Ministers' Conference of 1965 'to explore means by which Commonwealth trade might be encouraged and expanded'.[30]

The conference failed to satisfy the aspirations of either party, although it came close to drawing up a charter for economic co-operation between developed and developing countries, with particular reference to the problems of the latter. With regard to the British plan, members agreed only 'to consider the extent to which their governments in their public purchases might place orders in other Commonwealth countries where commercial and other considerations made this practicable'.[31] The Commonwealth African States were unfortunate in that the 1965 Commonwealth Prime Ministers' Conference had ruled out the possibility of a Commonwealth solution to commodity problems in general and cocoa[32] in particular, much to the disillusionment of Nkrumah. The Trade Ministers merely confirmed this decision. Instead of the positive policy sought by Commonwealth Africa, it was agreed only 'that there should be continued Commonwealth support for the United Nations Cocoa Conference'.[33]

Members had by now recognised that the Commonwealth was a sub-system of the wider international economic framework and that little could be achieved by trying to solve economic problems that cut across Commonwealth connections.

The Commonwealth and development

It was in the field of development that the Commonwealth experienced its greatest positive transformation. Between 1958 and 1975 the organisation increasingly addressed itself to development issues as the North—South conflict deepened and the socio-political balance of its membership shifted in favour of the developing countries. The Commonwealth's support of development started at the bilateral level, with no central co-ordinating body, with the association providing only a forum for discussing the issues.

Britain paved the way for increased intra-Commonwealth development co-operation by launching the Commonwealth Assistance Loans Scheme during the 1958 Commonwealth Economic Conference at Montreal. Canada also announced an aid programme for Africa, the Commonwealth African Technical Aid Scheme.[34] These two plans were bilateral in nature; there was no central Commonwealth co-ordinating authority.

At the Prime Ministers' Conference of 1960 Nkrumah urged the developed Commonwealth countries to increase their flow of aid to Africa in order to strengthen relations with Western countries. This led to the unanimous recognition that an aid programme, similar to the Colombo Plan in Asia, should be drawn up for Commonwealth Africa. The result was the establishment of the first broadly based plan of Commonwealth development in Africa — the special Commonwealth African Assistance Plan. The aim was to focus attention on the existing bilateral aid efforts of member States rather than to create a multilateral aid fund. Britain, Canada, Australia and New Zealand, often supported by India and Pakistan, were the main contributors.

The Commonwealth's role in development was greatly improved when the Secretariat was established in 1965. Although member governments were cautious in their endorsement of a development role for it, by 1966 the Secretary General, Arnold Smith, had been able to persuade member governments that a firmer commitment to development was needed if the Commonwealth was to have any success in promoting development. This was endorsed by the Prime Ministers' Conference of 1966.[35]

A modest but significant step was taken in 1967 with the decision to initiate a programme of technical assistance co-operation, financed by Britain, Canada and New Zealand and co-ordinated by the Secretariat. It facilitated the meeting of technical assistance needs on a 'third country' basis, financed under bilateral programmes through arrangements made by the Secretariat.[36]

Experience with this limited programme demonstrated the need to expand the Secretariat's role, broaden its scope and increase its administrative commitments and responsibilities. This led to the Commonwealth's first institutionalised multilateral fund controlled by the Secretariat and subscribed to, on a voluntary basis, by all members: the Commonwealth Fund for Technical Co-operation (CFTC), endorsed by heads of governments at the stormy Singapore conference in January 1971.

All Commonwealth governments make annual contributions to the fund. Canada, Britain, Australia and Nigeria provide a quarter of its resources.[37]

The CFTC was organised into three programme divisions — General Technical Assistance (GTA), Education and Training, and Export-market Development — a small headquarters Technical Assistance Group (TAG) and a division responsible for finance and personnel services. The rationale of the CFTC was to provide technical assistance to developing member governments on a mutual basis, i.e. bringing recipients and donors together to participate *as* both donors and recipients rather than keeping them apart in line with standard international and previous Commonwealth programmes.[38]

GTA provided from within the Commonwealth countries the technical expertise requested by the developing members, either in an advisory capacity or on an operational level, to fill posts for which qualified nationals were not yet available. GTA accounted for about 60 per cent of total CFTC expenditure, with an estimated three hundred experts in the field by 1977 covering various professional and technical fields.[39]

By the end of that year twenty-four developed or developing countries had participated in GTA as donors, with the developing countries accounting for about 45 per cent of the experts in the field.[40] The largest contributors were Britain, India, New Zealand, Canada, Sri Lanka, Ghana, Australia and Bangladesh, in that order. These eight countries accounted for more than 90 per cent of GTA experts in man-months in the field. The problems encountered by the developing members outside the Indian subcontinent in releasing badly needed technical experts to serve in other developing countries is well known and has been recognised by the CFTC.[41] However, twenty developing countries were able to participate in the scheme between 1972 and 1977 despite the fact that 80 per cent came from India, Sri Lanka and Bangladesh. In Commonwealth Africa seven countries — Ghana, Sierra Leone, Uganda, Nigeria, Kenya, Malawi and Lesotho — managed to release experts for GTA work, mainly in medicine, education, transport and communications, insurance and banking, legal professions, tourism, agriculture, economic planning and public administration.[42]

As recipients of GTA experts, however, Commonwealth African States accounted for 37 per cent of the total, with experts coming mainly from Britain, India, Sri Lanka, Australia, Canada, New Zealand and Jamaica.

The Education and Training programme, which began in 1972, accounted for 24 per cent of the expenditure of the CFTC. It was run by and for the developing countries. It supported the training of personnel from developing Commonwealth countries almost exclusively in other Commonwealth developing countries, and generally in the same region. This helped to keep costs down and it enabled the trainees to be trained in conditions similar to those in their own countries.[43]

Table 4.1 Commonwealth Fund for Technical Co-operation: nationality of expert or consultant, general technical assistance (man/months)

Field of assistance	Botswana	Lesotho	Swaziland	Malawi	Zambia	Kenya	Uganda	Tanzania	Nigeria	Ghana	Sierra Leone	Gambia
Medical				12.0		12.0			24.0	36.0		12.0
Education							0.5			4.0		30.0
Transport and telecommunications												
Insurance and banking										18.0		12.0
Legal										27.0		
Public administration										26.0		
Feasibility studies						0.8				33.8		
Accounting	0.8											
Agricultural and rural development								1.0				
Resources												
Environment												
Industries						N.A.						
Tourism												
Economic policy												
Economic planning							24.0					
Statistics	0.3											
Fiscal and taxation												
Others							24.0		0.8	0.8		
Total	1			12		13	50		25	146		54

Table 4.2 Commonwealth Fund for Technical Co-operation: education and training, by country of training, African group (man/months)

Trainee's country/organisation	Where trained												Total	% of grand total
	Botswana	Gambia	Ghana	Kenya	Lesotho	Malawi	Nigeria	Sierra Leone	Swaziland	Tanzania	Uganda	Zambia		
1. Botswana				164.0		5.0	84.0					72.0	320	79
2. The Gambia			174.5	1.3		0.5	844.5	414.5	3.0	0.3		1.3	1444	99
3. Ghana				14.5			33.3		12.0		1.0	1.0	62	56
4. Kenya	1.5		2.0	201.0		0.5	13.8	0.3	21.0			1.8	280	90
5. Lesatho			24.0				84.0		3.0	96.0	144.0	181.0	497	90
6. Malawi				226.3					45.0	48.0			319	83
7. Nigeria				2.0					15.0	24.0			41	93
8. Sierra Leone		0.8	38.8	5.5			52.5		3.0			13.0	114	49
9. Swaziland	20.0			0.5					18.0	342.0			381	100
10. Tanzania			12.0	121.0			5.0						144	26
11. Uganda			1.4	231.0			6.9						239	83
12. Zambia			36.0	237.3					36.0		288.0		597	89
13. HAC			0.3				0.3				6.0		7	100
14. FABC			4.0										4	100
15. RHB														
16. UBLS	N.A.		0.8				0.8				0.8		2	100
17. WABC													3	100
18. WABS											3.0			
19. Total	22.0	1.0	294.0	1204		6.0	1125	415	162	510	443	273	4454	
20. % of grand total	100	100	99	98		100	100	100	91	99	88	100		

During the 1976–77 financial year the programme supported 582 projects connected with education and training.[44] Commonwealth African States participated significantly. All were donors and recipients, except Lesotho, which sent trainees to other developing countries but did not receive any for training itself. Kenya, Nigeria, Tanzania, Uganda and Sierra Leone were the largest contributors in Commonwealth Africa. The largest number of trainees in Commonwealth Africa came from the Gambia, Zambia, Lesotho, Swaziland, Botswana and Malawi.[45]

The third CFTC programme, export market development, was the most specialised and accounted for 17 per cent of the fund's expenditure. It arranged programmes commonly known as 'Buyer and seller meet':[46] an export promotion device which enabled potential buyers to meet the sellers. It was of particular interest to countries with diversified product markets.[47]

The CFTC was gradually establishing itself as a centre for Commonwealth development when, in 1973, the oil crisis, and OPEC's huge success in altering the terms of trade, demonstrated to the developing countries that development could be achieved only by a fundamental restructuring of the international economic system. This demand for a New International Economic Order (NIEO) was first expressed at the sixth Special Session of the United Nations in 1974. Its significance as a new development lay in the qualitative change of emphasis from the piecemeal and reformist approach of the 1960s to a comprehensive and radical one which placed international questions of trade, aid, investment and monetary relations within the Third World perspective of 'real' and sustained economic development.

These international developments naturally had an impact on the Commonwealth with its membership of more than thirty developing countries. Not surprisingly it was the developing States that introduced NIEO issues into Commonwealth discussions, the Kingston conference of heads of state in 1975. The developing members saw their role, 'without apology', as representing the interests of all developing countries, Commonwealth and non-Commonwealth. To them it was an extension of the diplomacy of the 'Group of 77' in the negotiations for new and just rules of international exchange in goods and services, although they believed that much understanding and co-operation could be achieved in the Commonwealth, which was relatively insulated from the tendentious arena of the United Nations.

Britain's Premier, Harold Wilson, as recognised leader of the developed Commonwealth,[48] accepted the moral and political need to restructure the international economy[49] while disagreeing fundamentally with the policy commitments of the developing members as articulated by Burnham, Gowon and Manley. To Wilson, the NIEO had to take place in a growth-oriented international trading system.[50] He believed that without an emphasis on growth 'joint efforts to bring order into trade in commodities will be frustrated'.[51] He was sceptical, therefore, of the comprehensive plan[52] for commodities supported by all developing members, and of indexation,[53] a technical pricing system intended to relate the prices of primary commodities to the rate of increase or decrease in prices of manufactured products. Wilson introduced instead a six-point plan which, he believed, would promote economic interdependence.[54]

Although the developing Commonwealth countries welcomed the commitment to change in the direction of the NIEO, they found his practical proposals too deeply embedded in the reformist policies of the 1950s and 1960s. L. F. S. Burnham, in a separate plan, stressed the need for global considerations rather than individual national approaches. He criticised Wilson's growth philosophy, which, he said, would not automatically provide the jobs and opportunities for human development which the developing countries needed. To him there could be no 'talk about commodities without talking about the transfer of real resources'.[55] He maintained that the comprehensive approach to commodities and indexation[56] should form the framework for any discussion of a radical shift of resources from the wealthy nations to the poor.[57] On these issues he won the support of all the developing member countries.

What was actually at issue in the conflict between the British plan and the objectives of the developing countries was the conflict between international economic planning and the free interplay of market forces, and the differences over whether the new order should be based exclusively on the demands of the developing members or whether equal treatment should be given to the interests of the developed countries. These differences were temporarily resolved by the conference's recognition of 'the need to take immediate steps towards the creation of a rational and equitable new international economic order', and by the decision to accept Burnham's suggestion that a small group of experts from Commonwealth countries should be invited to draw up a programme aimed at closing the gap between the rich and poor countries.

The first report[58] of the Ten Wise Men, as they came to be known, was considered by Commonwealth Finance Ministers on the eve of the seventh Special Session of the United Nations. The UN gave general endorsement to this interim report and resolved that it should be a Commonwealth contribution to the work of the UN seventh Special Session.

During the UNCTAD meeting in Nairobi in May 1976 Commonwealth members held meetings of their own, but although Britain had supported the Commonwealth reports her representatives lined themselves up with the hawks of the old order — Japan, West Germany and the United States — in resisting one of the major proposals for a conference to discuss the setting up of a common fund for commodities.

Conclusion

The Commonwealth's role in development is doubly constrained in its operations. There is the first level of bilateral economic relations among Commonwealth countries where the Secretariat's role is restricted to consultation rather than changing the quantity, direction and politics of aid that developed members give to the developing members. There is also the second level of multilateral aid where the Secretariat is vested with tremendous influence in executing the development programmes, mainly through the CFTC. The Secretariat has been able to develop a constructive role for itself at this level. Its expansion depends, however, on the amount of money member governments are prepared to contribute to the fund. Most of the resource-flows between developed and developing members occur at government-to-government level and still by-pass the Secretariat.

Notes

1 Harold Macmillan, *Mr. Macmillan and Africa* (Conservative Political Centre), 1960, p. 11.
2 Afro-Asian Conference communiqué, in George McTurnan Kalin, *The Afro-Asian Conference*, 1956.
3 *Ghana Today* supplement, 5 June 1963, p. 3.
4 *Ibid.*, p. 5.
5 Nigeria, H/R Debates, 31 August 1961, p. 234.
6 J. K. Nyerere, 'A United States of Africa', *Journal of Modern African Studies*, 1.1, 1963, pp. 4–6.
7 Chimelu Chibe, *Integration and Politics among African States* (Uppsala), 1977, p. 364.

8 J. K. Nyerere, 'For Commonwealth and/or African Unity', *Common-wealth Journal of the Royal Commonwealth Society*, November/December 1961, Vol. IV, No. 6, p. 254.

9 Tom Mboya, 'Pan-Africanism and the Commonwealth: are they all in conflict? in Ali Mazrui's *The Anglo-African Commonwealth: Political Friction and Cultural Fusion*, 1967, p. 148, Appendix IV.

10 *Ibid.*, p. 152.

11 *Ibid.*, p. 253, and Nyerere, 'For Commonwealth and/or African Unity', *op. cit.*, p. 254.

12 Balewa, *Mr. Prime Minister, op. cit.*, pp. 84–5.

13 H.C. Debates, 27 November 1958.

14 Ghana Debates, 12 December 1958, col. 389.

15 Mboya, *op. cit.*, pp. 148–9; Balewa, *Nigeria, the Commonwealth and Africa, op. cit.*, pp. 84–5; Nyerere, 'For Commonwealth and/or African Unity', *op. cit.*, p. 253.

16 Cmnd 539, 1958.

17 *Ibid.*

18 *The Montreal Conference*, 1958, p. 10.

19 *The Times*, September 1958, in *The Montreal Conference, op. cit.*, p. 17.

20 H.C. Debates, 22 March 1961, Vol. 637, col. 447.

21 *Ibid.*, col. 477.

22 *Ibid.*, col. 477.

23 In both these years, however, South Africa ended up drawing more than the $280 million (Bell, *The Sterling Area in the Post-war World, op. cit.*, p. 60.).

24 *Ibid.*, p. 61.

25 About 30 per cent of South Africa's imports came from Britan and she exported 30 per cent of her goods to Britain.

26 R. W. Green, 'Commonwealth Preference: Tariff Duties and Prefer-ences on UK Exports to the Preferences Area', *Board of Trade Journal*, 11 June 1964, Table 1.

27 Commonwealth Finance Ministers' Meeting, Final Communiqué, 21–22 September 1966.

28 Commonwealth Economic Consultative Council, Final Communiqué, 22–23 September 1965.

29 Commonwealth Finance Minsters' Meeting, Final Communiqué, September 1966 and September 1967.

30 Meeting of Commonwealth Trade Ministers, Final Communiqué, 1966, *op. cit.*

31 *Ibid.*

32 Commonwealth Prime Ministers' Conference, 1965, Final Communiqué.

33 Trade Ministers' Conference, 1966, *op. cit.*

34 Commonwealth Economic Conference, 1958, Final Communiqué.

35 Commonwealth Prime Ministers' Meeting, 1966, *op. cit.*, p. 427.

36 Commonwealth Prime Ministers' Conference, 1969, Final Communiqué.

37   Commonwealth Fund for Technical Co-operation, *Commonwealth Skills for Commonwealth Needs*, p. 2.
38   *Ibid.*, p. 1.
39   Anthony Tasker (Managing Director of CFTC), *The Commonwealth Fund for Technical Co-operation*, 1977, p. 6.
40   Commonwealth Fund For Technical Co-operation, *Commonwealth Skills and Commonwealth Needs, op. cit.*, p. 2.
41   *Ibid.*
42   Table 4.1.
43   Tasker, *op. cit.*, p. 8.
44   *Ibid.*, pp. 8—9.
45   CFTC Statistics, Table 4.2.
46   Tasker, *op. cit.*, p. 12.
47   *Ibid.*, p. 13.
48   Derek Ingram, *The Imperfect Commonwealth*, 1977, p. 96.
49   Cmnd 6061, p. 1.
50   *Ibid.*, p. 1.
51   *Ibid.*, p. 3.
52   *Ibid.*, pp. 3—4.
53   *Ibid.*, pp. 3—4.
54   *Ibid.*, p. 5.
55   L. F. S. Burnham, Agenda Item 4. *World Trade and Commonwealth Trade*, p. 6.
56   *Ibid.*, p. 15.
57   *Ibid.*, p. 10.
58   *Towards a New International Economic Order: Interim Report by a Commonwealth Experts Group* (Commonwealth Secretariat).

5

Monetary relations, 1957—72

Ghana's independence in 1957 was followed closely by the formal declaration of sterling convertibility in 1958 and the end of dollar discrimination in 1959. The combined effect of these developments on the sterling area and on Anglo-Commonwealth African economic relations was overwhelming. It had always been the aim of British policy to reinstate sterling as a full international currency, respecting the rules of convertibility and multilateralism. Indeed, looking back, many politicians, financial experts and government officials believed that a floating exchange rate would have provided a quicker and easier solution to the pound's problems and would have saved the country from 'some of the indignities and uncertainties of stop—go economics'.[1]

The Chancellor of the Exchequer, R. A. Butler, actually wished 'to make the pound convertible at a floating exchange rate'[2] in 1952. Under the scheme he had in mind, most of the sterling balances would have been frozen. In the event the scheme was vetoed by the Prime Minister, Winston Churchill.[3] The collapse of this plan meant that Britain had to accept the fixed exchange rate regime, with a higher reserve ceiling than would otherwise have been necessary. This called for closer co-operation with Commonwealth—sterling countries.

By a combination of measures adopted by Commonwealth—sterling area members aimed at conserving sterling reserves, and by the systematic application of broadly deflationary fiscal and monetary policies in Britain in the 1950s, sterling's international position greatly improved. Gradually, but consistently, trade relaxation and modest convertibility were attempted. In May 1953 the West European countries concluded an arbitrage agreement which facilitated the free transfer of sterling held outside the sterling area without the usual governmental control;

in March 1954 a uniform payments sytem was introduced for non-resident sterling which removed British exchange control from non-residents using sterling for transaction purposes. Further steps were taken in 1955, when Britain started to support the market for security sterling by equalising the exchange rate between security sterling and transferable sterling.[4]

Full convertibility was finally established on 27 December 1958 and dollar discrimination was greatly relaxed in May 1959. The bestowal of formal convertibility on all current account sterling held by non-sterling residents transformed the entire international payments system. This chapter examines the effect of convertibility, the end of dollar discrimination and African independence on Anglo-Commonwealth African monetary relations.

The background to monetary independence, 1957–61

The Radcliffe Report on the working of the monetary system was produced immediately after the government's announcement of convertibility in 1958. It reiterated Britain's policy of maintaining sterling as an international currency and the sterling area payments arrangements that were necessary for the success of this policy.[5] Although dollar discrimination had ended, Britain still needed the co-operation of the sterling area countries, particularly in the crucial area of reserve holdings. From 1957 to 1961 African countries still supported the sterling area, and refused to introduce radical policies through concern for the stability of their new currencies and the implications for foreign investment.

The key questions for the African countries were whether they would continue to peg their currencies to the pound, use sterling for transactions purposes and continue to hold their reserves in sterling; and whether, even if they decided to remain in the sterling area, they would break free of the colonial sterling exchange standard by reducing the sterling reserve backing to their currencies. For Ghana and Nigeria these questions were resolved within the central bank framework, for Zambia and Malawi through the framework of the Federal Reserve Bank of Rhodesia and Nyasaland, and for the rest of the African countries through the currency board system.

Ghana

When Nkrumah's administration achieved independence on 6 March 1957 his government was still committed to the pursuit of the sterling area's objectives. During the debate in parliament on the Bank of Ghana Ordinance, Gbedemah, the Finance Minister, defended this position on practical and economic grounds, as Britain was still Ghana's main trading partner.[6] The country's relationship with sterling was clarified by Nkrumah in a major policy statement on the eve of independence.[7] He was no longer prepared to accept a static relationship with Britain, despite Ghana's continued membership of the sterling area. He demanded an agreement to guarantee the price of cocoa in the world market as compensation for her contribution to the dollar pool.[8]

Given Nkrumah's new policy of pursuing economic as well as political independence, this seems contradictory. If the proposal had been accepted it would have delayed Ghana's monetary independence, because 'the management of the Ghanaian economy' which 'produced the gold and dollar earnings for the Sterling Area' was deeply rooted in the colonial sterling exchange standard, colonial fiscal and commercial policies and the investment of the marketing board reserves in British securities. It is difficult to see how such a policy could have been reconciled with Ghana's new international image and her desire to follow an independent path of development.

Furthermore his insurance proposal was conceived on the mistaken assumption that dollar discrimination would continue and that it could be used as a lever against the real beneficiaries of the system. Sterling, as we have seen, was made convertible in 1958 and dollar discrimination ended in 1959. Thus although Ghana's co-operation was still needed, the immense problems of the 1950s had eased, mainly because of the area's improved balance of payments. It therefore reduced the urgency of the situation and made acceptance of Ghana's demands unlikely.

In the meantime Ghana was to remain in the sterling area and pursue a cautious monetary policy as a short-term means to her long-term end of monetary independence. The important factor was surely the sterling balances, which were over £200 million. In November 1957, in anticipation of the second Five Year Plan of 1959, Gbedemah stated that Ghana would use some of her sterling balances to speed up development, although the government would prefer to hold them in reserve and raise capital from Britain and the West.

With the failure to raise this capital, and the fall in the price of cocoa, Ghana was forced to turn to the reserves. But they were still widely distributed among different British securities with varying dates of maturity. They were hardly related to the government's liquidity requirements, which depended upon the seasonal fluctuation of the chief export commodities. In January 1958 Gbedemah stated that new advisory panels would be set up with the co-operation of United Kingdom financial institutions to control the future investment of all existing government funds.[9] He stressed that the maturity dates of the reserves held on government account should be synchronised with the capital expenditure estimates under the new Five Year plan, while those of the Cocoa Marketing Board should, as far as possible, be linked to the incidence of seasonal deficits.

The new government also expressed a desire to diversify its sterling reserves because of its policy of establishing new trade and aid relationships. For instance, in August 1958 the government initiated a policy of buying gold from the mining companies operating in Ghana as part of the policy of strengthening the currency and building up separate non-sterling reserves.[10]

During the first few years of independence, however, Ghana moved cautiously in reappraising its sterling connection. Modifications, the authorities thought, were necessary, but not a radical disengagement. The government was convinced that the changes it wanted could be achieved within the sterling system. In fact the link with sterling was so strong that the government opened the first overseas branch of the Ghana Commercial Bank at Cheapside in London to take care of the London reserves of Ghanaian organisations.

Nigeria

A central bank had been established in 1958, before political independence, and like Ghana Nigeria decided to work within the sterling system for a while. Her sterling balances stood at £216 million in 1959. The Finance Minister, Eboh, restated Nigeria's continued sterling commitment in February 1959.[11] However, Nigeria was also committed to the development of a truly independent money and capital market. There were arrangements in May 1959 to float an internal loan on behalf of the government.[12] Treasury bills were also introduced on 9 February 1959 to reduce dependence on the London market.[13] The government also hinted that banks, commercial organisations and statutory corporations should be prepared to repatriate their sterling funds when the facilities were available.

These policies marked the beginning of Nigeria's mobilisation of its sterling balances. Even at this early stage large sums of money were brought back from Britain for investment in the internal loan programme. It was the federal government's intention to mobilise £19 million or more towards financing its development plan by a series of loans. The first, of £19 million, was raised in 1959 and the second, of £10 million, in 1960. These were subscribed to by the marketing boards, commercial banks, post office savings bank, insurance companies, co-operative societies and the central bank.[14]

As a further stimulus towards indigenous money markets the government offered private and public corporations favourable treatment under the income tax laws if one-third of the income of their funds was derived from Nigerian securities by 1 April 1963.[15] No new pension or provident fund was to be approved for tax exemption unless a minimum of half their investment income was derived from Nigerian securities.[16]

These measures contributed to a decline in the sterling balances, from £216.5 million in 1959 to £147.5 million in 1961.[17] For the period between 1957 and 1961, however, Nigeria operated cautiously within the sterling area. Her reserves were spread over a wide field of gilt-edge securities issued by the British government and local authorities.[18] The Exchange Control Bill of 31 August 1961 specified that payments to non-sterling countries required prior exchange control permission, whereas the freedom to transfer funds to and from the sterling area was protected as in the past.[19]

Zambia and Malawi

Like Nigeria and Ghana, Northern Rhodesia and Nyasaland pursued diversification within the sterling area even before they achieved independence as Zambia and Malawi, through the Reserve Bank of Rhodesia and Nyasaland. The bank was established in 1956, and it took over the assets of the Central African Currency Board. When Northern Rhodesia and Nyasaland began to press for independence the sterling area was not a major issue. Their major concern was to establish individual central banks within the Commonwealth and sterling area.

For the period 1957—64, however, Zambia and Malawi had a common monetary system with Rhodesia. This created fewer problems for Britain than had arisen in West African decolonisation, because of the special relationship with the settler community which actually controlled the financial affairs of the federation. The Reserve Bank was instrumental in the expansion of local money markets.[20] The federation, under Rhodesian leadership, accepted membership of the sterling area.[21] Moreover, since the Rhodesian pound was fixed at par with the pound sterling, it was clear that any change in the external value of sterling would immediately raise difficult policy questions for the federation.

Sierra Leone, Gambia, Kenya, Uganda and Tanzania

In these countries no fundamental change occurred in monetary relations with Britain. They were still dependent countries working within the established currency boards. The only area of development was in the fiduciary issue, which had been made flexible since 1954, as the British government had allowed the colonies to invest part of the funds of their currencies in locally issued securities.[22] The West African Currency Board was now responsible only for Sierra Leone and Gambia. Sierra Leone obtained a fiduciary issue from the board which held £2 million of long-term local stocks.[23]

In East Africa the East African Currency Board continued to take an active part in the economic affairs of the three countries. The fiduciary issue was increased to £20 million in December 1957, and the EACB was authorised to acquire local Treasury bills to provide the three governments with short-term finance.[24] By 1960 the administration and method of working had greatly changed. The board was transferred from London to Nairobi, and started to provide seasonal finance for export crops, and to act as a banker of last resort to the commercial banks; the fiduciary issue was also increased to £EA24 million.[25]

With no basic changes in the political situation, and the currency boards still in operation, the connection with sterling was much stronger than in the central bank countries. True, there were already signs of reserve mobilisation in the issuing of Treasury bills, and the creation of fiduciary issue, but in the main their reserves were still vested in British securities, and they respected all the pound sterling's international roles.

The politics of reserve mobilisation: disengagement and monetary diversification, 1961–66

This period witnessed many changes in Anglo-Commonwealth African monetary relations. Most of Commonwealth Africa was now independent, and the flexibility of the sterling area system after convertibility was beginning to put the pound under strain as members ran down or diversified their reserves. Britain attempted to shore the currency up with a combination of economic policies aimed at curbing excess home demand, keeping down the rate of inflation and improving the balance of payments.

Commonwealth Africa's sterling reserves dwindled rapidly, mainly on account of the need to mobilise the balances for economic development, disengage from the dependent sterling system by building up local money and capital markets, and diversify into other currencies for commercial and investment purposes. Sterling reserves also declined because of the fall in commodity prices in the 1960s. Ghana and Nigeria became important holders in the 1950s because of the boom in the price of cocoa. Between 1955 and 1962 alone the price index for commodity products had fallen by 10 per cent.[26] Cocoa prices slumped to an all-time low of Nc 276–280 per ton in 1965 as compared with Nc 704–708 per ton in 1958.[27]

Faced on the one hand with this downward trend in commodity prices and on the other with a shortage of external capital, the Commonwealth African States took steps which inevitably affected the pound sterling: they mobilised their reserves and disengaged from sterling, setting up their own monetary institutions and diversifying into other currencies. As a result the net sterling balances declined from a record high of £755 million in 1954 to £254 million in 1966.[28] The reserves of Ghana and Nigeria declined more rapidly, leaving Zambia with a net £80 million of sterling reserves as the leading sterling holder in Commonwealth Africa. Some form of stability was provided by the delayed dissolution of the Central African Federation and by the delay in forming central banks in East Africa.

At the institutional level, the establishment of central banks had been firmly accepted by all Commonwealth African countries. Ghana and Nigeria radicalised their monetary relations after 1961–62; Sierra Leone established a central bank in 1964 and ran down her reserves through budgetary deficits; Zambia

Table 5.1   United Kingdom liabilities in sterling (£ million)

End of period	Total overseas sterling countries	East, Central and West Africa	Australia, New Zealand and South Africa	India, Pakistan and Ceylon	Carribbean	Far East
1945	2,327	204	294	1,352	53	142
1946	2,300	215	247	1,305	56	191
1947	2,192	249	228	1,208	52	196
1948	2,108	307	356	939	54	192
1949	2,111	336	463	774	55	195
1950	2,497	426	640	787	64	279
1951	2,585	531	548	782	64	391
1952	2,482	593	429	648	72	423
1953	2,715	658	537	644	86	432
1954	2,822	755	485	652	101	420
1955	2,764	743	313	704	97	459
1956	2,730	720	371	541	111	490
1957	2,608	671	447	354	124	470
1958	2,519	652	383	228	125	507
1959	2,704	630	471	255	113	592
1960	2,478	529	285	198	116	678
1961	2,631	464	450	180	126	701
1962	2,675	427	452	138	148	749
1963		397	654	212	189	662
1964		451	748	192	208	673
1965		425	538	191	213	731
1966		404	482	141	227	770
1967		341	460	115	236	707
1968		364	447	198	278	714
1969		441	381	274	243	854
1970 (June)		504	146	281	274	925

Source. Bank of England *Economic Quarterly* and Bank of England *Quarterly Bulletin*, various years.

and Malawi established central banks after the collapse of the Federation; and the East African countries, Tanzania, Kenya and Uganda, established separate central banks in 1966 after the failure of the federation plans. Everywhere the tendency was to break out of the dependent sterling system through the creation of central banks and the pursuit of independent monetary policies.

Radical action in Ghana and Nigeria

These countries were the most important sterling holders in Commonwealth Africa in the 1950s. As we have seen, both started gradual disengagement between 1957 and 1961. However, they pursued different policies, largely reflecting their different approaches to development. Ghana was sceptical about the role of private enterprise, and although modest beginnings were made in the establishment of a money market through the issue of Treasury bills there was hardly any sustained plan to replace her sterling connections with indigenous private financial institutions which would control her sterling reserves. Her reserves were depleted by the more direct policy of converting them to immediate capital goods for development.

Nigeria believed firmly in private enterprise and the need to substitute national for foreign control over it. She made great efforts to develop indigenous financial institutions, which led to substantial drawing on her sterling reserves, apart from the normal policy of converting reserves into capital imports.

Ghana started to disengage from sterling in 1961. On 5 July the direct connection with the London money market was terminated by the introduction of exchange control regulations. Before July the level of interest rates in Britain had a direct bearing on interest rates in Ghana. This was no longer possible, as exchange control approval could be withheld if it was 'in the national interest to require investment in Ghana'.[29] The policy was partly political, as it was in keeping with Ghana's status as a Republic'.[30]

Thus one of the strongholds of the sterling system — the freedom to transfer funds without control — had been abandoned. From now on all countries were to be treated equally in foreign exchange matters. The 1961 Bill also gave the government 'the powers to mobilise when necessary the foreign currencies held by Ghana residents, whatever nationality they were'.[31] Implicit in this was the end of the extra-territorial character of the expatriate banks and other commercial institutions which had traditionally held separate sterling reserves.

These measures coincided with the beginning of radical politics. Nkrumah had judged the economic system of the 1950s inadequate for Ghana's economic development. In the Seven Year Plan of 1964 he attempted to make planning and socialism the framework of Ghana's development. The aim of mobilising external funds was not achieved: the domestic resources to finance expenditure of £104 million fell far short of that figure, and the price of cocoa continued to fall. The government had to finance the greater part of its external development plan from its own resources. This was made possible by deficit financing, i.e. borrowing from the Bank of Ghana, by the issue of Treasury bills and sales of government stocks, by loans from the IMF, and finally by drawing directly on Ghana's reserves.[32] But each of these methods naturally represented a call on the reserves. Furthermore the Bank of Ghana Ordinance (1957) was amended to give the central bank powers to extend long-term credits to the government.[33]

It was these measures that led to the sharp decline in Ghana's sterling reserves, which in turn precipitated a crisis of confidence over the government's financial policies. Nkrumah was quick to point out the distinction between colonial Ghana's accumulated reserves and independent Ghana's marginal reserves: in the latter case the reserves had been used to promote social services and welfare schemes.[34] Nevertheless it was clear that the payments was precarious. On 14 March 1963 the administration of exchange control was removed from the Bank of Ghana and transferred to the Ministry of Finance and Trade. An Exchange and Control Committee was appointed to deal with all policy matters in connection with exchange control.

As the situation deteriorated more emphasis was placed on trade with the centrally planned countries of Eastern Europe which did not require foreign exchange.[35] In the 1960s Ghana was forced to disengage from many aspects of the sterling system because of her foreign exchange crisis. On 8 March 1965 the government introduced a new currency which did not use sterling as a unit of account for its external value. It was decided instead to base the currency on a parity of 1.03678 grams of fine gold.[50] The independence of the currency was demonstrated in February 1967 when the cedi was devalued by 30 per cent, some nine months before the sterling devaluation of November 1967.

Nigeria. As we have seen, Nigeria placed far more emphasis on the development of a local money and capital market than Ghana, thus weakening both the close financial links with British money and capital markets and the reserve role of sterling in Nigeria. This remarkable activity in developing a local money market was not confined to the sale and purchase of government securities. In April 1959, for instance, the Nigerian Cement Company had pioneered private-sector interest in a money market by offering the public 174,898 £1 ordinary shares. The shares were quickly oversubscribed by more than £30,000 — a large percentage going to indigenous institutions and private individuals. This led to the opening of a local stock exchange.[36]

It was in 1962, however, with the introduction of the new development plan for 1962–68, that fundamental changes were made in monetary relations with Britain. That year Nigeria announced major policies to promote the new development plan. By this time the central bank had completely taken over the responsibilities of banker to the government and an effective working relationship had been established with the commercial banks. Significant steps were taken also in the creation and strengthening of the money and capital markets for the issue of Treasury bills and federal government stocks and the Lagos stock exchange.[37]

This policy had two major effects on the government's sterling area membership. Firstly, it enabled the central bank to provide the seasonal expansion of credit required by redistributing bills of exchange held by the commercial banks and marketing boards. The federal government envisaged that indigenisation of the credit base would make Nigeria independent of the London money market, with substantial savings in foreign exchange.[38] Secondly, it provided the government with a sound argument for deploying sterling from Britain to reinforce the investment base that was being developed locally. The government maintained that it would consider investing its own reserves in Britian only if they were not required for immediate use in Nigeria; and such investments, including those of public corporations, commercial banks and other commercial concerns, should be centralised and managed by the central bank. To this effect, the statutory corporations, companies and marketing boards were advised to ensure that, apart from minimum working balances required to finance day-to-day commitments overseas, all their surplus funds should be repatriated.[39] Nigeria was determined to have her own local financial market to promote economic development. The change was followed moreover by the decision to hold 10 per cent of the country's reserves in gold and 10 per cent in US dollar securities.[40]

All these policies led to a dwindling of its sterling balances. Whereas in 1959 Nigeria had a total of £222.98 million reserves, in 1962 when the measures were announced they had gone down to £142.93 million (part of the decline was also due to direct conversion of reserves into capital imports), and by 1966 she had only £84.45 million.

It was also decided to end lesser impediments to a fully manoeuvrable monetary policy: the minimum level of foreign exchange reserves was tied to the nation's import bill of four months; the fiduciary issue was extended to 40 per cent; the unit of account function of sterling as the external value of the currency was terminated, and the Nigerian pound became tied to 2.58828 grams of fine gold. It was hoped that this last would indicate what adjustments should be made from time to time in the official exchange rate between the Nigerian pound and other currencies.[41]

Sierra Leone and the Gambia

When Ghana and Nigeria established central banks the West African Currency Board continued to operate in the remaining colonies of Sierra Leone and Gambia. By 1961, however, Sierra Leone was about to achieve independence and faced the choice of whether to remain in the WACB or to issue a separate currency and establish a central bank of her own. The precedent had already been set in Ghana and Nigeria, so it seemed that the establishment of a central bank was only a question of time.

J. B. Loynes was given the task of examining the problems of the future currencies of the two countries.[42] In this case, as in his earlier report on Nigeria, he commended the virtues of the WACB and the traditional link with sterling. On Sierra Leone, Loynes advised that in view of its economic growth and status as an independent country it should have its own distinct currency under its own authority and responsibility. He advised against the establishment of a central bank, preferring instead what he called a 'monetary authority' or 'monetary institute' which, he said, should be a forerunner to any future decision to set up a central bank; 'the country's banking system, reinforced by the London connection, already provides an adequate and efficient service to the government and the public'.[43]

On the Gambia, Loynes maintained that, with the termination of the WACB in Sierra Leone, the Gambia should be given a special currency and board in Bathurst. However, the currency should remain convertible into sterling at a fixed parity, and the board should keep the necessary reserves to put this beyond doubt; furthermore the currency should remain fully backed by sterling.[44]

The Gambia accepted most of these recommendations and a

year before its independence in 1965 established the Gambian Currency Board. The board issued a distinct national currency on 5 October 1964;[45] it became actively involved in various forms of fiduciary lending, the financing of the marketing of ground-nuts and the extension of credit to the government. The board also undertook various activities akin to those performed by central banks in other African countries. But the currency was still backed by a minimum of 70 per cent of its total sight liabilities by sterling.[46]

In Sierra Leone, following the Ghanaian and Nigerian examples, the government established a central bank in 1964 and justified it on political grounds.[47] In the event, however, the bank had very modest goals: to issue and redeem currency; to maintain external reserves to safeguard the international value of the currency; to act as a repository for government funds; to advise the government on financial matters; and to promote monetary stability.[48] There was a modest provision for fiduciary issue and for the issue of Treasury bills. Although this was to pave the way for financial crisis in the mid-1960s, it did not immediately affect the reserves, owing to the need for caution and the fact that, unlike Ghana and Nigeria, Sierra Leone did not have large sterling reserves at independence. The government's sterling balances stayed level at around £13 million between 1962 and 1965.[49] Furthermore the free payments system, designed to attract foreign capital, necessitated careful monetary arrangements.

The Bank of Sierra Leone issued the first Treasury bills in November 1964.[50] From this period onwards the bank continued to provide the government with credit facilities, and at the end of May 1967 it had extended credit amounting to £7.6 million.[51] With increasing participation by the bank in the government's policy of economic expansion, the country's reserves soon ran into difficulties. The budget deficit led to rising domestic inflation and a substantial loss of foreign exchange. By the end of 1966 the reserves were only about £8 million.[52]

The military government of 1967—68, faced with the task of trying to restore the pre-1966 level, realised that there was 'a direct correlation between deficit financing and the loss of foreign exchange reserves',[53] a view which was endorsed by the new civilian Finance Minister, Dr Fornah, in July 1968.[54]

As in Ghana, the crisis in the balance of payments and reserves was due in large part to massive budgetary deficits. The foreign reserves were gradually being 'run down to the point where they barely provided adequate backing for the Leone'.[55]

An IMF mission which visited the country in September 1966 identified difficulties in the budgetary position which had led to the crisis. A stand-by agreement was signed for a period of one year with effect from 1 November 1966. The IMF agreed to lend Sierra Leone $7.5 million to support the foreign exchange reserves.[56] In return the government was to accept a degree of fiscal discipline, in its domestic economy.[57]

The military government made a modest start in narrowing the deficit through the application of the IMF's recommended deflationary measures. It was the new civilian government, through the resourcefulness of the Finance Minister, Dr Fornah, that managed to bring the foreign exchange crisis under control. By June 1968 the reserves had risen to £17.5 million.[58]

The problem of the East African Federation: implications for reserves and monetary policy

By the mid-1960s sterling's role in West Africa was in rapid decline. For various reasons Ghana, Nigeria and Sierra Leone had all run down their reserves. What remained were mainly working balances to finance imports and to make payments in the settlement of currency problems. Sterling's reserve role was shored up by the continued use of the services of the East African Currency Board until 1966 and in Central Africa by the continued operation of the Reserve Bank of Rhodesia and Nyasaland in Zambia and Malawi until 1965.

In East Africa the early hopes of federation in 1960 delayed the transformation of the East African Currency Board into a central bank, but did not prevent the gradual modification of the colonial exchange standard of the board; this started in 1955 with the creation of a fiduciary element in the money supply. East Africa, unlike other parts of Commonwealth Africa, carried out significant changes in its monetary relations with Britain within the currency board framework. The EACB was able to move from its traditional role as a mere automatic moneychanger to an institution which was able to promote development by the issue of Treasury bills, by lending money for crop finance and by acting as banker to the commercial banks.[59]

Indeed, the report of the EACB for the year ending 30 June 1964 maintained that the credit extended to the three countries was £EA35 million, of which £EA 25 million was reserved for government proper and £EA 10 million for rediscounting and advance operations in respect of crop finance.[60]

During the early 1960s, however, the requirements of the three governments in terms of actual cash was much lower than their spending estimates; some were even satisfied that their short-term needs did not require any direct call on the board's facilities. Notable among them was Kenya, which resorted to borrowing direct from companies and other sources and made no immediate use of Treasury bills.[61]

However, conflicts of interest soon developed between the board and the three governments over the use of the board's reserves to promote economic development. Tanzania had become independent in 1961, Uganda in 1962 and Kenya in 1963, and although Kenya remained temporarily satisfied with the *status quo* the other two countries badly needed capital for development. In the absence of alternative sources, the EACB came under pressure to expand its credit to them.[62] The board resorted to the practice of exerting a stabilising influence on the governments' borrowing plans. With an eye to the problems that deficit financing had created in West Africa, it also insisted that to set in motion a more elaborate system of credit creation might result in accelerated expenditure 'followed by restrictions on current payments abroad and other damaging consequences'.[63]

Meanwhile, with the great interest in political federation in the three countries, demands were made by their governments to transform the board into a federal central bank. In 1962 Tanzania obtained the services of Erwin Blumenthal, a senior official of the Central Bank of West Germany, to report on the currency situation and advise on how a central bank could be established. Blumenthal recommended the creation of a two-tier federal central bank which would embody some of 'the sound principles of the Board'.[64]

By 1964 interest in political federation had faded, making the likelihood of a federal central bank remote. In September 1964, with the agreement of the three governments, the Finance Minister of Tanzania, Paul Bomani, requested the IMF to advise the three governments on the form a central bank should take. The IMF mission, headed by Jan Mladeck, visited East Africa in 1965 and had discussions with the three governments, on a separate basis from 4 to 13 February.[65]

Predictably, the negotiations broke down on the sovereignty issue and the desire by all three governments to maintain effective supervision of payments in and out of their countries.[66] On 10 June 1965 all three Finance Ministers announced that their governments would establish separate central banks and issue separate currencies. The Finance Minister of Tanzania maintained that the failure of political federation meant that it would be difficult to have a federal central bank which would serve the interests of each State. Uganda argued that an East African currency and central bank could develop only within the framework of semi-autonomous national banks linked with a central reserve bank performing specific functions.[67] Kenya took the view that if a federal central bank should be established, then the bank must be centrally managed.[68]

Despite these differences, the Tanzanian Minister explained that it had been agreed that 'the necessary arrangements for the creation of central banks and currencies should be closely synchronised in all three territories';[69] they should continue to form part of the sterling area; the new currencies should be at exact parity with the present East African currency; and that they should be freely convertible with each other.[70] More important, the three governments decided 'to impose exchange control between East Africa and other Sterling Area Countries to forestall an unhealthy movement of capital'.[71]

With the advent of the three central banks in 1966, fundamental changes were introduced in the traditional relationship with the sterling system. For example, under the Bank of Tanzania Act, 1965, exchange control was to be imposed against sterling; the profits of the bank were to be paid into the consolidated fund for domestic development; the par value of the currency was to be expressed in terms of gold; the lending powers of the central bank were to be increased; the maintenance of external reserves was to be measured in terms of import requirements (four months being regarded as the minimum); and reserves would not be confined to sterling but would include gold and convertible currency.[72]

However, between 1961 and 1966 (before the central banks were established) the East African Currency Board was able to preserve a semblance of stability on the sterling reserves. The board's sterling reserves stayed level at $136.3 million in 1961, $152.6 in 1964 and $134.7 million in 1966.[73]

Zambia and Malawi

In Zambia and Malawi sterling reserve stability was facilitated by the delayed dissolution of the federation with Rhodesia and the fact that the banking system continued to be linked to the federal reserve bank until June 1965. The federation was dissolved in 1963 but throughout that year and 1964 the federal reserve bank continued to act as an agent for the three governments for the issue of Treasury bills.[74]

Zambia achieved independence on 24 October 1964 and Kenneth Kaunda, the Prime Minister, immediately announced that a central bank would be formed to take over the functions of the Bank of Rhodesia and Nyasaland.[75] This echoed the position in Malawi, where in July 1964 a new law provided for the setting up of a reserve bank with a capital requirement of £500,000 sterling.[76]

In Zambia and Malawi there was no debate as to whether there should be central banks, partly because it had already been shown conclusively that the central bank revolution in Africa was irreversible, but partly also because both countries already enjoyed the advantage of a central bank in the Bank of Rhodesia and Nyasaland. The Bank of Zambia was set up in August 1964 and began to issue Treasury bills on the government's behalf in October. This was done originally through private placings and later by public tender. The Banking Act came into force on 1 March 1965, and the full separation of the common currency area took place in June 1965, separate exchange control legislation being established in each territory.[77]

Of the two countries only Zambia showed signs of improving its sterling reserves to any significant extent. Malawi's central bank reserves stayed constant at around $25 million between 1965 and 1970. Those of the Bank of Zambia rose from $80.3 million in 1965 to $513.8 million in 1970. Zambia's high level of reserves was due to the boom in the price of copper, her major foreign exchange earner. Thus by the mid-1960s she had replaced Ghana and Nigeria as the single most important sterling holder in Commonwealth Africa.

The Rhodesian crisis, the politics of monetary pressure, and the end of the sterling area

The trend towards mobilisation of Commonwealth African reserves was extremely difficult for Britain to check. It was no longer possible to impose a ceiling on imports from non-sterling countries or compel the African States to hold what was regarded as an adequate level of sterling.

Meanwhile sterling's international position was increasingly under pressure from balance of payments instabilities stemming from the diversification of reserves by most holders. The Labour government of 1964 introduced a series of measures aimed at putting the economy right and bringing the payments into balance — a 15 per cent surcharge on all imports except food, tobacco and basic raw materials; an export rebate scheme, the establishment of a Commonwealth Exports Council, consultations with industry on a plan to deal with productivity, prices and incomes.[78]

It was not enough, however, to stop the run on the pound or to restore confidence. Even the Chancellor's autumn budget of 11 November 1964, which reduced social benefits and introduced an export rebate tax and import deposits, could not save the day. In 1965 the government developed a combination of economic policies, both domestic and foreign, to curb home demand, keep inflation down and improve the balance of payments. The April 1965 budget was delationary in its overall effect, and provided for stricter control on foreign aid and investment.

Meanwhile the Rhodesian crisis erupted in November 1965 and Britain was faced with the real possibility of the dissolution of, or mass withdrawals from, the Commonwealth, coupled with threats of monetary pressure if she acquiesced in Ian Smith's unilateral declaration of independence. This crisis, occurring in the midst of the wider sterling one, aggravated the problems of her policy-makers.

Many African States threatened to withdraw from the Commonwealth before 11 November 1965 if Britain failed to stop the Rhodesian Front Party. The conflict was reinforced by the Organisation of African Unity's resolution calling on members to sever diplomatic relations with Britain if she failed to bring down the Smith regime by 15 December.

Britain reacted swiftly by threatening to suspend the economic advantages enjoyed by Commonwealth Africa in Britain, through preferences, aid and investment. This was a pre-emptive move, for although in reality only a handful of African States were prepared to make the break, the government feared that they could trigger off similar action by the moderate ones.[79] Britain responded by explaining through High Commissioners that sanctions would be counter-productive.[80] Tanzania and Ghana, undeterred, broke off relations when the OAU deadline was up. Nyerere picked out the failure to freeze Rhodesia's sterling balances, under the sanctions policy, as evidence of British complicity.[81]

Undoubtedly Britain was less disposed to extend the Rhodesian crisis to the delicate area of monetary relations at a time when sterling was under great pressure in the foreign exchange markets. It was twenty-two days after UDI before the government introduced the Reserve Bank of Rhodesia Order, 1965, to take over the assets of the rebel government. There was strong opposition at Westminster against the political use of the sterling reserves, mainly because of Britain's position as an international banker with a problematic currency.[82]

The government had to act swiftly, however, because of pressure from the African governments. An oder-in-council of 14 December 1965 sought to obtain information about the assets of the Rhodesian Bank and to transfer the powers of the Reserve Bank of Rhodesia to officials sympathetic to British policy. A board of six officials was appointed to safeguard the assets against the rebel government.

Tanzania and Ghana, having followed the OAU's call, lacked the economic power to bring effective pressure to bear on Britain. It should be remembered that at the time Ghana was suffering a serious shortage of foreign exchange and an adverse balance of payments. She was also contemplating negotiations with Britain and other Western countries for a rescheduling of her medium-term commercial debts. Her financial position was far weaker than in the 1950s when she had held massive sterling balances.

Nor was Tanzania strong. She had relied on Britain for most of her technical and financial aid. She could not use her meagre sterling reserves as an effective weapon, especially as some of them were still managed on a collective basis by the East African Currency Board.

Co-ordinated pressure on Britain was further undermined by the refusal of the other Commonwealth African States to sever relations. Zambia, which held about a quarter of Africa's sterling balances, tried to persuade the other members to remain in the Commonwealth and maintain relations with Britain. Kaunda wrote to African heads of state explaining his reservations on the OAU resolution. He emphasised Zambia's special position and her dependence on Britain in any attempt to bring down the Smith regime.[83]

It was not long (by mid-1966) before Zambia changed her orientation and revived the idea of a Commonwealth break, with threats of massive sterling mobilisation if Britain failed to put down the rebellion. Undoubtedly Kaunda had become disillusioned with Britain's handling of UDI, particularly as the so-called sanctions policy was already beginning to affect Zambia's economy, with no sign of Smith surrendering. It was no longer a question of severing relations: Zambia would leave the Commonwealth if Britain failed to act effectively. It is important to note that Zambia was having difficulties with Britain over her claims for compensation, amounting to £40 million, for her part in the policy of sanctions. Britian was prepared to offer only £7 million.

There were several indications that Zambia was prepared to use her economic weight in the Commonwealth, her control over British copper supplies, and her large sterling holdings, to insist on the use of force. Britain's Prime Minister, Harold Wilson, recognised the country's vulnerability:

Zambia was, in a real sense, part of the third constituency. Britian was utterly dependent on her copper supplies. Had they been cut off, either by the Rhodesians or by a Zambia made sullen by our refusal to use force, we would have had two million unemployed within a matter of months.[84]

The first threat that Zambia might apply monetary pressure was reported to have come in July 1966. There were persistent reports that she might demand payment for her copper in dollars or other hard currency and steadily reduce her portfolio of sterling holdings.[85]

At this stage, however, Zambia found it difficult to abandon Britain's settlement arrangements and the aid that was being promised. She still hoped that effective action would be taken against Smith; and in any case the use of sterling to apply pressure would not have solved the fundamental problem of UDI, however much it damaged sterling's international position and weakened Britain's economy. The Finance Minister of Zambia, Mr Arthur Wina, announced, therefore, on 21 July that it was not his government's policy to increase sterling's international problems.[86]

Meanwhile Zambia's political relations with Britain continued to deteriorate over the aid programme and the sanctions policy. On 18 August 1966 Wina told parliament that Zambia was converting some of her sterling reserves into gold and dollars.[87] The policy of diversifying her sterling balances went hand-in-hand with the threat to pull out of the Commonwealth. Britain realised that as long as that threat continued, Zambia might be tempted to reduce her holdings of sterling at a time when Britain needed all the support it could get from overseas holders.

The government therefore doubled its aid to Zambia and tried to tie this new offer to membership of the Commonwealth. It told Kaunda that the £14 million aid would be given only if there was no change in relations with Britain or the Commonwealth.[88] Judith Hart, Minister for Overseas Development, confirmed that Britain's policy would be to reconsider the £14 million if Zambia left the Commonwealth.[89]

These diplomatic moves were followed by an important meeting between the Chancellor of the Exchequer, James Callaghan, and Mr Wina, in London. Zambia's reserves and the threat of withdrawal from the sterling area were the major subjects of discussion. Mr Wina pointed out, however, that if Zambia decided to withdraw, Britain would be informed well in advance. He added that political considerations of Zambia's continued membership of the Commonwealth need not necessarily affect her membership of the sterling area.[90]

Although Wina later told reporters that Zambia would not be influenced by financial deals, serious consideration was being given to the economic cost of pulling out of the Commonwealth. Lusaka was coming round to the view that the loss of £14 million, with no alternative in sight, would affect the economy adversely. Zambia's attempt to draw a distinction between accepting the £14 million and the right to decide whether to pull out of the Commonwealth was heavily compromised, as Britain would not have it that way. To Britain a threat to the Commonwealth was a direct threat to British interests. Zambia was left almost in the lurch as she failed to persuade other African countries to pull out of the Commonwealth. Nyerere and Nkrumah broke off diplomatic relations with Britain but remained in the Commonwealth.

On 1 February 1967 Zambia and Britain announced that the aid agreement of £13.85 million had been signed after it had been made clear that Zambia would remain in the Commonwealth and the sterling area.

The disintegration of the sterling area

Britain was able to contain the monetary problems emanating from the Rhodesian crisis, but the difficulties facing sterling were much more extensive as the currency came under increasing pressure in the foreign exchange markets. The government was forced to devalue in November 1967, an act which initiated the disintegration of the sterling area.

In Commonwealth Africa only Sierra Leone, Gambia and Malawi devalued along with sterling. The decision was due to their slow rate of economic diversification. Britain was still the dominant force in their external economic relations. Nigeria, Ghana, Tanzania, Kenya, Uganda and Zambia refused to follow, however, viewing devaluation as a unilateral British policy which would impede their own economic diversification.

Nonetheless the devaluation of 14.3 per cent constituted a loss to all Commonwealth African States as their sterling reserves depreciated accordingly. For those that did not devalue, it affected their trade with Britain, to the extent that Nigeria, Kenya, Tanzania and Uganda refused for a while to honour sterling's traditional transaction role by demanding payment in local and other currencies for their exports. In Britain commodity traders protested to the government about the difficulties of trading with those countries, particularly as there was no forward cover for their transactions.[91]

Sterling's devaluation did not immediately affect the total holdings of Commonwealth Africa. From December 1967 to March 1968 there was actually an increase, from £341 million to £365 million. In fact the sterling area as a whole experienced an increase of £130 million.[92]

It was a temporary respite, however, for another crisis broke out in March 1968. Sterling area countries withdrew some £324 million from their holdings in anticipation of another devaluation. This led to two historic developments: the Basle facility contracted by the developed countries to defend sterling, and bilateral agreements with all sterling area countries to preclude a sudden withdrawal of their remaining balances.

The central banks of twelve[93] developed countries provided Britain with $2 billion in stand-by credit through the Bank for International Settlements to finance any further withdrawals. The facility was to have a ten-year life, with drawings to be permitted during the first three years (1968–70). Repayments were to be made during the sixth and tenth years (1973–77).[94] Bilateral agreements were entered into with the sterling area countries on 25 September 1968 in which the United Kingdom undertook 'to maintain the sterling value in terms of the US dollars eligible for guarantee'. The guarantee applied to the whole of each member's reserve balances except for a portion of 10 per cent of its total reserves. In the event of any future devaluation of the pound each country would receive a payment in sterling to restore the dollar value of the guaranteed position of its reserves.

In return for the guarantee the sterling area countries agreed to hold a specified proportion of official sterling reserves, the 'minimum sterling proportion'.[95] The agreements were to remain in force for three years, with provision for extension for a further two by mutual agreement. All Commonwealth African countries, except Botswana, Lesotho and Swaziland, entered into these agreements on 25 September 1968. The BLS countries followed in 1969 and 1970.[96] In the agreements with the BLS countries provision was made for the special position of the South African rand. BLS countries were to have their reserves only in the rand or the pound and should limit transfer of sterling assets into the rand to the amount needed for day-to-day business.[97]

The Basle agreements marked the beginning of the end of the sterling area. Now, for the first time, Britain realised that sterling's reserve role could not be defended by traditional means.[98] The Basle measures helped to stabilise sterling as the reserves of the Commonwealth African and other holders increased in the knowledge that a devaluation would not adversely affect their holdings.

The agreements were renegotiated in September 1971 and extended until 1973. On 23 June 1972, however, the sterling area was unceremoniously brought to an end when the pound was floated as a precaution against speculative outflows; exchange controls were introduced for the first time on capital transactions between United Kingdom residents and residents of the overseas sterling area. Residual forms of the old relationship lingered. Sterling was still the main trading currency of the Commonwealth African countries, and a greater percentage of their external reserves was still held in sterling than in other currencies. In fact Nigeria became one of the most important holders after the oil boom of 1973. Countries like Sierra Leone, Gambia and Malawi continued for some time to peg their currencies to sterling by floating along with Britain.

The Basle agreements were extended in October 1973 for another six months. Because sterling was moving downwards, this unfavourably affected the dollar rate of exchange at which the balances were guaranteed. Hence Britain had to pay more to sterling holders. The new one-year agreement of 1974 attempted to redress the balance. The guarantee was expressed in terms of a basket of currencies and not simply in terms of the dollar, and there was a reduction in the minimum amount of sterling which members were required to hold to qualify for the guarantee.[99]

However, on 12 November 1974 the Chancellor of the Exchequer, Denis Healey, announced the termination of the programme in his budget because of the oil exporters' surpluses.[100] With the end of the Basle agreements and the dissolution of the sterling area, British—Commonwealth African monetary relations ceased to be determined by a collective policy of preserving sterling's international role. The special privileges enjoyed by Commonwealth—sterling area members in the open payments policy of Britain were withdrawn. The remaining monetary relations have to do with the continued involvement of Britain with trade, aid and investment in Commonwealth Africa.

Notes

1   R. A. Butler, *The Art of the Possible*, 1971, pp. 158—9.
2   *Ibid.*, p. 158.
3   *Ibid.*, p. 159.
4   Strange, *Sterling and British Policy, op. cit.*, pp. 64—5.
5   Cmnd 827, 1959, p. 240.
6   Ghana Debates, 5 February 1957, col. 859.
7   Ghana Debates, 5 March 1957, col. 28.
8   *Ibid.*
9   *The Banker*, January 1958, p. 61.
10 *The Banker*, August 1958, p. 541.
11 H/R Debates, 9 February 1959, p. 63.
12 *Ibid.*, p. 67.
13 H/R Debates, 9 February 1959, p. 86.
14 Nigeria H/R Debates, 6 April 1961, p. 174.
15 *Ibid.*, p. 180.
16 *Ibid.*
17 *Commonwealth Development and its Financing*, Nigeria, *op. cit.*, p. 48.
18 H/R Debates, 23 February 1959, p. 483.
19 H/R Debates, 31 August 1961, p. 253.
20 The United Nations, Economic Commission For Africa, *Economic Bulletin For Africa* (Addis Ababa), Vol. 1, No. 1, 1961, p. 69.
21 Statement of Bank of Rhodesia, in A. R. Conan, *The Rationale of the Sterling Area*, 1961, p. 112.
22 Report by J. B. Loynes on the *Problems of the Future Currencies of Sierra Leone and the Gambia, op. cit.*, p. 30.
23 *Ibid.*, p. 19.
24 East African Currency Board, *Annual Report* (London), 1957.
25 EACB, *Annual Report* (Nairobi), 1960.
26 *UN Economic Bulletin for Africa*, 1964, p. 3.
27 Republic of Ghana, 1965, *Statistical Year Book* (Accra), p. 168.

28 See Table 5.1.
29 Ghana Debates, 24 October 1961, col. 92.
30 Ghana Debates, 13 July 1961, col. 267.
31 *Ibid.*
32 Ghana Debates, 8 October 1962, col. 161.
33 Ghana Debates, 23 October 1961, col. 151.
34 Ghana Debates, 2 October 1962, Vol. 29, col. 20.
35 Ghana Debates, 22 October 1963, col. 176.
36 UN *Economic Bulletin for Africa*, 161, *op. cit.*, p. 69.
37 Nigeria Debates, 29 March 1962, col. 495.
38 *Ibid.*, col. 497.
39 *Ibid.*, col. 502.
40 *Ibid.*, col. 503.
41 *Ibid.*, col. 506.
42 Report by J. B. Loynes, *The Problem of the Future Currencies of Sierra Leone and the Gambia, op. cit.*
43 *Ibid.*, p. 8.
44 *Ibid.*, p. 10.
45 *Gambia Currency Board Report, 31 December 1965* (London), 1965.
46 *Ibid.*
47 Budget Speech, 12 July 1962 (Government Printer), 1962, p. 2.
48 R. F. Saylor, *The Economic System of Sierra Leone*, 1967, p. 180.
49 Sierra Leone H/R Debates, 28 March 1966, col. 20.
50 *Budget Speech*, Hon. R. O. King, 31 March 1965 (Government Printer), 1965, p. 15.
51 *Statement on the Budget for 1967/68* (Government Printer), 1967, p. 3.
52 *Ibid.*, p. 1.
53 *Ibid.*, p. 8.
54 *Budget Speech*, 8 July 1968, *op. cit.*, p. 11.
55 Budget Speech, 1967/68, *op. cit.*, p. 8.
56 *Ibid.*, p. 1.
57 *Ibid.*, p. 2.
58 *Budget Speech*, 8 July 1968, *op. cit.*, p. 11.
59 Ervin Blumenthal, 'The Present Monetary System and its Future', in Hedley Smith, *Readings on Economic Development and Administration in Tanzania* (Tanzania), 1966, p. 86.
60 *EACB Report for the Year ended 30th June 1964* (Nairobi), 1964.
61 *Ibid.*
62 *Ibid.*
63 *Ibid.*
64 Blumenthal Report, *op. cit.*, p. 97.
65 *EACB Report, 1963, op. cit.*, p. 3.
66 *Ibid.*, p. 3.
67 *EACB Report*, 30 June 1965, *op. cit.*, p. 5.
68 *Ibid.*, p. 5.
69 Paul Bomani, radio broadcast, 13 July 1965.

70 *Ibid.*, p. 123.
71 *Ibid.*
72 Bank of Tanzania Act, 1965, No. 12 of 1966, 6 January 1966.
73 *International Financial Statistics*, IMF.
74 Northern Rhodesia, *Economic Report*, 1964 (Government Printer), p. 132.
75 *The Banker*, No. 465, November 1964, p. 738.
76 *The Banker*, No. 462, August 1964, p. 531.
77 Republic of Zambia, Ministry of Finance, *Economic Report* (Lusaka), 1965, p. 43.
78 Harold Wilson, *The Labour Government, 1964—1970: a Personal Record*, 1971, p. 19.
79 Wilson, *The Labour Government, op. cit.*
80 *The Times*, 8 December 1965.
81 *The Observer*, 12 December 1965.
82 H.C. Debates, 14 December 1965, Vol. 722, col. 1167.
83 *The Times*, 9 December 1965.
84 Wilson, *The Labour Government, op. cit.*, pp. 182—3.
85 *The Daily Express*, 21 July 1966; *The Guardian*, 21 July 1966.
86 *The Guardian*, 21 July 1966.
87 *The Guardian*, 19 August 1966.
88 *The Daily Telegraph*, 17 September 1966.
89 *The Financial Times*, 16 September 1966. Judith Hart also reiterated, in Parliament, this view of linking aid to Zambia's Commonwealth membership. (H.C. Debates, 8 November 1966, Vol. 735, col. 112.) Kaunda had written an article in *The Sunday Times*, 4 September 1966, threatening to withdraw from the Commonwealth.
90 *Financial Times*, 16 September 1966.
91 H.C. Debates, 13 March 1968, Vol. 760.
92 Bank of England *Quarterly Bulletin*, March 1969, p. 115.
93 Austria, Belgium, Denmark, Japan, Holland, the USA, Sweden, Switzerland, West Germany, Norway, Italy and Canada.
94 Cmnd 3787, 1968.
95 It was reckoned that the minimum sterling proportion for most Commonwealth African States was 40 per cent.
96 Cmnd 4224, 1969, and Cmnd 4415, 1970.
97 *Ibid.*
98 Cmnd 3787, 1968.
99 *Bank of England Report and Accounts*, year ended 28 February 1974, p. 21.
100 H.C. Debates, 12 November 1974, Vol. 881, col. 248.

6
Trade relations, 1957—75

Dollar discrimination strengthened trade ties between Commonwealth Africa and Britain, elevating the defence of sterling to a
central place in trade policy on both sides. However, independence and the end of dollar discrimination in 1959 led to a
progressive reduction in the African countries' trade with
Britain and a reappraisal of trade policy. For Commonwealth
Africa 'development' came to overshadow sterling's problems as
the central issue. Trade was seen as a means of earning foreign
exchange for the immediate purpose of promoting domestic
economic development. This policy had three major dimensions:
the diversification of trade links in search of new markets,
whether sterling suffered in the process or not; pressure on
Britian and other developed countries to adopt a special trade
policy towards developing countries which would provide more
foreign exchange for development; and the protection of existing advantages in British markets when they were threatened by
British membership of the European Economic Community.

  There were conflicts of interest between Britain and Commonwealth Africa on each of these objectives. As the centre of
the Commonwealth—sterling area Britain had no particular
interest in diversification. Trade was still important, of course,
to ensure monetary stability and for domestic economic reasons;
nor did she want to lose the advantages she enjoyed in the
markets of Commonwealth Africa. At the same time British
governments were determined to protect their trade with the
EEC, and for this reason recognised the need to respond to the
demands of Commonwealth Africa and other developing
countries for a special trade relationship. The political interaction between Commonwealth Africa's trade objectives and
those of Britain are examined in this chapter.

The impact of independence

Dollar discrimination and Commonwealth preference

The picture that emerged as the first African country achieved independence simultaneously with the end of dollar discrimination showed Britain as overwhelmingly the most important trading partner of Commonwealth Africa. Her predominance was greater in imports than in exports, because, as we have seen, the policy of trade discrimination in the sterling area encouraged the export of goods to non-sterling countries to earn hard currency. Commonwealth Africa's imports from Britain as a percentage of total imports was about 32 per cent. The average for exports was about 38.6 per cent.

The improvement in Britain's trade with the United States led to an extensive liberalisation of dollar imports in May 1959.[1] A wide range of goods were freed entirely from control. Commonwealth Africa responded with massive trade liberalisation with dollar countries. In Nigeria, for instance, in January 1959 many goods originating from dollar countries were put on the same licensing basis as goods from sterling countries, leaving only foodstuffs, motor cars and petroleum products under control.[2] Ghana announced a similar policy in July 1959.[3] These countries had been sceptical about dollar discrimination; they welcomed liberalisation as a step towards the ideal policy of 'no discrimination in trade'.

At independence the preference system remained the only Commonwealth instrument for promoting intra-Commonwealth trade. However, preferences were never fully applied to all of Commonwealth Africa. Only Sierra Leone, the Gambia, Zambia and Malawi gave Britain reciprocal preferences. The other countries enjoyed one-way preferences on a variety of exports to Britain. Preferences on British goods were precluded in Kenya and Uganda by the Congo Basin treaties, in Tanganyika by its trusteeship status, and in Nigeria by an Anglo-French agreement of 1898 which granted equal commercial rights to both parties in Nigeria and French West Africa.[4]

In 1961 it was reckoned that about half Britain's exports to the Commonwealth preference area entered free of duty, and more than half of British goods to the area enjoyed some measure of preference.[5] With regard to African countries that offered reciprocal preferences, some 17 per cent of British exports to Sierra Leone entered duty-free in 1961 and 90 per cent enjoyed some measure of preference;[6] in the case of

Malawi and Zambia one-third of British exports entered free of duty, and almost 96 per cent of all British goods enjoyed some measure of preference.[7] Most Commonwealth African exports entered Britain duty-free, apart from a limited range of commodities subject to revenue duties.

The reciprocal preferences in Sierra Leone, Zambia, and Gambia lasted for only a brief period after independence because of intensified pressures against reciprocal preferences from developing countries. Sierra Leone abolished British preferences in 1965, Zambia in 1966 and Gambia in 1973. Malawi alone continued to grant preferences to British goods until the Lomé Convention was signed in February 1975.

In the event, the preference system failed to prevent the diversification that took place after the end of dollar discrimination. In fact the value of Commonwealth preferences depreciated with the formation of the General Agreement on Tariffs and Trade and its policy of freezing all existing preferences. Thus with the progressive liberalisation of tariffs, under GATT auspices, Commonwealth countries experienced a fall in the value[8] of their preferences. The value of Commonwealth preferences also suffered with the formation of the European Free Trade Area in 1959.[9]

The politics of trade diversification by Commonwealth Africa
Trade liberalisation and political independence freed Commonwealth Africa from the constraints of the sterling area system. Their main concern now was to diversify trade links so as to earn foreign exchange for development. Diversification was greater in the countries that did not grant reciprocal preferences than in those that did, although, among the latter, Zambia achieved considerable diversification. In Botswana, Lesotho and Swaziland the strong South African presence meant that Britain was never the major trading partner.

This section is divided into three parts, covering the trade policies of the non-reciprocal preference countries, Ghana, Nigeria, Tanzania, Kenya and Uganda; the reciprocal preference countries, Sierra Leone, the Gambia, Malawi and Zambia; and the southern African countries, respectively. The object is to show the trend and extent of diversification and to suggest explanations. Special attention has been paid to the cases of Ghana and Nigeria. As the first two independent African States they laid down the basic rules which governed all Commonwealth African trade diversification.

The non-reciprocal preference countries   Ghana became independent in 1957 but did not liberalise trade with dollar
countries until 1959, following Britain's announcement. The
government's commitment to diversification was shown, however, by the proposal to send five economic missions abroad to
explore the prospects of increasing trade and attracting foreign
capital to Ghana.

It was on the occasion of the first trade and payments agreement on 12 November 1959 (with Israel) that the government
spelled out its external trade policy.[10] The Finance Minister
stressed the government's commitment to multilateral trade,
and identified four basic principles of policy: (a) non-discrimi-
nation; (b) non-dependence; (c) diversification, and (d) the
protection of exising export markets.[11]

Ghana experienced a balance of payments crisis in 1961
which forced the government to introduce import restrictions
in 1962; this arrested the deficit temporarily as imports from all
sources declined from ¢ 338 million in 1961 to ¢ 282 million in
1962.[12] The financial situation was desperately unstable, however; the government had to announce a foreign exchange
conservation programme in March 1963.[13] In addition far more
emphasis came to be placed on trade with the centrally planned
economies, although in practical terms the government found it
difficult to restructure trade away from the West.[14] Imports
from the USSR and East European countries were very small.
The greatest percentage increase was in 1965—66 when the
USSR and Poland increased their share of the Ghanaian market
from 4.6 and 2.3 per cent to 6.75 per cent and 4.4 per cent in
1966 respectively. Britain continued to be the most important
single source of imports between 1960 and 1966. Her share of
the market dropped, however, from 37 per cent in 1960 to
28.6 per cent in 1966. The major new partners were the United
States and West Germany.[15]

In 1965 the Ministry of Trade was split into two departments,
one dealing specifically with foreign and the other with internal
trade. The formation of the new Ministry of Foreign Trade led
to a thorough examination of Ghana's trade relations. It was
concluded that the selling of cocoa to the centrally planned
economies prevented Ghana from earning the foreign exchange
vital for development. Nkrumah affirmed that it would be
discontinued.[16]

The economic policies of 1961—65 affected Ghana's trade
relations with Britain. Although the UK remained Ghana's most

important trading partner, there were clear signs of a progressive decline. After 1965 Britain's role was considerably reduced. In 1967 she supplied only 29.7 per cent of Ghana's imports, in 1970 only 23.3 per cent.

Thus by 1970 Ghana had considerably diversified her import trade. But not towards the centrally planned economies. Nkrumah had slowed that process by insisting on hard-currency payment. The National Liberation Council, which overthrew him, strengthened this policy. Imports from the USSR and Poland actually declined in absolute terms, from 14.6 million NȻ in 1966 to 8 million NȻ in 1967 (USSR), and from 3.4 million NȻ in 1966 to 2.9 NȻ in 1967 (Poland). The main targets in Ghana's diversification policy were the United States, Western Europe and Japan. The United States became the second most important market for Ghana's imports, followed by West Germany and Japan.[17] The same was true of exports, where Britain's position was reduced from 20.9 per cent in 1967 to 18 per cent in 1970. Diversification was towards the United States (9 per cent), West Germany (7.2 per cent) and Holland (8.3 per cent).

Nigeria's independence in October 1960 came after the announcement by Britain of the end of dollar discrimination. Unlike Ghana, her trade policy had been liberalised before independence. She was thus able to pursue an independent foreign trade policy from the start under which all countries were 'to be treated equally'. Unlike Ghana also, Nigeria did not experience a major balance of payments crisis and the consequent financial instability. Her diversification policy was determined purely on nationalist and commercial grounds.

Like Ghana, at independence, Nigeria announced that an economic mission would be sent overseas 'with the aim of increasing the awareness in the world of the economic potential of Nigeria'. This mission gave trade a priority. A comprehensive statement on trade policy was made by the Finance Minister, Okotie Eboh, in March 1962. He stressed five major determinants: first, diversification of exports; the aim here was to increase export capacity from primary to secondary products; second, the development of new markets and the strengthening of advantages in old ones: this led to the signing of several bilateral trade agreements; third, the securing of stable prices for Nigeria's exports at a fair and reasonable level; fourth, the reduction of dependence upon imported goods, particularly consumer goods, and fifth, the reduction of the drain in invisible transactions.[18]

The combined effect of these policies led to a drastic decline in trade with Britain. The percentage of exports to the UK slumped from 49 per cent in 1960 to 25.9 per cent in 1970.[19] Before the oil boom, cocoa, palm oil, palm kernels, timber, palm oil, ground-nuts and ground-nut oil accounted for about half Nigeria's exports. Britain was the single most important market for most of these products, with the exception of ground-nuts, where France, Holland and Italy surpassed her in the late 1960s, and in timber, where her lead was narrowed by Holland and Italy. After the oil explosion, petroleum became the most important foreign exchange earner, accounting for over 90 per cent of the value of all exports.

Britain continued as the single most important source of Nigeria's imports, but her lead was reduced from 43.2 per cent in 1960 to 30.7 per cent in 1970. With the suspension of dollar discrimination, the United States made significant inroads; from 5.1 per cent in 1960 her share of the market rose consistently each year to 15.5 per cent in 1966, a position which she held thereafter. West Germany and Japan also increased their exports to Nigeria.

Tanzania, Kenya and Uganda achieved independence well after the policy of dollar discrimination had ended. Ghana and Nigeria had set the pace and pointed the way to trade diversification; Tanzania, Kenya and Uganda followed. They differed from Ghana and Nigeria in the sense that at independence there was a higher level of intra-regional trade within the East African Community than was the case among the West African Commonwealth countries. There was the prospect therefore that diversification could take the form of regional trade expansion. Although the United States was Uganda's largest market, Britian remained the largest single trading partner for Kenya and Tanganyika.

In Tanzania sisal, cotton, coffee, diamonds, cashew nuts and tea accounted for more than 60 per cent of exports. Britain was the single most important customer. Sisal, the major foreign exchange earner, dropped in price catastrophically from sh. 1700/- per ton in 1964 to sh. 765/- per ton in 1968,[20] mainly because of competition from polypropylene.[21] In 1963 it accounted for 35.7 per cent of Tanzania's export earnings; in 1969, for only 10 per cent.[22]

The lesson for Tanzania was the unpredictability of an international trading system over which she had very little control. Guided by the new policy of self-reliance, she stressed the need to produce commodities which could be consumed locally rather than to concentrate economic resources on exports. Despite this declaration, sisal was not replaced by domestic products. Instead coffee, cotton and diamonds became the major export products, although they too experienced some fall in output.

Tanzania was forced therefore to intensify trade promotion. Britain's share of her exports fell, however, from 29 per cent in 1966 to 25.7 per cent in 1969.[23] New markets were found in Japan, the USA and Western Europe. The same pattern was repeated with imports. Although Britain remained the most important supplier, her share fell from 35 per cent in 1966 to 26.6 per cent in 1969. Diversification was mainly towards the EEC, the USA and Japan.

In Uganda coffee, cotton, copper and tea formed 88.5 per cent of exports, coffee accounting for 52.8 per cent of the total. From 1962 to 1970 the United States was the leading importer of Ugandan products, mainly coffee. The United States consumes about half the world's coffee and was able to take up Uganda's expanding production. Britain increased her consumption of Ugandan coffee from 16.1 per cent in 1960 to 19.6 per cent in 1968. With regard to imports, Britain remained the single most important source, although her share fell from 32.9 per cent in 1961 to 22.6 per cent in 1970.[24] As in Tanzania, diversification was towards Japan, the United States and West Germany.

Kenya had a much more diversified export market than Uganda and Tanzania, with products ranging from tropical coffee, tea, sisal, cotton, maize, hydes and skins, pyrethrum, cashew nuts and oilseeds to temperate dairy products like butter, cheese and meat; she also produced semi-processed goods and petrochemical products. Coffee, tea, petroleum products, meat, pyrethrum and sisal accounted for about 70 per cent of exports. Britain was the most important trading partner in both imports and exports, although there was some increased expansion of trade with the EEC, Japan and the United States. Britain's share of the market fell from 43.7 per cent in 1960 to 30.2 per cent in 1973.[25]

The reciprocal preference area   Diversification in this group of States was slower, although in Zambia Britain lost her lead to Japan in 1973 and never fully established dominance in the Gambia until the mid-1960s.

Sierre Leone. Diamonds, iron ore, palm kernels, coffee and cocoa accounted for 95 per cent of exports, with earnings from diamonds claiming 65 per cent. Sierra Leone exported 78 per cent of her products to Britain in 1961, and 63 per cent in 1974.[26] After Britain, Holland was the most important export market, mainly for cocoa, followed by West Germany, Japan and America. Exports to Britain increased by only 90 per cent from 1961 to 1970, whereas exports to Japan, Holland and the United States increased by 800, 350 and 500 per cent respectively.

Diversification was greater in imports than in exports. Britain's share of the market dropped from 44 per cent in 1961 to 21 per cent in 1974. Japan, the United States and West Germany were the major beneficiaries. Between them they took 9.6, 9.1 and 6 per cent of the market respectively. Japan increased her exports by 200 per cent, America by 700 per cent and West Germany by 500 per cent; Britain by only 37 per cent. In fact, when Sierra Leone removed the preferences on British goods in 1965, British exports declined in value in absolute terms, whereas those of Holland, France and Japan rose rapidly.

The Gambia relied for more than 90 per cent of her exports on ground-nuts. Between 1962 and 1964 well over 50 per cent went to Italy. After 1964, however, Britain became the major consumer of Gambia's ground-nuts. Her share of Gambia's output showed a decline from 51.8 per cent in 1960 to 45.5 per cent in 1973.[27] Britain's share of Gambia's imports showed much more rapid decline, from 42.5 per cent in 1960 to 27.2 per cent in 1974. In common with other African countries, there was diversification towards Japan (6.9 per cent) Italy (5.3 per cent), the USA (4.9 per cent), West Germany (4.8 per cent) and France (4.1 per cent).

Zambia pursued real and sustained diversification in both imports and exports. Copper accounted for over 90 per cent of foreign exchange earnings and Britian was the single most important market in 1964, taking some 32.1 per cent of the total. By 1973, however, Japan emerged as the most important market, with 22.6 per cent. Britain's share fell to 19.6 per cent.[28] Japan indeed increased its consumption of the total world output of copper from 367,100 tons in 1961 to 1,201,800 tons in 1973, becoming the world's second largest consumer after the United States.[29]

With regard to imports, Britain remained the largest single supplier, although considerable progress was made by Japan, the USA and EEC countries. When Zambia removed Commonwealth preferences in 1966 Britain's share declined from 23 per cent in 1966 to 20.9 per cent in 1967.

Malawi was the only country that refused to revoke Commonwealth preferences until they were superseded by the Lomé Convention in February 1975. Britain increased her share of Malawi's imports from 21.4 per cent in 1964 to 24.8 per cent in 1973.[30] Rhodesia and South Africa were the major competitors. In 1973 South Africa accounted for 16 per cent of the total import market, chiefly in consumer goods.

Britain's share of Malawi's exports declined from 41.6 per cent in 1964 to 23.4 per cent in 1973. Tobacco accounted for some 40 per cent of exports. She also exported tea, ground-nuts, cotton and maize. The United States, Western Europe, South Africa and Rhodesia were the important areas of diversification.

The southern African States

Britain was never the main trading partner of the BLS countries. The geographical proximity of South Africa enabled the Republic to become the most important economic power in all three. Trade relations were strengthened by the common customs union established in 1910 and renewed in 1969.

Under the 1910 agreement Botswana, Lesotho and Swaziland received a fixed share of 0.28 per cent, 0.89 per cent and 0.15 per cent of total customs revenue collected; the balance of 98.7 per cent was taken by South Africa.[31] With the prospect of independence in the 1960s Britain initiated discussions with South Africa in 1963[32] for a review of the agreement. But South Africa broke off negotiations in 1965 pending a reappraisal of her relationship with the BLS countries in the light of the latter's rapid progress towards independence.

Negotiations were reopened in July 1968 and the new agreement was signed in December 1969.[33] Under it BLS received R17,010,000 in 1969—70, as compared with the R6,430,000 they would have received under the old agreement.[34] The 1969 agreement gave the BLS countries the right to protect their infant industries.

The fixing of the tariffs and duties remained the prerogative of South Africa, although the 1969 agreement provided for detailed consultations. Botswana was not satisfied with these arrangements and soon after independence commissioned a customs administration expert, F. Bishop, who was financed by the British government, to examine the possibility of setting up an independent customs department. Bishop's recommendation led to the establishment of the Botswana customs department within the customs union.

A high proportion of goods imported into the BLS countries originated from South Africa, which was able to compete effectively against overseas manufacturers because of her protected market. The main export products of BLS were meat, fruit, vegetables, sugar, pulp and waste paper, crude fertilisers and asbestos. Britain was the most important market for Botswana and Swaziland but South Africa dominated in the imports of all three countries. Botswana exported 67.8, 43.2 and 47 per cent of her output to Britain from 1973 to 1975 inclusive, as compared with 17.8, 37.5 and 23.5 per cent to South Africa. For the same period Botswana's imports from Britain were 5.5, 3.4 and 2.4 per cent as compared with 69.1, 75 and 79.8 per cent for South Africa.[35] This was also the case for Swaziland, where South Africa accounted for about 92 per cent of imports and Britain the greater part of the export market. In Lesotho, which is completely surrounded by South Africa, the Republic was the most important trading partner for both imports and exports.[36]

Britain's Commonwealth trade policy

As we have seen, with the end of dollar discrimination and the granting of independence, Britain's preponderance in trade declined sharply. However much they guarded their advantages in the British market, Commonwealth African States were determined to establish new export links with other countries. It was on imports, however, that the greatest diversification took place. Several factors accounted for this: the policy of dollar discrimination had largely controlled the imports of Commonwealth Africa outside the sterling area market, so that when the policy was abandoned the countries that had been discriminated against were able to redress the balance. At the same time British industry was becoming less competitive as a result of the very stop—go economic policies used to protect the pound. Thus it was not surprising that Britain's main competitors were able to pose a significant challenge to her traditional dominance in Commonwealth Africa.

African import diversification posed more problems for Britain than export diversification. The trade was still important to her domestic economy and to protect sterling's international position. Indeed, with the end of empire, trade promotion often dominated discussion of Britain's foreign policy. As the Plowden

Commission on the Representational Services Overseas in 1962 noted:

The survival of Britain, let alone her influence, depends on trade. The work of her representatives overseas must be increasingly dedicated to the support of British trade. Economic and political motives intertwine throughout our foreign policy and have always done so; but economic and commercial work has now assumed a position of fundamental importance. It must be regarded as a first charge on the resources of the overseas services.[37]

A debate developed in Britain about whether, and how, to reverse the decline of trade with the Commonwealth.[38] The Conservative government, realising the limitations of Commonwealth trade, had attempted to take Britain into Europe in 1961. In one parliamentary debate the Prime Minister, Sir Alec Douglas Home, stressed the need to come to terms with the changing interests of Commonwealth countries, the industrialisation plans of the New Commonwealth and the erosion of preferences. Subject to these limitations, however, the government believed that trade with the Commonwealth should be improved and affirmed the opportunities for increased trade with West Africa.

The Labour Party showed greater enthusiasm. Harold Wilson rejected the Conservative view of inevitable decline,[39] calling instead for a Commonwealth Export Council and outlining a ten-point programme for stepping up Commonwealth trade. He demanded that 'arrangements should be made for regular meetings to work through the development and capital investment programmes of each Commonwealth country'. According to this plan, Britain would ask Commonwealth countries for specific preferences in the awarding of contracts. As we have seen in chapter four, the Labour government of 1964 attempted to implement this programme by making Commonwealth trade the linchpin of its strategy in solving the balance of payments problem. The Commonwealth Exports Council was established and at the Commonwealth Trade Ministers' meeting of 1966 the President of the Board of Trade, Douglas Jay, put forward Wilson's ten-point plan of 1964.[40] Its rejection marked the last attempt to rely on the Commonwealth as a basis for British economic recovery. To Harold Wilson the message was clear:

I was acutely disappointed at the outcome. Despite the initiatives proposed by Douglas Jay ... there was virtually no willingness to improve intra-Commonwealth trading arrangements. ... There is in fact nothing under the sun more *laissez-faire* than Commonwealth trade.[41]

Trade and the problem of development

Britain was unable to contain the relentless diversification. One of the economic reasons behind it was the need to create additional demand for primary products which would yield higher prices and generate more foreign exchange for development. However, although diversification created new markets, the link between diversification and the terms of trade was weak. Commonwealth African and other developing countries' exports increased in absolute volume without a corresponding rise in prices. In fact the prices of most primary commodities declined sharply in the 1960s.[42] This created a problem for development and affected Commonwealth Africa's trade policy. With the resulting shortage of foreign exchange, on the import side, it forced many of them to enter into commercial credit agreements to sustain the necessary level of capital imports. On the export side, it led to a campaign for a special trade policy from the industrialised countries.

Commercial credits and the politics of debt in Ghana

In the absence of a large-scale inflow of foreign aid or sufficient export earnings to pay for imports, Commonwealth African countries, particularly Ghana, Nigeria, (in the 1960s) Sierra Leone and Uganda resorted to commercial credits to finance their development programmes.

Commercial credits are an important instrument of trade promotion between rich and poor countries. Individual foreign firms undertake to finance a project under an agreement guaranteed by their government. The firm advances credit for the cost of the project to the receiver government, which in turn guarantees the credit. The period of repayment is usually between four and six years; generally, such credits are repayable before the project starts to generate sufficient income to allow repayment on a self-liquidating basis.

Britain, acting through the Export Credit Guarantee Department, guaranteed most of the British firms' suppliers' credits to Commonwealth Africa. Because of the short-term nature of repayment, high interest rates and price inflation, suppliers' credits created debt problems for developing countries. By 1973 Commonwealth Africa was in debt to the tune of $326.8 million in suppliers' credits alone.[43] Ghana had the lions' share, with $214.9 million, Sierra Leone $45.3 million, and Nigeria $27.9 million. The other countries' debt from suppliers' credits was

Table 6.1 External public debt outstanding of Commonwealth African countries, 31 December 1973 (US $ millions).

Country	Disbursed only	Total	Including undisbursed				
			Bilateral official	Suppliers'	Banks	Multilateral	Other
Botswana	111.1	162.4	114.4	0.3	—	45.0	2.7
EAC	195.3	305.1	50.8	—	—	205.1	47.2
Gambia	10.0	12.7	9.3	—	—	3.4	—
Ghana	615.4	666.8	344.6	214.9	—	107.3	—
Kenya	401.4	596.1	300.2	13.5	20.9	227.0	34.5
Lesotho	7.6	12.8	1.3	—	0.5	10.5	0.5
Malawi	189.0	267.0	165.5	5.9	6.3	76.3	13.0
Nigeria	707.0	1101.2	482.7	27.9	18.7	568.2	3.7
Sierra Leone	89.3	122.7	43.8	45.3	2.4	27.5	3.7
Swaziland	34.4	34.7	22.7	3.5	—	8.5	—
Tanzania	424.6	793.9	588.9	0.2	18.6	160.9	25.3
Uganda*	172.3	235.2	153.5		2.8	58.2	20.7
Zambia	534.9	966.9	407.9	15.3	211.6	313.6	18.5

* Does not include suppliers credits.

Source. IBRD, *External Debt of LDCs*, world debt tables, Vol. I.

negligible, except for Zambia, with $15.3 million, and Kenya, with $13.5 million. Tanzania's, Swaziland's and Malawi's debt amounted to $0.2 million, $3.5 million and $5.9 million respectively; there were no suppliers' credit debts for the Gambia or Lesotho.

The debt problem was a major cause of strain in Ghana's relations with Britian. The Seven Year Plan of 1964 recognised the shortcomings of this method of financing imports and aimed instead at attracting 'soft' loans from international organisations and friendly governments; in addition some long-term foreign investment was expected in the private sector. In the event, however, there was a shortfall in the expected flow of resources under all heads and the government fell into the trap it had hoped to avoid, viz. it attracted a high percentage of suppliers' credits from both Western and Eastern countries. These credits were used to speed up industrialisation and improve the infrastructure.

The economic rationale of some projects was questionable at the time.[44] Between 1961 and 1965 Ghana was substantially in debt to the tune of some £307 million, with suppliers credits accounting for about £191.6 million.[45] Two-thirds were owed to Western countries and one-third to socialist countries. Britain accounted for the lion's share of the debt.

The problem became desperate in 1965, when the government invited the IMF to assist in renegotiating some of the debts. The IMF mission recommended, among other things, a temporary halt to the launching of new projects financed by suppliers' credits of a short or medium-term nature.[46] Debt repayment was running at an intolerable rate: £45 million in 1966/67, £43 million in 1967/68, followed by £45 million, £37 million and £26 million annually until 1970/71.[47]

It was the National Liberation Council, the military government that succeeded to Nkrumah's, which started real negotiations with Ghana's creditors to reschedule the debts. Responding to the NLC request for a study of the problem, the IMF replied that Ghana would need considerable foreign aid, and agreed to lend her a stand-by credit of £14 million for three to five years at 2–3 per cent interest.[48]

Following the IMF report, Britain agreed to convene the first meeting of Ghana's creditors to discuss the terms of negotiation. The attitude of the creditors was influenced by the fear that any substantial concession would be taken as a precedent by other debtor countries. Britain, acting as chairman, was in a difficult position. As the largest creditor she had an interest in avoiding default; but there was a limit to the terms that could be imposed if the country was not to face bankruptcy. In the negotiations, to the dismay of the NLC, Britain turned out to be the toughest negotiator.

The NLC argued that not all debts contracted by Nkrumah should be treated on the same basis, and stressed that there was an obvious case for re-examining the value of many contracts, viz. the frigate being built on Tyneside at a cost of £5 million, the VC10 ordered by Ghana Airways but not required, and the Drivici contracts which were alleged to be vitiated by corruption.[49] A series of tough and complicated meetings in which the IMF and IBRD played a supporting role resulted in two rescheduling agreements in 1966/67 and 1968.

The first covered all medium-term debts contracted before 23 February 1966 and falling due between 1 June 1966 and 31 December 1968. The amount involved was £56 million. Ghana was to start paying from July 1967, 20 per cent during the thirty-month period, and, after two and a half years' grace when only interest was to be paid, would begin repaying on 1 July the remaining 80 per cent in increments over an eight-year period. The individual creditors were left with discretion to determine the interest on the deferred principal, to be agreed on a bilateral basis. The agreement with Britain was signed in February 1967; it covered £25 million debts due until 1968, at 6 per cent interest rate.[50]

The second agreement covered the period of debt repayment between 1 January 1969 and 30 June 1972. Twenty per cent of the debt was to be paid during the period and the remaining 80 per cent spread over the period 1 July 1974 to 1 October 1981. Although Ghana asked for a maximum of 3 per cent interest on deferred amounts, she got only 6 per cent.[51] This added another £13 million to the total outstanding.

Britain and the other creditors regarded the second agreement as final. However, in 1969 the new civilian government headed by Busia demanded a new rescheduling, and stressed that a long-term agreement would help Ghana to improve her balance of payments and sluggish economic growth. Unlike the negotiating style of the NLC government the civilian Finance Minister, Mensah, affirmed that the creditor governments should share part of Ghana's predicament because of the suspicious circumstances surrounding some of the debts; he warned the creditors that even if there was a rescheduling Ghana reserved the right to re-examine some of the contracts.[52]

To start with, on 30 January 1970, the government terminated fourteen contracts signed between 1962 and 1965 with the Drivici group. It then asked for a composite refinancing loan for fifty years including a ten-year period of grace, at 2 per cent interest. It was particularly incensed at the additional interest at market rates which had to be met on the deferred payments.

Despite Mensah's hawkish position, Busia tried to cultivate a special relationship with the British government. During his many visits the debt problem formed a significant part of his discussions with Ministers connected with this issue. At the end of one of these visits, in September 1971, he welcomed Britain's attitude and expressed particular satisfaction with the decision to take back the £5 million frigate.[53]

A third rescheduling agreement was signed in July 1970. Ghana was granted 50 per cent relief on amounts due in both principal and interest, between 1970 and 1972, and each creditor was invited to consider three options: refinancing loans with a 61 per cent grant element; deferment for ten years without interest, which the creditors claimed would equal a grant element of 61 per cent; or additional aid, also with a 61 per cent grant element.[54]

Britain chose the first and decided to extend a £3.5 million refinancing loan. Serious disagreement developed, however, before it was accepted. Ghana maintained that the multilateral agreement of July allowed for relief on interest due on the debt which had previously been deferred. It was not until the following year that agreement was reached on Britain's terms.[55]

Busia's government was overthrown by the military National Redemption Council in January 1972, and on 5 February, the chairman of the NRC, Colonel I. K. Acheampong, unilaterally suspended payment of Ghana's debts.[56] He claimed that the creditor countries had persistently refused to view the solution of the problem from a developmental perspective. He announced that one-third of the principal would be repudiated outright, the accrued moratorium interest of $72 million on the principal emphatically rejected, that no obligations arising from the remaining contracts would be accepted unless the contracts concerned satisfied the conditions laid down, and that no repayment of any debt would be made for ten years. As a result the ECGD expected claims of up to £42 million. The department's total commitment to Ghana was £76 million.[57] Britain and several creditor countries reacted by removing cover from exports to Ghana.

Acheampong's repudiation put the creditors on the offensive. They were determined to press their claims and to talk him into another rescheduling meeting. Under their new offer Ghana was to be given five years' grace and would then repay the debts over fifteen years at 2½ per cent. Ghana was reluctant, however, to accept these terms. After months of delay an alternative was put forward which proposed a nil interest rate or one much lower than 2.5 per cent, but much longer grace and payments periods.[58]

Renewed negotiations took place in December 1973; in the communiqué that followed the creditors expressed sympathy for Ghana's economic predicament but were unable to accept all the proposals. Further talks were held in Rome in March 1974 which produced agreement. Ghana was given ten years' grace and payment was to be made in thirty-six instalments on 30 June and 31 December each year, starting on 31 December 1982 and concluding on 30 June 2000.[59]

Partly as a result of Ghana's experience, Commonwealth African and other developing countries realised that trade credits were an intolerable method of meeting their need for capital imports. They created debt problems and impeded economic development. The danger of default was equally clear to Whitehall, and one of the new aims of the Export Credit Guarantee Department was 'to help control the international credit race without jeopardizing the competitiveness of British exports'.[60]

Controlling the export credit race and protecting the competitiveness of British goods required a collective effort by all the major exporting countries. This has been very difficult to achieve, although there were institutions within the Western financial system attempting to co-ordinate export credit policies: the Berne Union, established in 1934 with a membership of private and public export credit institutions, the EEC co-ordinating group, established in 1960 with representatives from the Treasuries and export insurance companies of members, and finally the High Level Group created by the Trade Committee of the OECD in 1963.[61]

In the OECD attempts have been made to establish a ceiling for export credits and to reach agreement on credit terms for specific commodities.[62] When Acheampong repudiated Ghana's debts the High level Group of OECD met in 1972 to consider a common approach to suppliers' credits and see if guidelines could be drawn up for credit rating. In general, however, there has been an unwillingness to set up an institution with real authority to police the credit policies of exporting countries. Thus the debt problem is still a major cause of concern between developed and developing countries.

For Commonwealth Africa the problem was still how to satisfy the demand for capital imports in the face of downward prices in exports, low foreign investment and insufficient aid. The industrialised countries were urged to develop a special trade policy which would increase or stabilise the foreign exchange earnings of African commodities.

Commodity problems

Commodity problems have occupied Britain's attention since the decolonisation era, when the colonies needed favourable terms for their products to enable them to participate in the sterling area. Throughout the 1950s such issues centred on the Commonwealth and the specific commodity agreements which

Britain had signed as a consumer nation to help stabilise the prices of tin, sugar, wheat, etc. As we have seen, at independence the African States made commodity price stabilisation a primary objective and in 1964 joined other developing countries at the United Nations in convening a special conference to discuss trade and development.[63]

Ghana, Nigeria, Sierra Leone, Tanganyika, Uganda and Kenya voted with the other developing countries in supporting resolutions calling for preferential treatment for the products of developing countries, improvement in their terms of trade and the stabilisation of prices. All Commonwealth African States supported the Prebisch Report, which emphasised the need for a new trade policy towards the developing countries. Ghana's representative, Kojo Botsio, stated that what was needed was a 'new and harmonious system of international trade which will promote their economic development'.

The British government was sympathetic, but its policy was based on expanding world trade through growth.[64] Although Britain's representative, Edward Heath, supported the developing countries' demand, the government insisted on a pragmatic and flexible approach. According to Heath, commodities and the needs of poor countries should be treated on a case-by-case basis. Where Commonwealth Africa voted for all the resolutions, Britain voted for five, abstained on five and voted against five of the general principles; on thirteen specific resolutions she voted for seven, abstained on four and voted against one. The conference took no action on preferences.

Anthony Crossland reiterated the 1964 British programme during the second UNCTAD in 1968. It formed the thrust of British policy on commodities until 1975, when Harold Wilson moderately revised and adapted it to suit the new climate created by the developing countries' demands for a new international economic order.

The European Economic Community

Apart from trade diversification and the terms of trade, Commonwealth Africa was concerned also to protect its interests in the British market, which were threatened by the decision to join the EEC. With the decline in Commonwealth trade it had become an important trading partner for both Britain and the African countries.

Two features of the EEC, the Common External Tariff (CET) and the Common Agricultural Policy (CAP), threatened the latter's trade with Britain. UK pursuit of membership in 1961 raised the problem of having to apply the CAP and CET to Commonwealth African imports, removing their preferences in the British market. Whereas in the 1950s African policy had been to denounce the EEC without serious thought about coming to terms with it, Britain's decision to join compelled detailed assessment of how it affect trade and of how further EEC integration even without Britain would affect exports.

As we have seen, during the 1950s Britain put far more emphasis on co-operation with the Commonwealth, as the linchpin of the policy of defending sterling, than on Europe, which was discriminated against. Her response to European integration was lukewarm — support for military and security co-operation but in the economic sphere a preference for free trade which fell far short of total integration. When Europe, unimpressed, proceeded to form the EEC in 1958, Britain and six of the smaller European economies[65] formed the European Free Trade Area in 1959.

The Commonwealth saw no great danger in EFTA and endorsed it at the 1958 Commonwealth Economic Conference in Montreal. EFTA did not fully satisfy Britain's interests, however, and in 1961 she applied for membership of the EEC. The decision was influenced by economic, political and security considerations.[66] The question now arose as to how, within the Community, Britain could protect Commonwealth interests. According to her chief negotiator, Edward Heath:

... Commonwealth trade is one of the strongest elements in maintaining the Commonwealth association. ... I am sure that you will understand that Britain could not join the EEC under conditions in which this trade connection was cut with grave loss and even ruin for some of the Commonwealth countries.[67]

The response of Commonwealth Africa towards Britain's application was largely negative despite the trade discrimination they would suffer if they refused associate status. The African States rejected the EEC on political grounds and warned Britain not to disregard Commonwealth interests. Sierra Leone was the only country prepared to associate if Britain joined. Nigeria and East Africa rejected association with some qualifications, and Nkrumah rejected it for Ghana out of hand. For Commonwealth Africa the fundamental issue was the allegedly neo-colonial character of the Community's association policy and its harmful effect on African unity. As usual, Nkrumah set the pace:

The activities of the common market are fraught with dangerous political and economic consequences for the independent African states. The organization constitutes an attempt to replace the old evils we are striving to liquidate from our continent.[68]

Nigeria's reaction, although couched in the same language, was more flexible, as her leaders never endorsed Nkrumah's anti-neo-colonial policy. In 1961, after several representations to GATT, Britain and individual members of the EEC, the government concluded that the traditional forms of protest were ineffective and declared its intention to 'examine the possibility of closer economic cooperation with African states and association between Nigeria and the European Economic Community'.[69]

Sierra Leone actively sought association on the terms suggested under Part IV of the Rome Treaty. As the Prime Minister, Sir Milton Margai, explained:

We await Britain's final decision whether to join or not to join the European Community. If Britian joins, Sierra Leone will become eligible for association, and in that event we will apply for associate membership alongside the French speaking associated states whom I have consulted. If Britain does not join, we shall seek special trade agreements with the Community.[70]

Sierra Leone's stand was somewhat odd, since her chief export commodities — diamonds and iron ore — entered the EEC duty-free.

For Tanganyika, Kenya and Uganda the EEC was still a low priority because of their political status as colonies.[71] The same was true of Zambia, Malawi, BLS and Gambia. When in 1962 the EEC did become an issue for the three East African countries, political arguments had the edge over economic ones and it was the question of unity and federation that decided their position.[72]

In the face of opposition Britain argued that her membership of the EEC would protect Commonwealth interests. The government persistently maintained that the Commonwealth, being a loose association with diverse economic and political interests, offered no viable alternative to the cohesive and industrially successful EEC and that it could best be served by her joining.[73]

The government sent representatives to major Commonwealth countries in an attempt to persuade them to accept its position. John Hare visited Ghana, Nigeria and Sierra Leone. Britain did not bother much with the others, which, as colonies, she assumed would become associated under Part IV of the Rome Treaty. The communiqués issued at the end of Hare's visits did not state the policy standpoints of the countries involved,[74] although there were indications that he met tough counter-proposals from Nigeria and Ghana.

Britain tried to sell Part IV of the Rome Treaty to all Commonwealth African States, which would have put them on an equal footing with the French-speaking African associated States,[75] but, in the face of strong opposition to the reciprocity provisions of the treaty, held out the option of any other loose agreement with the Community which might suit them.[76]

To satisfy both Commonwealth African interests and the policies of the EEC, Britain proposed two options: either to grant free entry to the UK market alone for any Commonwealth country not associated with the EEC and then to fix the common tariff of the enlarged ECC at a level which would safeguard the interests both of that country and of the countries associated with the EEC; or to fix a zero or very low level for the common tariff.[77]

The negotiations seemed to be advancing well when the EEC endorsed the British view that, although Part IV was the ideal favoured for Commonwealth Africa, other forms of association should be offered,[78] and that further discussion would be necessary at a later stage to agree on the level of common external tariff on certain tropical products.[79] But then, during the crucial Commonwealth Prime Ministers' Conference of September 1962, Ghana, Nigeria, Tanganyika, Uganda and Kenya all opposed association as a neo-colonial device[80] which was bound to obstruct African unity.

However, although political factors played a significant role in their rejection of association, there were strong pressures in both Nigeria and East Africa for a special agreement with the EEC. This led to the belief that if association was rejected as neo-colonialism it should not prevent the establishment of separate agreements to protect their exports. This view was confirmed by Nigeria's Prime Minister when he announced his country's decision to open negotiations with the EEC in 1962.[81] Kawawa, East Africa's spokesman at the Conference, also said that 'despite rejection, East Africa would like to negotiate trade arrangements with the Community'.[82]

Meanwhile Britain's negotiations continued in Brussels until on 14 January 1963 President De Gaulle imposed France's veto. In Commonwealth Africa the outcome was ironic. Sierra Leone, the only country in favour of association, dropped her plans, while Nigeria and East Africa went ahead with theirs. The result was two separate agreements, between the EEC and Nigeria, and the EEC and East Africa. In both cases the negotiations were tortuous and complicated by the need to reconcile the conflicting claims of the Commonwealth relationship on the one hand and the EEC's special relationship with the francophone associated States on the other.

Nigeria's agreement with Europe (the Lagos Convention) was signed on 16 July 1966. It granted her exports free access to the markets of the EEC. But because of pressure from the associated States, which argued that Nigeria benefited from Commonwealth preferences, the EEC agreed to limit access by applying tariff quotas on four commodities — plywood, palm oil, groundnut oil and cocoa — which, the associated alleged, threatened their own trade with the EEC. Tariff quotas were calculated from an average of sales to the EEC during 1962—64 plus an annual increase of 3 per cent. In return Nigeria agreed to grant the EEC preferential treatment for twenty-six products, thus placing Britain and other Commonwealth countries at a disadvantage.

Britain protested to the Nigerian government when the text was made known. The Commonwealth Secretary, Arthur Bottomley, had warned Nigeria in August 1965 that if it discriminated against British trade 'the British government might be obliged to reconsider the treatment of imports from Nigeria to the British market'.[83]   Britain argued that the reciprocal preference granted to specific EEC exports operated against the principles of GATT and the spirit of UNCTAD, which disapproved of reverse preferences by developing countries to the products of industrialised nations. The government did not push its claims hard, however, because of the continued British interest in EEC membership and the fact that it was a British government which in 1961 had urged Commonwealth Africa to associate under Part IV. In the event the Lagos Convention was not ratified because of differences between EEC members and the federal government over the Biafran war.[84]

In East Africa the Arusha agreement with the EEC was signed on 26 July 1968 and approved by the European Parliament on 1 October. East Africa granted preferences to the EEC on fifty-nine products representing 15 per cent of imports from the EEC on a margin of 2—9 per cent. The East African products were granted free access to the markets of the EEC except for coffee,

cloves and pineapples, which were on a quota basis. New negotiations were held in late June and early July 1969 for a new
agreement which was essentially the same as that of 1968. A
few more products were added to the original fifty-nine imports
and the quotas for coffee, cloves and pineapples were slightly
expanded. This agreement was signed on 24 September 1969
and was to run parallel to the second Yaoundé agreement until
31 January 1975.

Meanwhile Britain made another attempt in May 1967 to
enter Europe but was vetoed again by De Gaulle. However,
when the Conservative Party reopened negotiations in 1970
terms were agreed in June 1971 and ratified by Parliament on
28 October. The treaty of accession was signed on 22 January
1972.

Britain's membership revived the question of Commonwealth
Africa's trade relations with the EEC. Whereas in the 1960s
African opposition to the EEC included Britain's application to
join because of what, it was thought, would happen to Commonwealth interests, in the 1970s all the African States accepted
the permanence of the EEC and British membership. The
vehement ideological opposition to the EEC, decked out in the
language of neo-colonialism, had petered out. Nkrumah, the
foremost critic, was no longer in office. Pan-Africanism remained
a long-term aspiration, accommodating the separate sovereign
States with their multifarious political and economic relations.
No African State had succeeded in achieving a complete transformation of the political economy inherited at independence;
all remained firmly within the Western international economy;
the diversification that had taken place was not towards regional
economic relations or socialist bloc countries but towards the
West.

Furthermore, the agreements signed by Nigeria and East
Africa with the EEC demonstrated that the EEC was prepared
to consider alternatives to the objectionable Yaoundé agreements. The Commonwealth was no longer a powerful economic
force; considerable diversification had taken place in trade, aid,
investment and monetary relations. This is not to say that
Commonwealth Africa supported the EEC uncritically. Recipro-
catiy was still opposed by all except Malawi, which decided to
apply for association under the Yaoundé terms. Ghana and
Nigeria in particular still distrusted the EEC's external trade
policy.

Commonwealth African States were given three options: a

Yaoundé-type agreement with francophone Africa, an Arusha-style agreement or a simple trade agreement. A separate Commonwealth African Group was formed[85] with the immediate purpose of negotiating with the francophone associates.[86] It held its first meeting in Lagos and established a secretariat for African Associables.[87] It also decided to send a delegation to Brussels for discussions with the Yaoundé associates.[88]

In April 1973 eleven Commonwealth African representatives met in Nairobi and discussed a joint approach to the negotiations.[89] The chairman, Dr Julius Kiano, pointed out that the three options had been proposed without consultation and might not meet all Africa's needs.[90] Meanwhile at a meeting in Rwanda between the Commonwealth States and the francophone associates, a communiqué was issued which stressed the 'similarity of views' between the two groups and called for continued exchange of views and information.[91]

The major points of difference were on the question of reciprocity and the European Development Fund. For the associates President Senghor of Senegal insisted that reciprocity, which was an integral part of the Yaoundé agreements, should be retained in any future trade agreement with the EEC to prevent Europe from invalidating the treaty.[92] Senghor believed that if any future EEC-African agreement was to be based on the principles of partnership and equality then Africa should reciprocate giving Europe's exports preferential treatment. This line of argument derived from his world view, which saw Africa and Europe as one entity. He believed that without reciprocity other powers would penetrate African markets and reduce the cohesiveness of Euro-African relations.[93]

The Commonwealth countries differed from this view. Although they wanted to promote trade with Europe they objected to suggestions of developing a distinct Euro-African system such as they had branded neo-colonialism in the 1960s. They saw reciprocity as giving an unnecessary preference to developed countries which not only offended against the provisions of GATT but worked against the UNCTAD demands for one-way preferences from industrialised countries. Most of them had also a tradition of non-reciprocity in trade relations. As we have seen, only Zambia, Sierra Leone, the Gambia and Malawi granted reciprocal preferences to Britain under the Commonwealth scheme, and the first three had even revoked them without retaliation from Britain. Perhaps it was not surprising that Malawi, which had never revoked her reciprocal preferences, was the only Commonwealth African country that was prepared to offer preferences to the EEC.

On the European Development Fund (EDF), the Yaoundé associates demanded that the pattern of the Yaoundé agreement should be followed, linking aid with trade. Otherwise, they reckoned, they might end up getting less aid than before, as countries that were not parties to the agreement would qualify for aid. They also insisted that an agreement to include the Commonwealth States should not result in less aid to associates.[94] Since Commonwealth Africa was not yet associated, they did not stress the aid/trade linkage, although they tried to allay the fears of the associates that steps should be taken to maintain their present level of aid from the Community.

The problem of reciprocity was solved by the EEC's Deniau memorandum. On trade, the document proposed the maintenance of a free trade area and ruled out preferences. It stated that associates might maintain or introduce customs duties or qualitative restrictions against the EEC which might be needed for budgetary purposes, development needs or for promoting regional co-operation. A new system for compensating associates for losses in export revenue was suggested.[95]

Meanwhile it was agreed that Commonwealth Africa and francophone Africa should form a common front with other African, Caribbean and Pacific countries to negotiate with Europe. The meetings of OAU heads of state and Ministers of Finance, Trade and Development in May 1973 produced an eight-point Charter for Economic Independence and a common front towards the EEC.[96] This was later strengthened, on the eve of the Brussels negotiations, at a further meeting in Nigeria of all the African, Caribbean and Pacific (ACP) countries. The OAU conferences set up a secretariat to work in Brussels with the existing Yaoundé and Arusha secretariats and appointed Wenike Briggs, Nigeria's Federal Commissioner for Trade, as spokesman in Brussels.[97]

At the preliminary meeting between the EEC and the ACP countries on 24 July 1973 the two groups stated their demands. Effective negotiations between the ACP States and the EEC started on 17 October and ended in January 1975. The negotiations therefore occurred against the backdrop of the oil crisis, the phenomenal rise of producer consciousness and the demand for a new international economic order. In themselves, these factors added strength to the ACP States' desire for unity. The African States advocated free entry of their goods to the markets of the EEC and a new and expanding European Development Fund whose management they would share and which would lay emphasis on industry. They also asked for the stabilisation of prices of their exports rather than earnings and relating the prices to the cost of industrial imports.

During the negotiations Britian and France clashed over the principle of reciprocity, which Britain opposed, and the policy on aid, which Britain insisted should be extended to non-associates like India, Pakistan and Bangladesh. France and other EEC countries felt that aid for the big Asian countries should be left to the wider international community at the United Nations because of the vast sums that would be involved. On this issue Britain found herself at loggerheads not only with ther Community partners but also with her traditional Commonwealth African partners. The latter felt that Judith Hart's proposals would reduce their own proportion of EEC aid.

Following Britain's tough line on aid, the Council of Development Ministers adopted a resolution stating that in principle the Community took seriously its financial and technical aid responsibilities to non-associates. But France maintained that even if the EEC accepted responsibility for a world-wide aid effort, priority must still be given to the Community's associates.[98]

The negotiations between the EEC and ACP States were long, difficult and complex. In between the formal negotiations the ACP countries themselves conducted working meetings in Addis Ababa and Dakar. There were sessions in Kingston, Jamaica, in July 1974 and in Brussels in January 1975. On 10 February 1975 the ACP countries met in Accra to review the final draft of the Brussels agreement. The agreement between the two groups was finally signed in Lomé, the capital of Togo, on 28 February 1975, and it became known as the Lomé Convention.

The Lomé Convention has five basic features: (1) trade agreements and trade promotion, (2) stabilisation of export earnings, (3) financial and technical co-operation, (4) industrial co-operation, and (5) the institutions of co-operation.

In the field of trade promotion almost all exports from the ACP countries were allowed to enter the EEC duty-free, except for agricultural products having joint marketing organisations, for which there were special arrangements, notably sugar.[99]

On stabilisation of export earnings, the convention introduced a new model in international commodity policy. It proposed to remedy the harmful effects of the instability of export earnings to enable the ACP States to achieve stability and sustained economic growth. To this end, the EEC proposed a system for guaranteeing stability of earnings from exports to the EEC of certain products on which their economies were dependent and which were affected by fluctuations in the world market.[100] The aim was not to change the terms of trade in favour of developing countries, as advocated by the ACP, but to guarantee falls in average earnings. The system works only after market forces have operated; it is a kind of social security.

Stabex, as it came to be called, covers twenty-nine products arranged in twelve groups: ground-nut products; cocoa products; coffee products; cotton products; cocoa nut products; palm, palm nut and kernel products; raw hides; skins and leather; wood products; fresh bananas; tea; raw sisal; iron ore.[101] Countries qualify for assistance when the commodity in question represents more than 7.5 per cent of the total receipts of the country concerned: the 'threshold of dependence'. This threshold is reduced to 2.5 per cent in the case of the least developed ACP States, those which are landlocked or islands, or those designated as least developed in the Lomé Convention.[102] The second criterion is that only exports consumed or processed in the EEC qualify. This rules out re-exports. However, Guinea-Bissau, Ethiopia, Rwanda, Burundi and Swaziland, which export very little to the Community, are exempt. Stabex applies to all their exports of the twenty-nine products.

For each product and for each ACP country a 'reference level' is drawn up each year, on the basis of export receipts over the four preceding years. When the earnings in any one year drop below this level by 7.5 per cent (2.5 per cent for the less developed States) the country involved calls on the EEC to pay it a sum corresponding to the difference. The recipient repays when its export earnings expand, except for the thirty-four least developed countries, which are exempted from repayment.

A few more products were added to the list in April 1977 — vanilla, cloves, pyrethrum, wool, mohair, gum arabic and ylang-ylang — and a few more countries were accorded Stabex for exports in all directions: Western Samoa, Seychelles, the Comoros, Tonga and Lesotho. Nigeria does not qualify because of the preponderance of oil in her total earnings. Among the Commonwealth African States classed as least developed, landlocked or island States are Botswana, the Gambia, Swaziland, Tanzania, Uganda, Zambia and Lesotho.[103] They qualify for Stabex under the 2.5 per cent threshold of dependence.

In the field of financial and technical co-operation there was to be no reduction in the EEC's financial aid to countries already associated under the Yaoundé agreement and other ACP States were placed on equal footing with them. Accordingly more money was provided under the new convention — a total of 3,390 million units of account.[104] This was made up of 2,100 million units of account for grants, 430 million units of accounts for loans on special terms, 95 million units of account for risk capital and 375 million units of account for Stabex.[105] A further 390 million units of account was made available for loans from the European Investment Bank's own resources. The ACP States participate in the administration of this aid and there is provision for special measures to help the least developed countries.

The Lomé Convention also provides for industrial co-operation.[106] Various types of programme are proposed, varying from development of research and technology to the establishment of contact between firms. These programmes are directed by a Committee on Industrial Co-operation, assisted by a Centre for Industrial Developments.

To administer the convention there is a Council of Ministers, assisted by a Joint Committee of Ambassadors. The convention also makes provision for a Consultative Assembly, composed on a basis of parity of members of the European Parliament and of representatives designated by the ACP States.

The Lomé Convention marked a new phase in Commonwealth African relations with Britain. The system which had been the framework of both Britain's and Africa's economic policies in the 1950s had not only undergone fundamental changes in the 1960s by way of diversification, but had now become integrated into a wider system of Afro-European relations. Commonwealth preferences had been abandoned and Britain was part of a wider Europe striving towards greater economic and political unity. Commonwealth Africa's relations with Britain in Europe also involved the participation of the Yaoundé countries, which were previously outside their politico-economic system. With their combined effort, and discovery of their common economic backgrounds, a new spirit was born which strengthened the forces of regional co-operation. The Economic Community of West African States (ECOWAS) was in fact an indirect consequence of Lomé.

The Lomé Convention itself has not solved the basic problems facing commodities in the world markets, nor has it addressed itself fully to the structural problems of economic imbalance and the asymmetrical relations between Europe and Africa.

In fact it has been seen by many writers (mainly radical) as perpetuating Europe's dominance over Africa. The emergence of the convention in 1975 represented an attempt by the Europeans (who remain a powerful bloc within the Western economic group) to stem the tide of radical demands by the developing countries for a new international economic order. The oil crisis clearly demonstrated the potential of producer power and the dependence of the industrialised countries on raw materials. It was hoped, therefore, by the EEC countries that, while not meeting all the demands of the developing countries for indexation and a comprehensive plan for commodities, Lomé could provide a model for future North—South relations. Some of these hopes are now being questioned by the ACP countries.

Notes

1 *The Banker*, July—August 1959, p. 407.
2 H/R Debates, 9 February 1959, p. 62.
3 *The Banker*, July—August 1959, p. 475.
4 *Britain and the Developing Countries: Africa*, COI Reference pamphlet 94, 1970, p. 9.
5 R. W. Green, 'Commonwealth Preferences on the Exports to the Preference Area', *Board of Trade Journal*, 11 June 1965, pp. iv—v.
6 *Ibid.*, p. xvii.
7 Zambia and Malawi were then members of the Central African Federation.
8 *The Kennedy Round: Estimated Effect on Tariffs*, UNCTAD (Geneva), Parts I and II, 1968, TD/6/Rev. 1, pp. 3—40.
9 Harry Johnson, 'The Commonwealth preferences: a system in need of analysis', *Round Table*, October 1966, p. 366.
10 Ghana Debates, 12 November 1959, col. 335.
11 *Ibid.*, col. 337.
12 Ghana Debates, 8 October 1962, col. 159.
13 Ghana Debates, 14 March 1963, col. 351.
14 Ghana Debates, 22 October 1962, Vol. 34, col. 177.
15 See Y. Bangura, 'The Politics of Economic Relations between Britain and Commonwealth Africa, 1951—75', unpublished Ph.D. thesis, University of London, 1978, appendix 5(1), for detailed figures.
16 Ghana Debates, 24 August 1965, col. 34.
17 Bangura, *op. cit.*, appendix 5(1).
18 H/R Debates, 29 March 1962, col. 521—33.
19 Bangura, *op. cit.*, appendix 5(2).
20 *Tanzania: Second Five Year Development Plan for Economic and Social Development*, 1 July 1969—30 June 1974, Vol. 1, p. xiv.

21   Cmnd 6061, 1975, p. 68.
22   Tanzania *Statistical Abstract*, various years.
23   Bangura, *op. cit.*, appendix 5(3).
24   *Ibid.*, appendix 5(4).
25   *Ibid.*, appendix 5(5).
26   *Ibid.*, appendix 5(6).
27   *Ibid.*, appendix 5(7).
28   *Ibid.*, appendix 5(8).
29   Cmnd 6061, p. 57.
30   Bangura, *op. cit.*, appendix 5(9).
31   P. M. Lander-Mills, 'The 1969 South African Customs Union Agreement', *Journal of Modern African Studies*, 1971.
32   *Report of the Establishment and Organization of the Department of Customs and Excise* (Gaberone), p. 3.
33   *Ibid.*, p. 6.
34   Lander-Mills, *op. cit.*, p. 276.
35   Bangura, *op. cit.*, appendix 5(10).
36   The BLS countries also send a large proportion of their male labour force to work in South Africa.
37   Cmnd 2276, 1964, para. 10.
38   H.C. Debates, 6 February 1964, col. 1356–82.
39   *Ibid.*, col. 1373.
40   Wilson, *The Labour Government, op. cit.*, p. 117.
41   *Ibid.*
42   Taking 1955 as a base, the United Nations calculated that the price index of commodities fell by 10 per cent in 1962. (*Economic Bulletin For Africa*, 1964, p. 3.)
43   Table 6.1.
44   A. Krassowski, *Development and the Debt Trap*, 1974, chapter five.
45   *Ghana: a Current Report, 3–11 April*, 1967, p. 4.
46   Ghana Debates, 10 September 1965, col. 717–18.
47   *West Africa*, 12 October 1968, p. 1191.
48   Krassowski, *op. cit.*, p. 124.
49   *West Africa*, 10 December 1966, p. 1410.
50   Cmnd 3247.
51   Cmnd 3944.
52   *West Africa*, 29 November 1969, p. 1455.
53   *West Africa*, 10 September 1971, p. 1063.
54   *West Africa*, 18 July 1970, p. 790.
55   Cmnd 4763.
56   *Speeches and Interviews by Col. Acheampong* (Information Department), 1973, Vol. I, pp. 20–8.
57   *West Africa*, 10 March 1972, p. 289.
58   *West Africa*, 1 January 1973, p. 3.
59   Cmnd 6039, 1974.
60   *Review of Export Credits Guarantee Department*, March 1972, p. 6.
61   Christopher Prout, 'Finance for Developing Countries', in Susan

Strange (ed.), *International Economic Relations of the Western World, 1959–1971*, Vol. 2 (RIAA), 1976, p. 378.

62 *Ibid.*, pp. 382–3.
63 *Proceedings of UNCTAD, 23 March–16 June 1964*, Vol. I, Final Act and Report, E/Conf. 46/141, Vol. 1, p. 4.
64 UNCTAD (1964), Vol. II, E/Conf. 46/141, p. 390.
65 Austria, Denmark, Norway, Portugal, Sweden and Switzerland.
66 J. D. B. Miller, *Survey of Commonwealth Affairs: Problems of Expansion and Attrition, 1953–1969*, 1974, pp. 309–17.
67 Cmnd 1565, 1961, p. 8.
68 *African Freedom Fighters and Unity*, address by Nkrumah to the Conference of African Freedom Fighters in Accra on 4 June 1962, p. 5.
69 H/R Debates, 1961–62, col. 604, p. 20.
70 Sierra Leone, H/R Debates, 29 November 1962, col. 438.
71 Joseph Nye, *Pan-Africanism and East African Integration*, 1965, p. 22.
72 *Ibid.*, p. 223.
73 Harold Macmillan, H/C Debates, 2 August 1961, col. 1484–5.
74 Cmnd 1449, 1961.
75 The French-speaking African States first became associated under Part IV in 1958 as colonies. At independence associate status was negotiated, culminating in the Yaoundé agreement of 1963. It retained the same provisions of the first agreement — free entry to the markets of the EEC for the exports of the associated States, the right to discriminate against the EEC for budgetary or balance of payment reasons and for the protection of infant industries; they also received aid from the European Development Fund and the European Investment Bank. But they were expected to grant reciprocal preference to the goods of the EEC. The 1963 agreement was succeeded by the 1969 Yaoundé agreement, with the same basic provisions.
76 Cmnd 1565, *op. cit.*, p. 10
77 *Ibid.*, p. 10.
78 Miscellaneous No. 25, 1962, *The United Kingdom and the EEC*, Cmnd 1805, p. 4.
79 *Ibid.*, p. 4.
80 Sierra Leone supported association.
81 *Mr. Prime Minister, op. cit.*, pp. 69–70.
82 Nye, *op. cit.*, p. 226.
83 *Commonwealth Survey*, Vol. II, No. 19, 14 September 1965.
84 *West Africa*, 12 October 1968, p. 2680.
85 *West Africa*, 5 March 1973, p. 298.
86 *West Africa*, 5 March 1973, p. 299.
87 *Ibid.*, p. 299.
88 *Ibid.*
89 Malawi was not represented.
90 *West Africa*, 23 April 1973, p. 549.

91 *Ibid.*
92 *West Africa*, 2 April 1973, p. 425.
93 For an excellent exposition of the politics of reciprocity see James Mayall, 'Africa and the enlarged EEC', *Millenium Journal of International Studies*, Vol. 3, No. 2, autumn 1974, pp. 127–32.
94 *West Africa*, 28 May 1973, p. 693.
95 To be discussed below.
96 *West Africa*, 28 May 1973, p. 693.
97 *West Africa*, 9 July 1973, p. 943.
98 *West Africa*, 24 June 1974, p. 765.
99 ACP–EEC Convention, *The Courier*, No. 31, special issue, March 1975, Title I, Art. 2.
100 *Ibid.*, Title II, Art. 16.
101 *Ibid.*, Art. 17.
102 *Ibid.*, Art. 17.
103 *ACP–EEC Convention, op. cit.*, Title II, Art. 24.
104 One unit of account = $US 1.5.
105 *ACP–EEC Convention, op. cit.*, Title II, Art. 92.
106 *Ibid.*, Art. 26–39.

7

Aid relations, 1957—75

As we have seen in chapter three, Britain's aid programme in the period of decolonisation was expected to achieve two objectives: to prepare the colonies for independence and to protect colonial participation in the sterling area. At independence British aid to Africa was no longer aimed at defending the *status quo* in the sterling system; dollar descrimination had ended and it was almost impossible to predict the monetary policies of the African countries. Britain still needed an aid programme, of course, for trade promotion and for the development of amicable relations with the new States to protect her residual interests. The former objective, aid as long-term trade promotion, required Britain to determine her aid programme in accordance with her balance of payments problems without much consideration to collective Commonwealth interests. The latter, the protection of her residual interests, was forced upon her as part of the price of decolonisation. These two aspects of the aid programme are examined in this chapter.

The evolution of British policy

In 1957, when Ghana achieved independence, Britain had yet to work out a coherent programme that would take into account, on the one hand, her own economic problems and, on the other, the new political situation and rising economic expectations of the African States. The government's aid programme still centred on the Colonial Development and Welfare Act. It was British policy, however, to wind up this programme at independence, since it had been designed essentially for dependent countries. The issue was further complicated by the outright denunciation of the scheme by Nkrumah on the eve of Ghana's independence. Buoyed up by the massive

Ghanian sterling reserves, he maintained that his 'foreign policy ... will not be dictated by the need to seek assistance from other countries'.[1] He affirmed that Ghana would not seek the continuation of CD & WA (which he saw as charity) but would encourage 'development expenditure' by Commonwealth countries 'on a basis of equality and mutual benefit'.[2]

Three arguments were advanced in support of a continued British aid programme to match the new situation. First, as the Chancellor of the Exchequer recognised in 1958, African independence was bound to put 'a strain on the reserves' and would limit Britain's domestic freedom of action.[3] To contain the rate of sterling reserve mobilisation by the newly independent African States, it was necessary to provide them with additional sources of capital for economic development. Second, it was reasoned that as Britain was a major trading nation there was rational self-interest in aiding developing countries to prevent a slide into slump, particularly as the decline in commodity prices made this a distinct possibility.[4] Third, there were those, like Harold Macmillan, who argued that Britain had an interest in providing Africa with aid to preserve stability in the face of the East—West conflict.[5]

It was against this background that Britain announced a new aid programme for both the colonies and the independent Commonwealth States at the Commonwealth Economic Conference of 1958.[6] Commonwealth Assistance loans were to be tied to the purchase of British goods and services.[7] Exchequer loans to the colonies were not tied, but the government recognised Britain's special commercial advantages in awarding such loans.[8]

The 1958 aid policy was clearly conceived with balance of payments problems in mind. The message was clear. If Britain was to take an active part in the development of the newly independent States, the balance of payments should not suffer in the process. When the scheme was launched in Montreal the Commonwealth African States did not recognise its serious limitations due to British determination to insure her own balance of payments. They welcomed it as a major contribution.[9] However, the Commonwealth Assistance loans proved difficult to disburse in Africa. They carried high interest rates with relatively short repayment periods. The rates were arranged at the current rate of borrowing from the UK Treasury with the addition of a ⅛ per cent or ¼ per cent management charge; the repayment was usually twenty-five years' maximum, with a seven year period of grace. More important, the tying of loans to the purchase of British goods left the Commonwealth African countries with limited room for manoeuvre in using them to support development.

By 1964 Sierra Leone had an overall commitment of £3½ million under the scheme. Between 1963 and 1965 she had spent only £550,000 and after 1965 found it almost impossible to disburse the rest.[10] The same was true of Uganda, Ghana and Tanzania, whose rate of loan disbursement declined as the years went by. Kenya had a small amount of Commonwealth Assistance (£575,000), so she gradually dispensed with it, although not without some difficulty, as the extent of her annual disbursement shows (Table 7.1). Only Nigeria had managed to disburse more than half her total commitments by 1968; even then she was some £14 million underspent.

There was clearly a need to revise the scheme to make it more acceptable. In its July 1960 report the Select Committee on the Estimates strongly asserted that the new Commonwealth States would require financial aid on a wider basis than that provided by the existing programmes.[11]

The government was therefore forced to introduce major changes in 1963; it announced that loans for periods of up to thirty years with periods of grace up to ten years would be made to developing Commonwealth countries. Where economic circumstances made it necessary, the government would be prepared to remove the burden of service charges by granting a waiver of interest, as well as the deferment of capital repayment for seven years. It was claimed that this latter concession would reduce 'from say 5½ per cent to below 3 per cent the effective rate of interest on a loan for twenty-five years'.[12]

The monetary constraints on Britain's aid policy: the balance of payments

Britain's aid commitment to developing countries was accepted by all governments, and the special problems of Commonwealth Africa were clearly appreciated. But underlying the need for aid to Africa and the Commonwealth was the problem of the economy and the balance of payments. At independence the link between aid and the balance of payments became all the more important since political control over the African countries had ended and their governments were eager to establish new economic contacts. Furthermore the British economy

Table 7.1 Issues from the Consolidated Fund for Development: loans made under section 3, Export Guarantees Acts, 1949–67 (Commonwealth Assistance loans) (£ '000)

Country	Overall commitment	1964–65*	1965–66*	1966–67*	1967–68*	1968–69†	1969–70†
Kenya	575	–	156	337	47	35	–
Tanzania	1,250	226	273	74	173	–	–
Uganda	2,400	1,167	191	5	29	–	–
EACSO and EAU	5,200	1,624	133	991	1,775	189	195
Ghana	7,164	1,854.5	180	50	30	17	–
Nigeria	20,800	3,815	6,904	3,401	2,209	1,264	1,465
Sierra Leone	3,500	550	–	–	–	–	–

* Actual expenditure.

† Provisional; estimates as at 31 March 1969.

Notes. EACSO: East African Common Services Organisation; EAU: East African University.

Sources. Ministry for Overseas Development, Select Committee on Overseas Aid, 1968–69, 1969–70, Bill 285.

was going through a period of crisis both at the domestic and the external payments level. By the mid-1960s it seemed that the liberal aid atmosphere which had been reflected in the 1963 White Paper would founder as a result.

However, between 1963 and 1966 the liberal aid policy was temporarily sustained as a result of the pro-Commonwealth policy of the new Labour government. Harold Wilson's plan for the regeneration of British industry and improvement of the balance of payments rested squarely on closer Commonwealth economic relations. The National Plan of 1965 was drawn up on this assumption.[13] Under these arrangements British aid was to be given a prominent role. The Labour government set up the Ministry for Overseas Development in October 1964 and centralised the administration of aid in one department under a Cabinet Minister.

The early orientation of the MOD reflected the idealism of the Labour Party in this field. The old moral argument for providing aid was resurrected and its relationship with the wider economic objective finely established.[14] The balance of payments constraint was rightly recognised, but at that stage the connection between aid and trade for balance of payments reasons was not yet explicitly stated. British aid was to be concentrated on 'those countries and regions where it will have the greatest effect on development in the long run'.[15] The only vital link with trade was long-term. The government believed that Britain had a vital role to play in Commonwealth development and insisted that aid should be freed from its political constraints.[16]

However, this euphoria was not to last as the balance of payments moved into massive deficit in 1966. It came to be widely felt that the aid programme constituted a strain on the balance of payments and that radical policies were required to control it.

Many politicians and academics felt that the sacrifices of the British people under the incomes policy and credit squeeze should be extended to the external level by cutting the aid programme.

The economic measures of July 1966 included therefore measures for the restriction of government overseas expenditure. Disbursements under the aid programmes were to be limited to £205 million in 1967/68 as compared with a target of £225 million in 1966/67.[17] This was to be achieved partly by cutting the provisional aid programme itself and partly by slowing down

Table 7.2 Disbursement of UK bilateral technical assistance to Commonwealth Africa, 1964–73 (£'000)

	1964	1965	1966	1967	1968	1969	1970	1971	1972	1973
Gambia	120	281	120	296	162	266	167	274	403	439
Ghana	307	315	379	464	646	910	933	894	1,047	1,263
Nigeria	1,189	1,320	1,556	1,811	1,571	1,898	1,499	1,614	2,502	4,999
Sierra Leone	166	190	276	332	371	408	417	353	394	684
Kenya	2,323	4,849	2,604	3,815	4,075	2,733	3,217	2,891	4,499	4,741
Tanzania	3,219	2,510	1,873	866	1,774	1,681	1,792	1,405	1,378	1,387
Uganda	1,956	2,155	3,048	1,480	2,386	2,154	2,025	2,342	1,969	1,626
EAC	3,123	3,527	3,329	2,205	2,354	1,476	784	1,251	1,972	2,972
Botswana	155	276	341	398	419	549	577	714	639	970
Lesotho	61	309	368	214	288	289	249	274	407	562
Swaziland	169	254	285	388	325	356	452	505	514	826
BLS	17	46	5	6	1	–	12	16	22	28
Malawi	1,195	1,113	1,283	1,370	1,677	1,734	1,685	1,742	2,822	2,160
Zambia	1,645	2,284	2,197	3,575	4,306	4,288	2,523	3,842	3,592	4,006
Total	15,645	19,429	17,664	17,220	20,355	18,742	16,386	18,117	22,160	26,663

Notes. EAC: East African Community.
      BLS: General aid to Botswana, Lesotho and Swaziland.

Source. British Aid Statistics, 1964–68; 1969–73

disbursements. Reductions were envisaged mainly in bilateral financial aid and were to apply to individual items in the course of normal aid negotiations with the recipient countries.

In the face of public criticism, and with no detailed statistical data to back their preferred policy, the MOD erred on the side of those who advocated cutting the aid programme to protect the balance of payments. The cuts inevitably affected Britain's aid to Africa. From £67,573,000 in 1965 it fell to £55,355,000 in 1966 and £54,603,000 in 1967; in 1968 it fell to £36,566,000.[18]

The impact of the reductions on relations with Commonwealth Africa was varied. For Botswana, Swaziland, Lesotho, Malawi and the Gambia, which received a high proportion of budgetary and technical aid from Britain, there was hardly any alteration in the existing pattern. The two types of aid had little effect on the balance of payments. For instance, an agreement was signed between Britain and Gambia in 1967 for £3,200,000 to be used for development and budgetary purposes.[19] In addition a grant of £90,000 was made available for uncompleted projects which were carried forward from 1966/67 and grants to the extent necessary to balance the recurrent budget were arranged, with a ceiling of £590,000 for 1967/68, £450,000 for 1968/69, £370,000 for 1969/70 and £280,000 for 1970/71.[20] This was in addition to technical assistance.

For Sierra Leone the restrictions coincided with an attempt to put the country's monetary house in order in the face of a massive balance of payments and budgetary deficit. Most of the excess public expenditure of this period was caused by the undue optimism on the part of Sir Milton Margai's government that foreign assistance would be forthcoming from Britain and other 'friendly countries'. This was what prompted the Minister of Development, R. G. O. King, to increase expenditure:

At the moment very considerable assistance is coming primarily from the United Kingdom and the United States, but indications are that not only will these two nations provide further and much bigger assistance, but that other nations will very likely be giving us appreciable assistance ... I have therefore very strong reasons for including in my proposals more projects than I know we have the financial ability or executive capacity to carry out at the moment ...[21]

Although the flow of finance from external sources was exaggerated — the government had to resort to contractor finance schemes — it was true that Britain was by far the most

Table 7.3 Gross disbursement of UK bilateral aid to Commonwealth Africa, 1964–73 (financial and technical aid) (£ '000)

	1964	1965	1966	1967	1968	1969	1970	1971	1972	1973
Kenya	14,391	16,692	10,460	7,618	4,395	10,756	11,099	9,820	10,638	11,668
Tanzania	6,509	4,991	4,169	1,223	1,181	1,762	2,030	2,120	1,725	1,498
Uganda	5,388	3,626	4,347	4,861	2,386	3,771	4,352	4,029	3,254	1,811
EAC	6,039	5,451	5,354	4,165	2,361	1,481	979	2,236	1,983	2,977
Gambia	874	1,392	834	799	173	813	399	583	922	940
Ghana	2,383	575	479	494	646	5,734	5,488	6,876	1,769	1,803
Nigeria	4,319	9,615	5,760	5,543	2,545	5,608	11,030	7,098	6,541	7,807
Sierra Leone	1,471	780	1,099	905	371	952	932	1,010	813	1,016
Botswana	3,187	3,455	4,648	5,236	5,658	4,874	2,795	4,405	3,354	3,309
Lesotho	1,935	3,170	3,858	4,030	4,202	3,717	653	3,054	2,404	1,855
Swaziland	2,365	2,765	3,302	3,154	2,557	4,357	3,129	1,462	3,838	3,434
BLS	104	469	250	208	262	–	12	16	205	314
Malawi	10,282	10,120	8,035	8,286	4,808	7,152	7,709	5,774	8,197	5,443
Zambia	7,128	4,472	2,760	8,801	5,021	5,667	2,569	5,418	4,210	5,849
Total	66,375	67,573	55,355	54,603	36,566	56,644	53,176	53,901	49,853	49,724

Notes. EAC: East African Community.
BLS: General aid to Botswana, Lesotho and Swaziland.

Source. British Aid Statistics, 1964–68; 1969–73

important donor before the July 1966 measures. Between 1961 and 1965 she accounted for 80 per cent of the aid received. By that time only France, West Germany, the United States and the World Bank had provided limited loans to Sierra Leone.[22]

When the cuts in the British programme were announced, the country was caught unprepared. Partly because of the assumption that British aid would continue at the existing level, the government had undertaken a programme of domestic public expenditure cuts recommended by the IMF. The immediate consequences were to speed up its external aid diversification. The new government had briefly renounced dependence on external aid altogether. The Minister of Finance, Dr M. S. Fornah, stressed at the time of taking office in 1968, after the one-year military interregnum, that donor countries were unwilling to offer substantial loans to developing countries: they would therefore have to bear a sizeable proportion of their development programmes.[23]

The lesson was the necessity of self-reliance; it led to an awareness that development capital, not only from Britain but from donor countries generally, was hard to come by. Everywhere the major donors were reducing their aid programmes, some because of balance of payments problems, others because of a general public disillusionment with the political and economic returns. In 1968 the second UNCTAD was emphatic in discerning a general downward trend in aid to developing countries.

The new conviction that development should not be based on shaky external foundations was embodied in Tanzania's Arusha Declaration.[24] Tanzania was prepared to mobilise her domestic resources to the maximum and to place less emphasis on foreign assistance. Nyerere was convinced that even if the pre-Arusha mode of development was accepted, the necessary foreign capital would not just be forthcoming.[25] Most of Commonwealth Africa turned to diversification as it became clear not only that total dependence on Britain was bad politics, but that Britain herself would be unable to offer all the aid that was required to finance their development programmes.

In Britain, the argument as to whether the balance of payments suffered as a result of the aid programme continued until the mid-1960s, when the MOD carried out a statistical analysis which changed the attitudes of the department, built up confidence for an expansion of aid and placed a new emphasis on the commercial aspect.[26]

The report reversed earlier conclusions. It maintained that for every £100 of British aid overseas, £62 returned to Britain. For Commonwealth Africa the general average was even higher, 74 per cent. This despite the low percentage of tied aid to East Africa and the southern African countries. The return for East Africa was 83.9 per cent, for Malawi 56 per cent, for Zambia 93.7 per cent, for BLS 49 per cent and for Nigeria 78 per cent.[27]

These high percentages were mainly due to the low level of switching in British aid to Africa as a result of the close trade relations of the 1960s; it was also partly due to the high level of induced imports, reflecting a high propensity to import from Britain; the reflection effect was high also in Commonwealth Africa because of Africa's increasing trade with Britain's other trading partners, especially the EEC.

From the report it appeared that about three-quarters of the aid offered to Commonwealth Africa came back to Britain. Thus, *prima facie*, the cost to the balance of payments was only 25 per cent of the total flow. The average amount of British aid to Africa from 1964 to 1973 was about £60 million; the real cost to the balance of payments was £15 million per annum. If one takes into account annual payment of amortisation and interest, which from 1964 to 1978 was running at an average of £13 million, this would reduce the cost to about £2 million. In fact since 1972 the repayment of amortisation and interest has been running at about £15 million a year.[28] On this argument there appeared to be no cost to the balance of payments.

On the basis of the report the Minister of Overseas Development declared that:

If one weighs up the effect on the balance of payment's position, both pro and anti, I come to the conclusion that the balance of payments position now in 1969 would be worse if we had no aid programme over the last ten years. Equally, I think were we to drop it suddenly now we would have a worse balance of payments in the 1970s.[29]

This view was echoed by Judith Hart, Reg. Prentice's successor at the MOD.[30] The conclusion that development aid had a positive impact on the balance of payments led to a stronger emphasis on the commercialisation of aid, particularly as the MOD had to demonstrate the usefulness of the programme to a sceptical public. Aid was to be an integral part of the export drive. The memorandum of the Minister of

Table 7.4 UK bilateral aid to Commonwealth Africa: amortisation and interest (£ '000)

	1964	1965	1966	1967	1968	1969	1970	1971	1972	1973	1974	1975	1976	1977	1978
UK gross bilateral aid	70,775	69,807	55,711	55,025	57,900	61,033	58,690	60,806	55,423	59,866					
Amortisation and interest	8,914	9,120	9,633	10,306	10,909	13,118	13,830	14,540	15,151	15,664	15,637	16,078	16,321	16,393	17,691

Source. British Aid Statistics.

Overseas Development to the Select Committee on Overseas Aid in 1968 spelled this out clearly. The Treasury also endorsed 'the desirability, within the necessary limitations, of increasingly concentrating' Britain's 'bilateral aid on those countries which offer the greatest potential markets'.

This policy was in marked contrast to the idealism of 1964, when the MOD laid emphasis on 'countries and regions where it will have the greatest effect on development in the long run', a policy which was seen by industrialists as out of tune with British interests. The Confederation of British Industry had been outspoken in its criticism of the government because of its alleged failure to keep industry informed about the aid programme and the inadequate commercial orientation in dispensing it.[31] This was certainly the situation from 1964– 66/67, as the Permanent Secretary of the MOD himself maintained that there was a tendency to pay insufficient attention to Britain's commercial interests.[32] But, as he further maintained, after 1967 the attitude of the MOD changed in terms of using aid as an instrument of British trade and the machinery of consultation between the MOD and the Board of Trade improved markedly.[33]

The implication of this new policy was that British aid was to be diversified and freed from the constraints of the Commonwealth system. The Foreign and Commonwealth Office was in fact optimistic that British aid would be less concentrated in the Commonwealth in the future: this was inevitable as the patterns of Anglo-Commonwealth economic relations changed.[34] But as the MOD discovered, it was easier to assert the restructuring of British aid than to abandon old partners, patterns and commitments. In practice it proved difficult to sacrifice the political philosophy of British aid to the new commercial objectives. Certainly, without the political committments, 'there would be less [aid] in some countries in Southern Africa and perhaps more in Latin America, because of the market potential'.[35]

In the meantime, however, the Commonwealth continued to receive a substantial share of British aid. Some 85 per cent went to the Commonwealth as a whole and some 30 per cent to its African members. Britain was unable to shift the emphasis radically, although as the MOD explained to the select committee in 1969, it 'had in fact already been taking account of commercial considerations in allocating the aid programme'.[36] Thus in Africa aid was increasingly concentrated on Nigeria,

Zambia and Kenya, which offered the greatest scope for British exports and investments. The high proportion to Nigeria was reflected mainly in technical assistance. Oil has enabled Nigeria to dispense with British financial aid, but she still needs technical expertise. Britain has been able to increase its technical aid scheme to Nigeria rapidly. Nigeria was sixth in the technical aid table in 1964; by 1973 she had become the largest recipient in Commonwealth Africa.[37]

Aid to Ghana, Tanzania and Uganda fluctuated wildly because of political problems. In 1966, after the overthrow of Nkrumah, Britain increased the flow to help the new regime tackle Ghana's urgent economic problems; there was a further increase when the moderate and pro-Western Kofi Busia became Prime Minister. However, with the advent of Acheampong and his unilateral repudiation of debts on commercial credits, aid to Ghana declined.[38] In the case of Tanzania, aid relations were cool from 1965 to 1970 because of the severance of diplomatic relations over Rhodesia in 1965 and Tanzania's decision to suspend pensions payments to British officials who served in Tanzania before independence. In Uganda, Amin's Asian policy and the nationalisation of British property in 1972 put him out of favour and led to the suspension of aid.

British aid to Sierra Leone and the Gambia was comparatively modest. A strong case could be made that Britain neglected these two countries; they were not strategically placed like the southern African States and lacked the market potential of Nigeria and Kenya. The total aid they received was far less than that extended to Botswana (a smaller population than that of Sierra Leone and about the same as that of Gambia) or Swaziland (far smaller in size and population than Sierra Leone and roughly the same size as the Gambia).

Aid to Botswana, Lesotho and Swaziland was comparatively higher partly because of the technical aid programme and partly because of the huge budgetary assistance offered to them. Aid to Lesotho was interrupted in 1970 when Chief Jonathan suspended the constitution in the face of apparent defeat in the general elections.

Meanwhile the six-year rule of the Labour government was brought to an end by a Conservative administration far more disposed towards the profitable employment of British aid. The Conservatives accepted the increasing commercialisation of aid and were prepared also to use the programme to support British private investments. On 26 April 1971 they introduced new measures to protect British company investments in developing countries and in the process tried to link aid to private investment;[39] there was an attempt to link the Commonwealth Development Corporation with the activities of British firms; to expand the provision of capital aid, through recipient governments, to local investment banks and development corporations for use in joint ventures in private British capital; and to link aid for basic infrastructure projects to particular private investment plans in the developing countries. It was stressed that such aid, which would be provided on a normal government-to-government basis, would cover infrastructure such as roads or power supplies essential to a private investment project and which the investor could not himself be expected to finance: and finally, to provide a pool of skilled labour, through technical assistance, thus indirectly assisting private investors who needed to recruit trained local staff.[40]

The extent to which these measures were successful is difficult to assess, partly because the Conservative government lasted only four years and partly for reasons already outlined in connection with the trade/aid dichotomy. There was clearly an awareness and readiness to restructure British aid and to make it more efficient in promoting trade and private investment, but Britain's political commitments in Africa dictated that the restructuring would be slow and difficult. These political problems will now be examined.

Political aid commitments

The political commitments in Britain's aid programme were an unavoidable part of the price of decolonisation. These commitments did not fall within the mainstream of aid policy, which, as we have seen, was profoundly influenced by balance of payments considerations. However, despite their relative independence, the implementation of the commitments was significantly influenced by the economic situation generally and commercial and monetary objectives in particular. There were four such commitments: first, the technical aid programme, with particular reference to the Overseas Service Aid Scheme (OSAS) and other supplementation schemes; second, budgetary aid to financially dependent countries; third, the Pensions Aid Scheme and its political ramifications in Tanzania; and, fourth, the Land Purchase and Land Resettlement Scheme in Kenya. The first was a natural outcome of the confusion and uncertainty which threatened the colonial service as many colonies approached or achieved independence; the second was a special problem for Britain as she had to continue to subsidise many newly independent African States because of their inability to raise sufficient revenue for their budgets; the last two enabled the Commonwealth African States to meet burdensome obligations to British citizens which could not otherwise have been met.

The Overseas Service Aid Scheme and other supplementation arrangements

In 1954, in recognition of the rapid advance of the colonies towards independence, the British government announced the establishment of the Overseas Civil Service to replace the Colonial Service.[41] The new service was designed to take into account the post-independence changes in the conditions of service of pensionable British officers as the new States developed their local civil services, and also the continuing need for expatriate officers in those States.[42]

According to British policy, the large number of colonial civil servants — about 15,000 — needed security and a reliable future, as most of them had entered the service on the assumption that the empire would outlive their careers. With inadequate alternative employment in the home civil service and huge costs to the British taxpayer if they were to return home without proper jobs, the British government felt it was necessary to act quickly.[43]

The need to protect the interests of colonial civil servants coincided with the problems the new States would have faced if these officers were to leave prematurely, because of the inadequate preparations to staff the colonies with experienced national administrators. In 1960 there were only 16,644 local officers in the colonies, as opposed to 25,004 expatriates in comparable posts. For Commonwealth Africa the figure was 12,091 locals as against 16,417 expatriates.[44] Commonwealth Africa therefore needed the services of the expatriates until their own nationals could take over from them.

The main problem, as it was conceived by Britain, was how to persuade the expatriates to stay on in the newly indpendent States. Two things seemed necessary: compensation schemes and agreements to safeguard their pensions.

The principles governing compensation were that at independence expatriates should be entitled to retire with compensation judiciously calculated; where they opted to continue in service compensation should not constitute an inducement to retire; retiring officers should be given compensation in a lump sum at the time of retirement; compensation schemes should also offer individual officers the right to serve so long as their services were required; and expatriates should be regarded as members of the British civil service.[45]

The Ghana scheme set the basic pattern for all subsequent compensation schemes. In 1955, with the attainment of internal self-government, Ghana, in agreement with Britain, introduced a scheme of compensation for pensionable British officers. Under the scheme it was open to expatriates, if they wished, to retire, at independence with their full pension and compensation. The scheme accelerated the rate of retirement because of the favourable inducements it offered. It proved costly to the Ghanaian government, which alone was responsible for the payment of pensions, compensation and inducement allowances.

This problem was partly mitigated in Nigeria by the introduction of Special Lists A and B.[46] Under Special List A the salaries, pensions and compensation due to any British expatriate were paid by Britain and recovered from Nigeria. The collapse of Special List A because of the British government's failure to guarantee expatriates a full career led for the first time to more direct financial participation by Britain through the provision of aid. Special List B was established, guaranteeing expatriates 90 per cent in advance of their entitlement to lump-sum compensation while they were still serving; Britain also agreed to reimburse half the cost of the allowance of the 90 per cent advance compensation with an interest-free loan to Nigeria.

In 1958 Sierra Leone announced compensation terms to encourage expatriates to continue in service. These were approved in 1960 and followed the Ghanaian and Nigerian schemes. A new feature was the stipulation that the lump-sum compensation should be payable, not immediately on retirement, but by eight annual instalments with an interest rate of 5 per cent.[47]

In all three schemes, except perhaps in the case of Nigeria's Special List B, Britain tried to pass on the financial responsibility to the new governments. However, the West African countries were relatively more advanced and the number of expatriates in their civil services was not as high as in East, Central and southern Africa. In East Africa there were 8,912 expatriate civil servants, compared with 5,284 in West Africa.[48] Faced with the next round of independence in East Africa, the British government 'fully realised that the new governments would not be able to meet the full cost of these programmes'.[49] The Secretary of State for the Colonies said in Parliament on 28 July 1960 that Britain was prepared to take over from the colonies the inducement pay and allowance of British expatriates, so that while the local government would be responsible for the local rates of the salary and other conditions of service, Britain would bear the cost of supplementary pay and allowance for the expatriates. These proposals were institutionalised in the Overseas Service Act of 1961.

Some 1,400 pensionable and 6,500 contract officers came within the scope of these arrangements, at an annual cost to the British government of between £13 million and £14 million.[50] Britain was prepared to offer a similar arrangement to Nigeria and Sierra Leone, but in both countries general public service agreements had been negotiated and compensation schemes settled.[51] It was reckoned that Nigeria rejected OSAS for political reasons as well. The fact that it was not offered to Ghana was seen as an insult in lumping Nigeria and the colonies together.[52] Ghana did not take part because it already had its own programme. In any case, as Kenneth Younger maintained, supplementation was unnecessary because Ghana was offering the market price to retain and recruit expatriates.[53]

Public Service Supplementation Schemes (PSSS) were arranged, however, with Sierra Leone and Nigeria in 1965 and with Ghana in 1967.[54] These schemes were for supplementing of the salaries of British expatriates working in those countries. A similar scheme was drawn up for expatriates serving in Zambia and Malawi who because of their original intention of settling in the country did not qualify for OSAS. It came into effect in 1966 and called the British Aided Conditions of Service Scheme (BACSS). Under this scheme, Britain was not responsible for any of the cost of compensation or pension payments. At the end of 1968 BACSS agreements covered 699 expatriates.[55]

Britain also concluded agreements with several Commonwealth African countries to extend supplementation to any employment in public and social service. They applied mainly to the universities of Zambia, Malawi, Ghana, Nigeria and Sierra Leone and expatriate teachers in Sierra Leone, Ghana and Nigeria. The schemes did not cover pensions or compensation, and Britain's contribution was determined in relation to shown needs and the aid available for such purposes.[56] Expatriate supplementation and other schemes negotiated with the governments of Nigeria, Sierra Leone and Ghana covered 1,870 officers at the end of 1968.[57]

The Overseas Service Aid Scheme and supplementation schemes accounted for more than a quarter of British aid to Africa and the Commonwealth. Little wonder, then, that with the formation of OSAS in 1961 the Conservative government established the first official institution to address itself solely to technical aid: the Department of Technical Co-operation.

These technical aid schemes did not directly affect the balance of payments; the officers' salary payments were made outside the country where they were serving, to a bank of their choice. It could in fact be argued that they helped the balance of payments indirectly by creating the right conditions for future spin-off exports. British culture (in the widest sense) was maintained and an orientation towards British goods prolonged. An exact computation of their impact on British exports is impossible, but the MOD certainly recognised the possible spin-off effects for commercial relations. The aid cuts of 1966 did not affect, therefore, the technical aid programme. The technical aid schemes were renewed in 1971 to run until 31 March 1976.

The Pensions Aid Scheme and its political ramifications in Tanzania

One of the most critical and emotionally charged aspects of the Anglo-African aid was the payment of pensions by the African States to British expatriates who had served prior to independence.

British government policy was that the African States should accept the responsibility for payments, since all new States took over the assets and liabilities of the colonial power. British policy was rooted in nineteenth-century international law, which discounted the developing countries' disapproval of European customary law and the asymmetrical colonial relationship on which British policy rested.

To guarantee the payment of these pensions the British

government persuaded the new States to sign Public Officers' Agreements. The central provisions of such agreements were that expatriates should enjoy equal rights with local officers as regards tenure and promotion; there should also be equal treatment as regards pensions, leave and passage, and conditions should not be less favourable than those in force immediately before independence; a pensionable officer who continued to serve on and after independence should continue to be entitled to retire at any time. Pensions should be paid in sterling (to a bank of the individual's choice) at the pre-independence rate of exchange between sterling and the local currency irrespective of any variation in the local rate; and expatriates should be eligible for transfer or promotion in the British civil service without prejudice to pension rights.

These agreements were heavily loaded against the new States; they were drawn up mainly to protect the favourable conditions of expatriates under the colonial system. In most Commonwealth African States no distinction was in fact drawn between expatriate and indigenous officers, even for accounting purposes. Thus when pensions were increased in Nigeria in April 1961 there was no discrimination against expatriate pensioners — a situation which was opposed by many Africans.[58]

To facilitate payment of the pensions the British government offered loans and grants to the new States. Without this assistance the public outcry and their financial difficulties would have rendered the pension schemes unworkable. The yearly pensions for all British expatriates amounted to £23 million, of which £10 million was paid by the overseas governments and £14 million by British.[59]

Tanzania however, found the pre-independence pension scheme was a burden and decided to terminate it on 18 June 1968.[60] It was estimated that about 3,000 expatriates were affected by this decision. The amount involved was £7½ million: £1 million for the pensions and £6½ million for loans provided by Britain towards Tanzania's liabilities for compensating part of their pensions.[61]

The party newspaper, *The Nationalist*, came out in strong support of the government's action and depicted the conflict in neo-colonialist terms, arguing that Tanzania was being forced to pay the agents of Britain who contributed towards the colonisation of the country.[62]

Despite British representations, the Tanzanian government

stuck to its position. Mr Jamal stated that Britain took almost eight months to respond to Tanzania's *aide-mémoire* of July 1967 and found the two concessions offered in July 1968 unacceptable.[63] Britain had proposed to supplement the existing compensation and commutation loans to the extent needed to meet future liabilities from the service of the remaining pensionable officers; it was estimated that the additional loan needed for this would amount approximately to £1 million over the next four years; she also agreed to a revision of the formula for calculating the new State's contribution to the pension scheme which would have the effect of increasing the British share in Tanzania from about £50,000 to about £200,000.[64]

In the face of Tanzania's determination the British government suspended its aid programme. A development loan of £7.5 million under negotiation was cancelled. Technical assistance programmes were to be allowed to run out but no new ones were to be initiated.[65]

Until 1970 Britain opposed all attempts to abolish the Public Officers' Agreement, despite persistent attacks from Members of Parliament, aid organisations like the Overseas Development Institute, and the pensioners themselves, who wanted more security, demanding the payments come under British administration. Britain insisted that any repudiation of the pension scheme would lead to an equivalent reduction in the development aid budget.[66]

On 11 March 1970 the British government decided, however, to bow to parliamentary and public pressure and announced a two-stage take-over of the pension payments. In the first stage the African governments would continue to pay the recipients from the reimbursements received from Britain. The final responsibility now lay with the British government, although administrative responsibility still rested with the African governments. Aid relations were resumed when in June 1970 a senior official of the MOD visited Tanzania and offered a loan for capital development and a full range of technical assistance. Tanzania accepted.

In 1973 the new Conservative government introduced legislation which gave it responsibility for the administrative and financial aspects of the scheme and covered both pre- and post-independence pensioners. The Bill provided, however, that through agreements with overseas governments they would repay Britain for post-independence services.[67]

The cost of reimbursement of the second stage of the pensions programme was £12 million in 1973 and 1974. This figure was expected to fall as the years went by. The final cost was esti-mated to be in the region of £200 million over some fifty years. Despite criticism from developing countries and aid organisations, Britain was firm on the decision to compute the scheme as part of its aid programme.[68]

The Land Purchase and Land Resettlement Scheme in Kenya

About forty per cent of total British aid to Kenya between 1962 and 1975 went towards land purchase and resettlement. As a percentage of British aid to Africa as a whole this was about eight per cent. From 1962 to 1965 two-thirds of aid to Kenya was for land purchase and resettlement, representing about eleven per cent of British aid to Africa.

The land problem had been at the forefront of Kenya's aid relations with Britain since decolonisation. During the colonial era 7.5 million acres of the Kenya Highlands were reserved exclusively for European use. Indeed, the political history of colonial Kenya 'was replete with petitions, del-egations, uprisings and demonstrations, reflecting a sizeable body of African opinion opposed to settler control of the "lost lands" '.[69] Without an acceptable resolution of the con-flict political independence would have strained both racial harmony and Anglo-Kenyan relations.[70] With the large Euro-pean settlement in Kenya the British government had a strong interest in preserving a multi-racial society where Europeans would play a large role in the spheres of politics and econ-omics.[71]

There were certainly fears of land nationalisation or a take-over move by Mau Mau nationalists, as they had vowed at independence. As African independence became inevitable, the crux of the matter seemed to be the method of financing land transfer from willing European sellers to African buyers. A start was made in January 1961 when the British govern-ment concurred with the Europeans in the transitional govern-ment in setting up the 'Yeoman and Peasant' scheme. Its objective was to settle 6,000 African families on farms designed to produce £100 a year net income and a further 1,800 families on Yeoman schemes designed to produce £250 a year net income.[72] The scheme was projected to cost £7.5 million.

After the constitutional conference of March 1962 the radical nationalist party, the Kenya African National Union, which had promised the Mau Mau nationalists the distribution of free land, entered into a coalition with the moderate Kenya African Democratic Union and accepted the proposals for a grand land purchase and settlement scheme to be financed by Britain. This was the One Million Acre Scheme,[73] announced by the Colonial Secretary, Reginald Maudling, in July 1962. It was designed to purchase 200,000 acres of land a year and to settle 70,000 African families on 1.5 million acres in five years.[74] The total cost was £25,091,000, of which Britain provided £21,420,000. The IBRD and CDC provided £2,471,000, and the remaining £1,200,000 was provided by the West German government. About 30 per cent of the British contribution was in grant form. The scheme was intended to remain in force until 1967 but was in fact ended in 1965.

In 1964 the Kenyan government asked Britain for a follow-up scheme at a more ambitious cost of £30 million. The request was difficult to meet owing to Britain's chronic balance of payments problems.[75] Meanwhile a temporary agreement was reached on a further £1½ million for the purchase of 100 European mixed farms in the Ol Kalou Salient pending the results of a fact-finding mission headed by Maxwell Stamp to examine the effect of the land aid scheme on the Kenyan economy.

The Stamp Report stressed that land transfer had not demonstrated any positive economic development and had caused a foreign exchange drain on the Kenyan economy.[76] The report recommended a continuing programme of land purchase but at a much reduced rate. This was a turning point, as following the report, land aid and development aid became linked in the form of a package deal to the benefit of the Kenyan economy and the interest of Britain's main aid programme.

The report formed the background to negotiations in November 1965 for an extension of the land purchase and resettlement scheme. A new scheme was announced for the purchase of 100,000 acres of European mixed farmland each year for four years commencing in April 1966. Britain made an interest-free loan of £18 million for the period between 1966 and 1970 of which £11.7 million was for economic development and £6.3 million for land purchase.[77]

A new programme was announced in April 1970 to succeed the Forty Thousand Acre Scheme. Britain offered £11.5 million aid to Kenya. Of this, £7.75 million was for various development proposals, including land consolidation and rural development; the remainder, £3.75 million, was for land purchase.

The aid was for a period of four years; £2.75 million was in grant form and the other £8.75 million a twenty-five-year loan at 2 per cent interest with a period of grace for capital repayment of seven years.[78]

By 1970 the land aid scheme had been brought into line with the mainstream of Britain's aid programme.[79] The emphasis was now on schemes which promoted economic development in Kenya and trade with Britain, and the amount of aid allocated specifically for land transfer depreciated. This new approach was repeated in the scheme of March 1973. £22 million was made available to the Kenyan government for commitment over the next three years; this included £5 million carried over from previous undertakings. Of the outstanding £17 million, £7 million was for land transfer, £6 million was in grant form for the purchase of land, and £1 million a loan for the Agricultural Finance Corporation. The balance of £10 million was a loan for other development projects.[80]

Budgetary aid to financially dependent countries

Britain's budgetary aid programme to financially dependent countries in Commonwealth Africa differed from the previous three programmes only in so far as it did not involve offering loans to help British citizens; it was a direct subsidy to the African governments to enable them to balance their recurrent budgets. But, like the other three aid programmes, budgetary aid was firmly rooted in the political economy of decolonisation: the need to provide sufficient capital for the new States to strengthen their political independence.

Malawi, the Gambia and BLS achieved independence without having established a taxable capacity which would enable them to raise sufficient revenue to balance their expenditures.[81] The need for budgetary aid was first recognised in the 1950s during the decolonisation era. After the war British policy towards the colonies was to keep expenditure strictly within revenue for as long as possible.[82] However, with the need to expand basic and recurrent services to match the growing demands of the nationalists for satisfactory standards of administration, it became almost impossible to maintain rigid control over expenditure.[83] For those countries without a taxable capacity or revenue-earning commodities the British government was compelled to step in to subsidise the deficit that emerged between expanded expenditure and limited revenue.[84]

The critical countries were Botswana, Lesotho and Swaziland.

In consultation with the World Bank, the British government appointed a mission to undertake an economic survey of the three countries.[85] It was the mission's report that provided the rationale for the development of a budgetary programme for financially dependent countries. The aim was to enable such countries to reach the take-off point, become self-reliant and eventually achieve stable political independence.[86]

With the submission of the report to Britain the programme of budgetary aid which started in the 1950s received public endorsement. The problem of what would happen if the three countries achieved independence before the deficit was 'over-topped by the steadier growth of revenue' was left unanswered. As it happened, political independence came before financial self-reliance, and Britain was forced to extend budgetary assistance to the independence period.

Malawi was the first Commonwealth African State to present Britain with this problem.[87] When the Federation of Rhodesia and Nyasaland was dissolved in 1963, Malawi's inadequate tax base and limited revenue yield could not match the growing expenditure of the government. In 1966 Britain undertook to provide budgetary aid, which for the period 1966—68 was to be within a maximum of £5.3 million a year.[88] From 1966 to 1973 she received some £22 million in budgetary aid. This was almost the same as the amount of capital aid for development for the same period.

Britain did not maintain the maximum of £5.3 million for 1966—68 agreed upon in the London financial talks, mainly because of the drastic steps Malawi took to end her budgetary dependence. Budgetary aid actually depreciated annually between 1966 and 1973. The depreciation was also a consequence of the fifty-fifty rule introduced by the British government as an incentive to governments receiving grants-in-aid to economise.[89] The rule allowed 50 per cent of the savings under the agreed ceilings to be added to the following year's development aid.

The Gambia faced similar problems at independence in 1965. Actually after 1958 the Gambia was unable to match revenue with expenditure of a recurrent nature. Opportunities for increasing revenue were limited; the tax base was not large, and apart from small trading companies there were only a handful of industrial enterprises to be taxed.[90] The MOD sent an economic survey mission to the country in 1965.[91] Its report was not optimistic about the possibility of raising sufficient revenue to correct the budgetary deficit in the near future.[92] Britain agreed to offer a four-year budgetary aid programme between 1967 to 1971, and stressed that a reduction would depend upon the export performance of Gambia's chief commodity, ground-nuts.

In Botswana, Swaziland and Lesotho, the take-off point envisaged in the British and IBRD report did not occur before independence. Britain therefore continued to provide budgetary aid. Between 1967 and 1973 all three countries received a total of £27,985,000. Of this, Botswana received £13,835,000, Lesotho £11,550,000 and Swaziland £2,600,000. Budgetary aid to Swaziland was for one year only after independence because of her relative wealth in terms of export commodities, asbestos, iron ore and timber.

Budgetary aid posed awkward and complex problems for Britain and the recipient countries alike. This type of aid is justifiable only in a colonial relationship where the distinction between the metropolitan and the colonial government is often blurred. At independence the recipient countries had to suffer the indignity of submitting their budgets to the MOD in Britain. They resented it,[93] and the donor did not want to be seen publicly controlling their economies.[94]

Both donor and recipients were pledged therefore to end the system. The Gambia indicated on receipt of the 1967/71 budgetary aid that it was a prime objective of policy to eliminate the need for it as quickly as possible.[95] For Malawi, Britain announced radical changes on 11 March 1971. The government explained that it was prepared to agree to fixed amounts of budgetary aid for the three year period 1971/72: 3.6 million kwacha in 1971/72, 2.6 million kwacha in 1972/73 and 1.6 million kwacha in 1973/74. It stated that these amounts would be adjusted to take account of Malawi's financial responsibility for primary and related payments to expatriate officers which she had already offered to meet from 1 April 1971.[96] Since the total of these pensions and related payments was likely to be about a million kwacha or more per annum, the need for budgetary aid was deemed to disappear before the end of the 1973/74 financial year.[97] Thus one means by which Britain got round the budgetary problem was the pensions and computation schemes she took over in 1971. This was, however, only one part of the solution. The other was expenditure control by the recipients.

The MOD sent an economic mission to Botswana in 1965

to look into the possibility of reducing dependence upon external aid due to budgetary deficits. Its report urged the adoption of three sets of measures: a programme of economic development which would raise the productive capacity of the country, a fiscal policy which would divert part of the increase in incomes towards meeting the recurrent budget deficit, and finally the utmost economy in public expenditure.[98]

In practice it was the third proposal, that was implemented in earnest, since these countries lacked the resources to raise immediate revenues. Thus in 1970 Lesotho announced a six-point fiscal programme for ending the budgetary deficits.[99] It was mainly because of these measures that Lesotho was able to dispense with budgetary aid in 1973/74. By similar programmes budgetary aid to Botswana was brought to an end in 1971/72. The Gambia was expected to achieve a budgetary surplus early in the fourth development period, which started in 1974/75, through strict budgetary control and economy in government expenditure.[100] The government in fact achieved a small budgetary surplus in 1972/73.[101]

Conclusion

From the period of independence to the early 1970s Britain found it difficult to restructure aid away from the Commonwealth towards areas of export potential. Much as this was a logical decision for an economy beleaguered by balance of payments worries, it was impracticable for a country that had just come out of the business of colonialism, with many residual commitments. It seemed, however, that in the post-1975 period Britain would be much freer to chart the course of its aid as most such political commitments were wound up or in other ways discharged.

Notes

1 Ghana Debates, 5 March 1957, Vol. 4, col. 26.
2 *Ibid.*, col. 10.
3 H.C. Debates, 15 April 1958, col. 51–2.
4 Cmnd 2736, 1965, paras. 15–18.
5 *Macmillan in Africa, 1960*, Conservative Political Centre (London), 1960, p. 11.
6 The Montreal Conference, 1958. (C.O.I.).
7 Cmnd 974, *op. cit.*, para. 16.
8 Cmnd 672, 1959, p. 9.

9 Nigeria H/R Debates, 9 February 1959, p. 59.

10 See Table 7.1.

11 *Fourth Report from the Select Committee on the Estimates,* Session 1959–60, para. 15.

12 Cmnd 2147, 1963, para. 44.

13 Cmnd 2764, p. 1.

14 Cmnd 2736, paras. 1–2.

15 *Ibid.,* para. 4.

16 *Ibid.,* paras. 1–2.

17 Cmnd 3180, *op. cit.,* para. 59.

18 Table 7.3.

19 Sessional Paper No. 7, *British Financial aid to the Gambia, 1967/68– 1970/71, and a Study of The Economy of Gambia,* 1967, p. 1.

20 *Ibid.,* p. 1.

21 *Speech on the Development Programme* (Government Printer), 1962, pp. 1–2.

22 *Peace For Progress: a Progress Report on Economic and Social Development* (Government Printer), 1965, p. 83.

23 *Budget Speech* (Government Printer), 1968, p. 3.

24 J. K. Nyerere, *Freedom and Socialism: a Selection of Speeches and Writings,* 1968, Parts II–III, pp. 238–41.

25 *Ibid.,* p. 239.

26 'Aid and the Balance of Payments', *Economic Journal,* March 1970, *ibid.,* p. 8.

27 *Ibid.*

28 Table 7.4.

29 Select Committee on Overseas Aid, Sessions 1968–69, H.C. 285, p. 12.

30 H.C. Debates, 27 November 1969, Vol. 792, col. 606–7.

31 Seventh Report from the Estimates Committee, *op. cit.,* q. 1057.

32 *Ibid.,* q. 1535.

33 *Ibid.,* q. 1377–8 and 1535.

34 Memorandum, Foreign and Commonwealth Office, para. 2, Select Committee on Overseas Aid, 7 July 1969.

35 Seventh Special Report from the Select Committee, *op. cit.,* p. 12.

36 *Ibid.,* p. 12.

37 Table 7.2. She now pays the full cost of those technical aid schemes.

38 Table 7.3.

39 Cmnd 4656, 1971, paras. 16–19.

40 *Ibid.,* p. 7.

41 Colonial No. 306, 1954.

42 Cmnd 1193, 1960, para. 3.

43 *Ibid.,* para. 3.

44 Memorandum, Secretary of State for the Colonies. Fourth Report from Select Committee on Estimates, Session 1959, Bill 260, p. 84.

45 Cmnd 1193, *op. cit.,* para. 9.

46 Specialist List A in Cmnd 978. Specialist List B in Cmnd 492, 1958.

47 Cmnd 1129, 1960, Annex, para. 2.
48 Fourth Report of Estimates Committee, *op. cit.*, p. 84.
49 Cmnd 1193, *op. cit.*, p. 7.
50 Memorandum, Secretary of State for Technical Co-operation. Estimates Committee, Tenth Report, 1964, Appendix B.
51 Cmnd 1193, *op. cit.*, p. 7.
52 O. A. Ojedokun, 'Nigeria's Relations with the Commonwealth, with Special Reference to her Relations with Britain, 1960–1966' (University of London, unpublished Ph.D. thesis), 1968, p. 200.
53 Select Committee on Estimates, *op. cit.*, q. 1835.
54 Cmnd 3994, 1969, para. 12.
55 Cmnd 3994, *op. cit.*, para. 11.
56 *Ibid.*, para. 13.
57 *Ibid.*, para. 14.
58 Nigeria H/R Debates, 13 April 1961, p. 496.
59 The Select Committee on Overseas Aid, Session 1968/69, *op. cit.*
60 Reported in Yashpal Tandon, 'Juristic Disimperialism: a Case Study of Tanzania's Dispute with the UK over the Pensions Issue', in Y. Tandon, *Readings in African International Relations*, Vol. I (East Africa), 1972, p. 222.
61 H.C. Debates, 20 June 1968, Vol. 766, col. 174–5.
62 Tandon, *op. cit.*, pp. 223–34.
63 *Ibid.*, p. 223.
64 *Ibid.*
65 H.C. Debates, 20 June 1968, Vol. 766, col. 174–5.
66 H.C. Debates, 26 July 1968, Vol. 769, col. 1251.
67 H.C. Debates, 1 March 1973, Vol. 851, col. 1763.
68 H.C. Debates, 1 March 1973, Vol. 851, col. 1798.
69 Garry Wasserman, *Politics of Decolonization: Kenya Europeans and the Land Issue, 1960–1965*, 1976, p. 17.
70 *Aid Policy in One Country: Britain's Aid to Kenya, 1964–1968* (Ministry of Overseas Development, London, 1970, p. 5. Nottidge and Goldsack: The Department of Settlement of Nairobi, *The Million Acre Scheme, 1962–1966*, p. 1.
71 G. Holtham and A. Hazlewood, *Aid and Inequality in Kenya*, 1976, p. 106.
72 *Ibid.*
73 *Nottidge and Goldsack, op cit.*
74 *Ibid.*
75 H.C. Debates, 4 December 1964, Vol. 703, col. 1028.
76 Reported in *Aid Policy in One Country: Britain's Aid to Kenya, op. cit.*
77 H.C. Debates, 28 July 1967, Vol. 751, col. 1193.
78 H.C. Debates, 15 April 1970, Vol. 799, col. 257–8.
79 H.C. Debates, 7 July 1971, Vol. 820, col. 419.
80 H.C. Debates, 9 March 1973, Vol. 852, col. 224.
81 Kenya received budgetary aid in 1964/65.

82   *Report of an Economic Survey Mission: Basutoland and Swaziland*, 1960, p. 218.
83   *Ibid.*, p. 218.
84   The provision of budgetary aid actually started in Botswana in 1956/57. (*Ibid.*, pp. 10 and 11.)
85   *Ibid.*
86   *Ibid.*, p. 14.
87   Cmnd. 3180, 1967, para. 352.
88   *Ibid.*, para. 351.
89   David Jones, *Aid and Development in Southern Africa: British Aid to Botswana, Lesotho and Swaziland*, 1977, p. 38.
90   Gambia. Sessional Paper No. 7, 1967 (Bathurst), p. 4.
91   *Ibid.*, p. 1.
92   *Ibid.*, p. 4.
93   Lesotho, *First Five Year Development Plan, 1970/71–1971/75* (Maseru), 1970, p. 33.
94   Cmnd 3180, 1967, *op. cit.*, para. 352.
95   The Gambia, Sessional Paper No. 7, *op. cit.*, p. 1.
96   Malawi, *The 1971 Budget Statement*, 11 March 1971, p. 16.
97   *Ibid.*, p. 16.
98   *The Development of the Bechuanaland Economy: Report of the Ministry of Overseas Development*, Economic Survey Mission (November), 1965, p. 1.
99   Lesotho, *Five Year Development Plan, op. cit.*, p. 33.
100 Standard Bank, *Annual Economic Review*, Sierra Leone and Gambia, August 1972, p. 10.
101 Standard Bank, *Annual Economic Review*, Sierra Leone and Gambia, November 1973, p. 11.

8

Investment relations, 1957—75

On the eve of independence, Britain's investment policy was still largely determined by the balance of payments and sterling's international position; this monetary constraint led to a substantial concentration of investment in the Commonwealth countries. This Commonwealth bias did not change when sterling convertibility had been restored or indeed when the pound was floated in June 1972 — although there were slight modifications in the 1960s to take account of persisting balance of payments difficulties. Most Commonwealth African countries, however, terminated the free payments system with sterling even before 1972 and sought to control the activities of foreign private investors, either by outright nationalisation or through partnership schemes. As the pattern of Commonwealth African attitudes towards foreign private investment unfolded — all of them wanted it in one form or another — Britain, particularly under the Conservatives, became convinced that the only effective way she could assist development was by strengthening the forces of private enterprise in such countries and guaranteeing the investments of British firms there.

The first part of the chapter examines the impact of sterling convertibility and African independence on Britain's investment policy. In part two an attempt is made to develop a typology of independent Commonwealth African policies towards foreign private investment; part three examines the balance of payments constraints on Britain's investment policy.

The impact of sterling convertibility and African independence on Britain's investment policy

By the time of sterling convertibility and the beginning of African independence the Commonwealth African States were well prepared to diversify their investment sources as Britain had advocated, and all were agreed that, since private foreign investment was necessary for economic development, it should be adequately protected. For the time being, however, they continued to look to Britain as the immediate source of capital and were keen to protect the advantages of Britain's open payments policy towards them through their membership of the sterling area. Indeed, even with the proclamation of sterling convertibility the British government still operated a system of free payments with the Commonwealth–sterling countries and continued to enforce exchange control restrictions against non-sterling ones.

This sterling-oriented investment policy was complemented by more positive fiscal measures. The Finance Act of 1957 introduced a scheme which gave companies trading abroad a degree of relief from income tax and profits tax in Britain. The Act also provided that companies with a large proportion of profits earned through overseas subsidiaries would be able to offset tax paid overseas against income tax and profits tax in Britain. This helped to avoid a disincentive to invest in developing countries who imposed higher tax rates in favour of those who imposed lower tax rates.

These fiscal measures were institutionalized in a series of double taxation agreements entered into between Britain and Commonwealth African countries, which avoided taxing twice the investment yields of foreign investors. Partly as a result there was a 54 per cent increase in British investment in Commonwealth Africa between 1958 and 1960 (£8.5 million in 1958 and £13.3 million in 1960). This was a modest improvement, however, because the total average increase for all countries receiving British private investment rose by more than 75 per cent (£144 million in 1958 and £249 million in 1960). British investment in Australia, New Zealand and South Africa rose by 66 per cent (£42.3 million in 1958 and £70.1 million in 1960).

This modest trend continued well into the 1960s. In other words, Commonwealth Africa's share of British investment remained small. Indeed, its overall share depreciated between 1962 and 1968, recovering only slightly between 1969 and 1971.[1] Africa's share of total British investment in the Commonwealth–sterling area followed a similar pattern, depreciating between 1962 and 1968 and improving only slightly between 1969 and 1971. However, British investment to the rest of the world rose consistently between 1962 and 1971. There was a sharp increase in 1967, partly due to the devaluation of the pound, which led to an immediate rise in the sterling value of British assets held in other currencies. British investments were £3,405 million in 1962 and £6,666 million in 1971. This was a manifestation of Britain's traditional role as a capital-exporting country of the first rank. In the case of Commonwealth Africa, British investment varied: from a peak of £325.3 million in 1962 it fell to £307.5 million in 1965 and £252 million in 1966; it rose consistently between 1967 and 1971 to a peak of £395 million in 1971.[2]

As a result of the growth of their markets and their policies towards foreign private investment, Nigeria, Zambia and Kenya emerged as the major Commonwealth African recipients of British private investment. The latter was concentrated in six major industries:[3] the distributive trades (£135.4 million) mining and quarrying (£67.2 million), food, drink and tobacco (£44 million), agriculture (East Africa mainly, £36.8 million), chemical and allied industries (£29.5 million) and manufactures (£22.6 million).[4] The total for these six industries was £353.3 million and represented about 84.4 per cent of total British investment in Commonwealth Africa.

Tables 8.3 and 8.4 show the level of net earnings of British investment in the major Commonwealth African States between 1961 and 1967. It fluctuated for all countries. Nigeria and Ghana showed high net earnings. The most important point to note is that no loss was recorded in any one year, although, as Table 8.4 shows, for 1967 there were several losses in a number of British companies. But overall they were offset when the earnings of other countries were taken into account. Table 8.5 shows the extent of disinvestment in Commonwealth Africa. From a balance of payments perspective it appears from the tables that this disinvestment was unfavourable, for in the long run the repatriation of profits and disinvestment might more than outweigh the initial favourable effect on the balance of payments. Table 8.6 shows the extent of unremitted profits, net acquisition of share and loan capital and provision for depreciation. The picture that emerges suggests that British companies operating in Commonwealth Africa financed a large part of their new direct investment out of unremitted profits.

Table 8.1 British overseas investment: net earnings by country and area, 1962–71 (£ million)

	1962	1965	1966	1967	1968	1969	1970	1971
Africa	325.3	307.5	252.0	275.7	288.9	328.0	351.0	395.9
Malawi		8.4	9.2	9.5	10.5	10.6	11.7	19.5
Rhodesia	103.3	62.0						
Zambia		7.8	14.5	20.8	25.6	28.9	32.2	30.5
East Africa	60.5	60.5	61.5	69.9	73.2	78.4	82.0	85.1
Kenya	47.0	43.2	42.3	50.2	53.7	52.1	60.7	60.5
Tanzania	7.7	9.3	10.8	10.9	10.1	10.4	10.8	6.7
Uganda	5.8	8.0	8.4	8.8	9.4	9.9	10.6	7.3
East Africa nsd								10.3
West Africa	161.5	166.8	166.8	175.0	179.6	210.1	225.1	254.8
Gambia	1.0	0.6	0.7	0.7	1.1	1.3	0.9	0.3
Ghana	53.2	53.4	55.5	56.6	59.0	68.6	69.9	73.0
Nigeria	92.8	94.7	91.2	95.0	93.6	109.5	129.7	154.6
Sierra Leone	14.5	20.1	19.4	22.7	25.9	30.7	24.6	25.0
West Africa nsd								1.9
Commonwealth developing countries nsd	5.9	10.9	15.7	19.3	23.4	24.2	26.4	24.1
South Africa and S.W. Africa	290.0	391.7	429.8	545.5	585.6	640.8	626.7	651.7
World	3,405.0	4,210.0	4,401.6	5,186.9	5,585.3	6,063.2	6,404.1	6,666.9
Developing countries	1,273.6	1,431.6	1,395.3	1,589.3	1,668.3	1,746.2	1,849.9	1,859.4
Developed countries	2,131.4	2,778.4	3,006.3	3,597.6	3,917.0	4,317.0	4,554.2	4,807.4
Commonwealth	2,048.9	2,427.8	2,451.1	2,836.6	3,013.0	3,013.0	3,369.2	3,365.2
Australia	520.4	712.9	761.1	894.4	966.4	1,077.2	1,114.8	1,137.5
Canada	484.0	531.4	549.1	661.0	686.9	722.0	713.9	671.0
New Zealand	108.5	137.1	144.3	135.1	139.7	147.7	159.3	155.7
USA	301.3	387.6	422.1	530.0	600.0	646.5	762.2	794.7
EEC	272.9	392.2	445.7	550.7	628.9	738.3	808.0	985.2

Source. Trade and Industry, 15 November 1973.

Table 8.2 Values of UK direct investments, by industry and by area and country (£ million)

	Agriculture, forestry, fishing	Mining, quarrying	Food, drink, tobacco	Chemical and allied industries	Metal manufacture	Mech. eng. & instrument engineering	Electrical engineering	Motor vehicle manufacture	Textiles, clothing, footwear
Africa	36.8	67.2	44.0	29.5	0.5	4.4	6.8	1.9	7.7
Malawi	8.8			—				—	
Zambia				4.8		1.2	3.1		
East Africa	22.9		9.9	4.0	—	—	—	—	—
Kenya		—	5.3	2.9	—				—
Tanzania		—			—				
Uganda	—	—	—	1.1	—	—	—		
East Africa									
West Africa		67.0	29.9	20.7		2.8	3.0	0.7	5.8
Gambia									
Ghana		43.1							
Nigeria			20.4	17.3		2.2			5.7
Sierra Leone	—	—			—	—	—	—	
West Africa	—								
Commonwealth developing countries	0.9	0.4	3.2						2.9
South Africa		75.4	68.3	58.6	50.8	47.7	74.8	15.5	34.9
World	441.5	557.6	1,104.2	683.9	142.7	263.4	498.0	93.4	298.6

	Paper, printing, publishing	Rubber	Other manufactures	Construction	Transport and communications*	Shipping	Distributive trades	Other financial institutions	Property owning and Managing	Other activities	Total
Africa	4.8	4.8	22.6	5.7	6.3	–	135.4	3.6	3.2	10.7	395.9
Malawi	–	–	–				5.4			–	19.5
Zambia							16.0			1.1	36.5
East Africa	1.6	–	6.4	1.3	2.7		28.0	1.0		5.8	85.1
Kenya		–	5.2	1.2			20.2	–	–		60.5
Tanzania			0.7	–			1.4				6.7
Uganda			–		–		0.8				7.6
East Africa nsd	–		–				5.6		–	–	10.3
West Africa	2.8	3.7	14.7	3.3	2.5		86.0	2.3	2.8	3.8	254.8
Gambia	–	–	–	–	0.3		–	–	–	–	0.3
Ghana	–	–				–	17.2				23.0
Nigeria	2.8	–	14.7	2.4		–	65.9	–	–		154.6
Sierra Leone	–	–	–	–		–	2.9			–	25.0
West Africa nsd	–	–	–	–	–	–	–		–	–	1.9
Commonwealth developing countries	–			3.6	17.3		3.3		1.4		40.5
South Africa	19.0		57.4	12.9	4.3		75.4	15.7		16.0	651.7
World	261.5	134.1	450.6	88.6	241.9	67.4	876.4	99.1	140.0	219.0	6,666.9

*Other than shipping

Table 8.3 British overseas investment: net earnings, by area and main country, 1961–67 (£ million)

	1961	1962	1963	1964	1965	1966	1967
Overseas sterling area	163.2	179.8	213.3	249.2	251.0	236.7	236.9
Ghana	7.9	5.8	4.2	7.3	5.9	4.9	4.8
Kenya	1.3	1.7	3.0	2.5	4.1	4.8	4.4
Nigeria	4.2	2.0	6.4	7.8	8.3	7.6	5.1
Sierra Leone	3.3	4.0	4.9	5.4	3.3	3.5	3.0
Uganda		0.3	0.4	0.2	0.4	1.2	0.6
Zambia					0.9	2.7	3.9
All areas	249	274	330	370	400	427	438

Source. Board of Trade Journal.

Table 8.4 British overseas investment: profits, losses and net earnings, by area and main country, 1967

	Net earnings		Profits and interests		Losses	
	No. of concerns	£ million	No. of concerns	£ million	No. of concerns	£ million
Commonwealth Africa	336	24.1	262	26.4	74	2.3
East Africa	113	6.4	98	6.6	15	0.3
Kenya	80	4.4	69	4.6	11	0.2
West Africa	147	12.9	98	14.7	49	1.8
Ghana	31	4.8	16	5.0	15	0.3
Nigeria	94	5.1	63	6.6	31	1.5
All areas	3,820	437.9	3,017	483.8	803	45.9
Developing countries (h)	1,549	135.8	1,212	150.3	337	14.5
Developed countries	2,271	302.2	1,805	333.5	466	31.4
Commonwealth total	1,910	208.0	1,590	225.7	320	17.7

Source. Board of Trade Journal.

Table 8.5 British overseas investment: gross investment and disinvestment, by area and main country, 1967

	Gross investment		Gross disinvestment		Net investment	
	No. of concerns	£ million	No. of concerns	£ million	No. of concerns	£ million
Commonwealth Africa	213	21.9	144	21.4	357	0.5
East Africa	61	3.2	59	5.2	120	-2.0
Kenya	42	2.3	42	4.2	84	-1.9
West Africa	93	14.0	81	12.5	174	1.5
Ghana	20	4.4	21	1.5	41	3.0
Nigeria	56	6.8	50	9.3	106	-2.5
Commonwealth total	1,361	213.8	690	85.6	2,051	128.2
Developed countries of the world	1,723	319.3	767	101.6	2,490	217.8
LDCs of the world	1,051	137.9	657	74.8	1,708	63.1
All areas	2,774	457.2	1,424	176.4	4,198	280.9

Source. Board of Trade Journal.

Table 8.6 British overseas investment: net investment by component and provision for depreciation, by area and main country, 1967

	Total	Unremitted profits of subsidiaries	Net acquisition of share capital	Changes in indebtedness of parent company		Changes in related trade credit		Provision for depreciation
				Branches	Subsidiaries	Credit extended	Credit received	
Commonwealth								
Africa	0.5	7.0	-3.2	1.1	-4.5	-3.2	0.4	13.4
Malawi	0.8	0.5			0.1		–	0.6
Zambia	0.2	1.8			1.2			1.6
East Africa	-2.0	1.5	-0.4	-0.8	-2.2	-1.8	0.2	1.9
Kenya	-1.9	1.3	-0.2	-0.8	-2.1	-1.8	0.1	1.5
Tanzania	0.2	0.1			0.1	-0.1		0.3
Uganda	-0.3	0.1			-0.2			0.2
West Africa	1.5	3.3	–	1.8	-3.5	-1.8	0.1	9.3
Ghana	3.0	1.8	–	-0.3	1.5	1.6	–	1.8
Nigeria	-2.5	1.4	-0.2	1.2	-4.8	-3.3	0.1	5.7
Sierra Leone	1.1	0.1			-0.1	-0.2	–	1.8
All areas	280.9	189.5	46.5	26.1	18.8	11.8	-5.1	244.9
LDCs	63.1	48.6	7.2	15.7	-8.4	-6.0	-0.4	69.8
Developed countries	217.8	141.0	39.3	10.4	27.2	17.8	-4.7	175.0
Commonwealth total	128.2	84.8	19.0	19.6	4.9	-9.1	-3.8	122.7

Source. Board of Trade Journal.

Independent Commonwealth African States' policies towards foreign private investment

The uniform and unquestioned acceptance of foreign private investment in the decolonisation period was largely a function of the strategy of economic development adopted, with its strong emphasis on private enterprise and the market economy. In the 1960s clear divisions emerged, however, in the development strategies of the African States, which influenced their subsequent policies towards foreign investment. Four distinct groups emerged: States oriented towards public ownership; those which pursued indigenisation; the residual sterling bloc States; and those dependent on the Republic of South Africa. Ghana, Tanzania and Zambia belonged to the first group; Nigeria, Kenya and Uganda to the second; Sierra Leone, Gambia and Malawi to the third; and Botswana, Lesotho and Swaziland to the fourth.

Too much weight should not be placed on this simple typology, as these groups were not mutually exclusive. For instance, whereas Sierra Leone belonged to the third group there was a time when she introduced partial nationalisation schemes. Ghana experienced three different types of regime, from Nkrumah's socialism, through the liberal economy of the first military and Busia governments, to Acheampong's policy of self-reliance and partial nationalisation. Again, Zambia was not fully committed to public ownership although the series of economic measures introduced between 1968 and 1970 were a manifestation of preparedness to use the State to regulate economic development. All Commonwealth African States had partnership schemes with foreign private enterprise, pursued some aspects of indigenisation and used the State to protect the economy from foreign domination.

But the fourfold distinction nonetheless remains useful for analytical purposes. The first group of States ran into difficulties with Britain when they nationalised or restricted the expansion of British private investment. In the second group (with the exception of Amin's Uganda), despite indigenisation, British private investment continued to rise because of the countries' commitment to private enterprise; British capital was prevented from expanding in certain areas specifically earmarked for local entrepreneurs. The last two groups were well disposed towards British capital and private enterprise, and imposed hardly any restrictions on the expansion of foreign investment.

States oriented towards public ownership
The common denominator in this category was the increasing involvement of the State in the direction and management of the economy, stemming either from a political crisis, from total dependence upon one industry and the need to control it, as in Zambia, or from the realisation that the economic policies of decolonisation had not contributed to economic development.

Ghana   With the introduction of exchange controls to include sterling area countries in 1961, the publication of the Convention People's Party's Programme for Work and Happiness and the introduction of the Seven Year Development Plan of 1964, Nkrumah's government started to construct the socialist foundations of a new Ghana 'based on the public ownership of the means of production and distribution'.

A combination of political, economic and historical factors led to this momentous change. Ever since Nkrumah entered politics he had been committed to the ideal of continental unity, a commitment which stemmed from his belief in the importance of the continuing struggle against colonialism. His writings on political economy basically reflected the problems of colonial economic dependence. However, the tactical compromise he made in 1951 when his party entered into a partnership government with British colonial officials led to a moderation of his policies and a partial abandonment of radical action against British colonialism. During this period the party's energies were absorbed by the gains made in, for instance, local government reforms and the rapid Africanisation of the civil service. The fact that large sterling reserves had accumulated as a result of high cocoa prices also blunted the government's opposition to the colonial economy.

However, Nkrumah's quest for continental unity went on unabated. On many occasions in the 1950s he uncompromisingly advocated African unity, and took positive steps in that direction by launching several pan-African conferences. His quest was always posed in the context of the struggle against colonialism and imperialism. This was effectively stated in one of his most powerful speeches during the conference of heads of state in Addis Ababa in 1963 in which he sharply censured Western exploitation of Africa's raw materials, calling on his fellow heads of state to establish a political union of Africa.[5] It was against this background that his theory of neo-colonialism was developed, which, he believed, was a system that effectively subjugated African States: although in theory they had all the outward trappings of sovereignty they were in reality neo-colonial dependencies because their economic systems were dictated and directed from outside. One of the instruments of neo-colonialism, he argued, was the use of foreign capital 'for the exploitation rather than for the development of the less developed parts of the world'.[6]

The struggle against 'neo-colonialism' necessitated the establishment of socialism because of the lack of an independent entrepreneural class in Ghana; in his view the local entrepreneurs tended to co-operate with neo-colonialism.[7] The Seven Year Plan of 1964 recognised five sectors co-operating side by side:[8] State enterprises, enterprises owned by foreign private interests, enterprises owned jointly by the State and foreign private interests, co-operatives and small-scale Ghanaian private enterprises. The government did not intend to nationalise private foreign investment, but the 'public and co-operative sectors of the productive economy should expand at the maximum possible rate'.[9] Many public corporations were established to provide a nucleus for the eventual socialisation of the economy. The new policy with its ideological opposition to neo-colonialism stemmed the flow of foreign investment to Ghana. The only major influx was the American-financed Volta project. The Kaiser Corporation agreed to construct and operate an aluminum smelter at Tema for a total of £44 million. In addition the US government agreed to offer a loan of £9.6 million towards the Volta dam and hydro-electric station at Aksombo. British private investment remained almost static. Between 1962 and 1965 there was an increase of only £0.2 million (£53.2 million in 1962 and £53.4 million in 1965).[10]

Nkrumah's policy was reversed by the military government of 1966 — 69 and by the Busia administration of 1969 — 72. Both administrations attempted to dismantle most of the public corporations and to restructure the economy from the ideology of central planning to free enterprise, with more sympathy for private foreign investment. J. A. Ankra was determined to fight Nkrumah's ideology of 'turning Ghana into one vast public service machine'.[11] The State Enterprises Secretariat was converted into a form of holding company to enable individual enterprises to operate on an autonomous basis. Kofi Busia pursued these policies with even greater passion, declaring himself unalterably opposed to socialism and public ownership. As a result there was a relatively modest increase in British investment. From £55.5 million in 1966 when the military came to power, British investment rose to £68.6 million in 1969. Under Busia it increased to £73 million in 1971.[12]

This situation was reversed again, however, by the advent of Acheampong in 1972 and his proclaimed policy of self-reliance. This was not a return to Nkrumah's socialism, although its practical implementation resembled some aspects of Nkrumah's belief in the role of public enterprise. Acheampong's public statements on assuming office clearly demonstrated a swing to the forces opposed to the private enterprise policies of the NLC and Busia administrations.[13] On foreign investment, he sharply criticised the repatriation of profits and dividends and affirmed the need to build an independent national economy in which 'growth and development are not ends in themselves but means towards the satisfaction of the social needs of the people as a whole'.[14]

On this basis the government acquired 55 per cent of the mining and timber industries and other manufacturing concerns. Anglo-Ghanaian relations were generally strained by these measures, especially as they were applied simultaneously with the repudiation of debt on Ghana's medium-term credits.

Tanzania   Like Ghana and the other African States, Tanzania accepted private enterprise and the mixed economy in the early years of independence on the assumption that economic development would be largely dependent upon the flow of foreign capital; attempts were therefore made to attract it. Only after the failure of overseas capital to materialise, at least in the required amounts, and the realisation that Tanzania would have to finance most of her development plan from domestic resources, did her leaders revive their latent convictions to socialise the economy.

In the first Five Year Plan of 1964 Julius Nyerere recognised the limitations of planning and accepted the need to attract foreign investment.[15] Fiscal and financial incentives were provided by the government. This liberal initiative did not attract enough capital to finance the government's development plan. The flow of private investment from Britain did not improve to any appreciable extent. Indeed, the external capital contribution envisaged in the plan did not materialise. The 1964 plan forecast 22 per cent of central government expenditure and 48 per cent of total investment expenditure from local sources; the result was actually 65 per cent of central government capital expenditure financed from domestic sources, and 70 per cent of the total investment spending from within Tanzania.[16]

The lesson was that Tanzania would have to rely more on her local resources and that public ownership and planning were necessary to regulate and develop them; this was the policy of self-reliance and socialism, which was firmly established as a political doctrine in 1967. The Arusha Declaration represented a revolt against the country's past dependence on foreign capital.[17] The objective was to build an egalitarian society in which the State would have effective control over the principal means of production. Tanzania did not rule out a continuing contribution by foreign investment to economic development, but the government stipulated that outside capital should not be allowed to dictate its pace.[18] A series of nationalisation schemes were carried out in February 1967. All banks, food processing companies, life insurance companies and the National Insurance Corporation were nationalised; furthermore the government established the State Trading Corporation for external and wholesale trade. The government announced its intention of taking a controlling share in another list of foreing companies.[19] All other areas were open to private investments.[20]

As the major investing power in Tanzania, Britain was hit hardest by these measures, particularly in banking, insurance, trade and manufacturing. Nyerere reiterated that although Tanzania had 'rejected the domination of private enterprise' the government would 'continue to welcome private investment in all those areas not reserved for government in the Arusha Declaration'.[21] Tanzania's orientation towards socialism and nationalisation, however, effectively deterred private investment from entering the country. In 1968, one year after Arusha, British private investment actually declined from £10.9 million in 1967 to £10.1 million. By 1971 it had fallen to £6.7 million.[22]

In 1972, in a further round of nationalisation, a large number of British companies were taken over. The British government reacted strongly, persuading the World Bank to withdraw a £4.3 million loan for tea development.[23]

Zambia   Unlike Nkrumah in Ghana and Nyerere in Tanzania, Kaunda based his development objectives not on socialism but on Humanism,[24] which rejected capitalism but was interpreted as being a stage higher than socialism.[25] The significance of this political ideology lay not so much in its alleged superiority as in the fact that it provided a useful justification for Kaunda's residual belief in private enterprise.[26] Zambia's rejection of capitalism led, however, to the introduction of partial State enterprises at the expense of foreign private investors. The problem started with Kaunda's realisation that despite liberal exchange control measures to encourage foreign investors to plough their profits back into the country they 'were obsessed with making hay while the sun shines and expatriated increasingly large portions of their profits'.[27] Zambia was thus compelled to introduce radical changes in her foreign exchange regulations to prevent the mass repatriation of profits. Under the new scheme, investors were allowed to remit dividends abroad only when they did not exceed 30 per cent of equity capital and when this 30 per cent in turn did not exceed half of the profits.[28]

A series of partial nationalisation schemes were carried out between 1969 and 1970. The first was of the copper mines, which earned over 90 per cent of the country's foreign exhange. This was the exploitive type of investment which belonged to the colonial era when the rules governing the extraction of minerals were made solely by the colonial power and the mining companies. The mineral rights had been passed on in perpetuity by the British South African Company to the Anglo-American Corporation and Rhodesian Selection Trust. Independent Zambia could not take them away without amending the constitution, which required a national referendum in which there should be a 51 per cent affirmative vote.[29] After the referendum of June 1969, the copper mines were nationalised in August, the State taking 51 per cent control.[30] The countries mainly affected were Britain, America and South Africa.

Further measures aimed at controlling the foreign element of Zambia's economy were taken in 1970: foreign investors were excluded from all retail trade, now to be undertaken by Zambians, State companies and co-operatives; State companies and entirely Zambian-controlled companies were to operate all transport services; wholesale trading was to be confined to Zambian businesses and State companies;[31] foreign investors were expected to move from distributive into productive industries. The State further acquired a 51 per cent share of the banks and several manufacturing industries. The United Bus Company of Zambia and all building societies were completely taken over, and the State insurance company was to be enlarged to become the sole insurance company in Zambia.[32]

Although British investors lost some of their holdings to individual Zambians and the State, the inflow of capital from the UK continued to increase, thanks to the government's assurances that it would continue to honour its commitment to partial forms of private enterprise and also because of its fair compensation terms. British investment rose from £25.6 million in 1968 to £36.5 million in 1971.[33]

Indigenisation: Nigeria, Kenya and Uganda

These States were firmly committed to private enterprise, in which foreign investment was expected to play a substantial role. They refused to endorse any radical ideology that would jeopardise private capital and attempted instead to substitute national private enterprise for foreign private investment through participation schemes. As in countries oriented towards public ownership, here too the State was instrumental in controlling foreign investment, although it was done for the benefit of national individual entrepreneurs. By and large it was the private sector that was expected to provide the impetus for rapid development. Apart from basic public utilities, which were nationalised, all other industries were open to private enterprise. Although British investment was periodically affected by acts of indigenisation, unlike the 'public ownership' States, British investors still considered it worth putting money into the 'indigenisation' States.

Nigeria   The First Republic believed in national private enterprise and attempted to 'Nigerianise' the financial and monetary system by establishing a Lagos stock exchange and money and capital markets. It was expected that these financial institutions would assist the local development of private investment, and thus make the country less dependent on foreign investors.[34] On the industrial level, however, the shortage of immediate local capital meant that there would be a continuing need for foreign investment if economic growth was to be maintained and improved.[35]

Nigeria refused to be drawn into the socialist mode of development, which its leaders considered a recipe for political instability. Indeed, the Finance Minister was disturbed by the constant calls for nationalisation by the opposition party which culminated in the nationalisation debate of 27 November 1961.[36] The government seized the opportunity to restate its views: other than the public utilities which were already in public ownership, it would leave all industries to private enterprise. Instead the policy would be to 'Nigerianise rather than to nationalise', which meant increasing the participation of Nigerians in the ownership and direction of industries.[37]

Despite the government's open-door policy, the level of foreign investment did not reach the plan target of £33 million. It was estimated in 1964 that the foreign private capital inflow was about £10 million in 1962 and £15 million in 1963. These figures were substantially lower than the levels attained in previous years — £24 million in 1959, £19 million in 1960 and £30 million in 1961.[38]

However, this setback did not prevent either of the two military leaders who came to power after 1966, Ironsi and Gowon, from supporting development schemes based on private enterprise and the attraction of foreign investment. During Gowon's tenure of office the policy of indigenisation was given sharper focus and a new sense of urgency. In the second National Development Plan of 1970, drawn up with an eye to the experience of the Civil War, the government stressed the need to speed up indigenisation.[39]

In order to give effect to this policy, the Nigerian Enterprises Promotion Decree was passed in February 1972. The decree set out in its first schedule twenty-eight industrial and commercial ventures which were reserved exclusively for Nigerian entrepreneurs and associations; they included retail trading, banking, rice milling, the bottling of soft drinks, hairdressing, road haulage, newspaper publishing and printing. In schedule two there were twenty-five activities in which Nigerians were given an equity participation of not less than 60 per cent. Notable among them were wholesale distribution, brewing, the manufacture of soap and detergents, fish and shrimp trawling and processing, and paper conversion. In schedule three Nigerians were given an equity participation of not less than 40 per cent. This schedule covered mainly capital goods.[40]

Between May 1973 and October 1974 the commission had fixed prices for the ordinary shares of twenty-four companies. During the same period over 54 million ordinary shares of K50 each were transferred to Nigerian entrepreneurs and associations.[41] The government also acquired 55 per cent of the equity of all the companies producing crude oil.[42] There were eleven oil companies, the largest being Shell-BP.

Indigenisation did not radically affect the inflow of capital, because of the government's commitment to private enterprise and its willingness to protect the areas scheduled for foreign enterprise. Foreign investors were confident that the government's policy would facilitate their own investment plans. The conviction was reinforced by the fact that indigenisation did not take the form of nationalisation, with all the problems usually associated with delayed compensation; it was, rather, a policy in which indigenous entrepreneurs bought shares from the foreign companies through the State. The government even attributed the scheme's success partly to 'the co-operation of the alien companies affected'.[43]

British private investment in Nigeria rose at an unprecedented rate, mainly because of the flourishing oil industry and the government's massive development programmes after the oil price revolution of 1973.

Kenya   Kenya's development philosophy was based on the KANU manifesto, the constitution and the policy statement of 1965 which spoke of 'African Socialism'.[44] It rejected 'Marxism' and '*laissez-faire* capitalism' as outmoded, emphasising instead the need to develop within 'the traditional African system' of 'political democracy and mutual social responsibility'. But it should be 'a working system in a modern setting fully prepared to adapt itself to changing circumstances and new problems'. This policy of adaptation necessitated the acceptance of technical and financial assistance, technological know-how and foreign investment.[45] Thus Kenya's 'African Socialism' respected private enterprise and the full participation of foreign capital in the development process.

Foreign investors were given a free hand to invest and repatriate profits. Measures were also taken to protect them from competing manufactures from overseas. Customs duties were raised to protect domestic industries; raw materials could be imported free of duty; investment allowances were granted and constitutional guarantees offered of fair and prompt payment to forestall fears of nationalisation.[46]

The 1964 − 70 Development Plan stressed the government's commitment to private enterprise.[47] Kenya's leaders believed, however, that private African participation was necessary in every aspect of the economy. The Document on African

Socialism and Planning appealed to foreign investors to accept the 'spirit of mutual social responsibility' by offering shares to Africans who wished to buy them, by employing Africans at managerial levels as soon as qualified people could be found, and by providing training facilities.[48]

Unlike Nigeria, however, which had ample resources and oil revenues to speed the process of indigenisation, Kenya's programme was pursued at a moderate rate: 'foreign investment is likely to be a growing rather than a shrinking one'.[49] Indigenisation did not adversely affect British private investment. Indeed, Kenya is regarded as one of the most promising areas for investment in Africa. British investment rose from £42.3 million in 1966 to £60.5 million in 1971.[50]

Uganda   Uganda's policy towards foreign investors has had a chequered history. Between 1962 and 1970 the government of Milton Obote welcomed foreign capital. Between 1970 and 1971 there was a brief move to the left with the government's publication of the 'Common Man's Charter' of partial nationalisation. Between 1971 and 1972 this policy was reversed, but after 1972 the Asian crisis and strained political relations with Britain led to a series of nationalisations in which the State was used in a holding operation to transfer British investments to Ugandan citizens.

In May 1970 Obote's administration announced a series of measures for the compulsory acquisition of a controlling interest in virtually all financial, insurance, oil distributing, transport, manufacturing and agricultural industries, and the total exclusion of private enterprise from export and import trading.[51] The Common Man's Charter took its inspiration from the Arusha Declaration, but at the practical level it was similar to the 1968 − 70 partial nationalisation schemes of Kaunda in Zambia. It differed only to the extent that the State's intervention in partnership with foreign capital was not a holding operation for the development of indigenous investment but a move on the Tanzanian pattern towards eventual public ownership of industry.

Although 'only in a few instances were the measures effected ... the pronouncements did much to erode the confidence of private investors'.[52] In January 1971, eight months after the May 1970 measures, Obote's government was overthrown by Idi Amin, who evoked the partial nationalisation policy.[53] The new government announced its intention of taking a

monopoly control over certian undertakings which were of
critical importance to the economy. They included electric
power, water supplies and the export marketing of cotton,
coffee and tobacco. The government was to participate on a
minority basis in commercial banking and insurance, basic
iron and steel production, sugar production and the processing
of petroleum products.[54] Private capital was free to invest in
all other business activities, with or without government participation; and the government's policy was to be free of any
'doctrinaire political ideologies'.[55] It was not long, however,
before this liberal attitude collapsed in the wake of the Asian
crisis in 1972 and Amin's take-over of Asian-owned property
after notice had been served on Asians to leave Uganda. Britain
reacted angrily and within a short time political and diplomatic
relations had sunk to a low ebb. Amin resorted to the State
take-over of a large number of British companies pending
their sale to Ugandan soldiers and civilians sympathetic to
government policy. Some twenty-one companies and nineteen
tea estates were acquired by January 1973, and eighty-seven
companies were denied renewal of their trading licences under
the terms of the 1972 Decree on Properties and Business.[56]
British investment dried up rapidly, and with no prospect of
effecting 'prompt, fair and adequate' compensation the British
government cancelled a £10 million loan and terminated technical assistance.[57]

The residual sterling bloc States: Sierra Leone, Gambia and Malawi

Like the indigenisation States, the 'residual sterling bloc'
States believed in private enterprise and indigenisation, and
accepted the role of foreign investment in development. But
their fragile economic base and limited capital resources meant
that, much as they might want indigenisation, they would
still have to reckon with a sizeable foreign presence in the
private sector.

What distinguished these countries from others in Commonwealth Africa was their close link with sterling up to and
even for a while after the official end of the sterling area in
June 1972. Malawi, Sierra Leone and the Gambia continued
to peg their currencies to sterling and insisted on maintaining
— much to the advantage of British investors — a free payments
system with Britain at the expense of non-sterling countries.[58]
Although they advocated economic diversification, Britain

was still the most important economic force in their trade and investment.

Another feature was their low-key approach to international politics, which they believed should be related to their development needs. The importance of attracting foreign investment meant a less contentious stand on foreign affairs and the avoidance of political ideologies. Thus a year after the Gambia's independence the Governor General spoke of the need to project the economic needs of the State in foreign policy.[59] The link between foreign policy and development was underlined also by Sierra Leone's post-independence leaders. For instance, in 1967 during one of the country's most critical financial periods, the military leader, Andrew Juxon-Smith, expressed the hope that the 'country's foreign policy will aid the development of the country'.[60] In Malawi Hastings Banda had been a militant opponent of alignment with Communist countries, which he believed would be disastrous for foreign investment. He was prepared to maintain relations with Rhodesia and South Africa under a policy aimed at maximising receipts of foreign capital irrespective of conventional norms in Africa.[61]

The residual sterling bloc countries had an open-door policy towards foreign investment. In Malawi schemes such as industrial licensing, incentives, tax rebates and financial drawbacks were initiated to attract foreign investors.[62]

Similar measures were taken in Sierra Leone. The first Prime Minister, Sir Milton Margai, laid the foundations of the country's commitment to private enterprise by insisting on an open-door policy.[63] The government introduced the 1960 Development Act, which offered development companies 'tax holidays' of two to five years, duty-free importation of machinery and raw materials, and sites for new industries.[64] This policy was reaffirmed by the 1968 government of Siaka Stevens.[65]

Various schemes with foreign participation were taken up by the 'residual sterling bloc countries' without the political drama such policies aroused elsewhere. For instance, although Malawi did 'not believe in the nationalisation of industry' the government stressed that it would 'promote participation between government and the private sector' in certain sectors where it would benefit both investors and the government.[66] In November 1968 the State acquired a majority holding in the largest wholesale firm in the country. Although Bookers' reacquired control in 1970, the State-owned Malawi Development Corporation (MDC) retained a substantial interest.[67]

The government, acting through the MDC, extended its activities into transport, industry, banking and other financial concerns.

In December 1969 the government of Siaka Stevens departed from the pattern established by Sir Milton Margai's administration in 1961, which had ruled out nationalisation of mining, by acquiring a controlling 51 per cent interest in all the mines of Sierra Leone.[68] The companies affected were Sierra Leone Selection Trust, a subsidiary of Consolidated African Selection Trust, which mined diamonds; the Sierra Leone Development Company, a subsidiary of William Baird's of Glasgow, which mined iron ore; Sherbro Minerals, a subsidiary of Pittsburgh Plate Glass of America, which mined rutile; and the Sierra Leone Ore & Metal Company, wholly owned by Allusuisse of Switzerland, which mined bauxite.

But by the mid-1970s the government had decided to restrict nationalisation to the first two companies because of complaints of financial losses and the subsequent collapse of Sherbro Minerals. By 1973 the State's controlling interest of 51 per cent was restricted to Sierra Leone Selection Trust, as the SLDC also ran into financial difficulties.[69]

Apart from this deviation, Sierra Leone continued to attract foreign investment: there was steady co-operation with foreign investors in partnership schemes with citizens and the State in banking, insurance, commerce and transport.

The effect of the three States' policies cannot be effectively measured, but they cannot have been other than minimal because of the limitations of their markets. In the Gambia, for instance, British private investment was almost negligible: £1 million in 1962 and £0.3 million in 1971.[70] In Sierra Leone there was a modest increase, from £14.3 million in 1962 to £25 million in 1971.[71] In Malawi, British investment rose from £8.4 million in 1965 to £19.5 million in 1971.[72]

States dependent on the Republic of South Africa: Botswana, Lesotho and Swaziland

BLS achieved independence between 1966 and 1969, and, like all Commonwealth African States, shared the long-term goals of rapid economic development, social and economic justice and eventual economic independence. Elsewhere these goals promoted varying degrees of economic nationalism against the former imperial power. In the case of the BLS countries, however, their nationalism was directed not against Britain but against South Africa, which enjoyed a dominant presence in their economies. In fact, up to a point, economic relations with Britain were considered vital to political independence and survival in the face of the expansionism of the Republic.

Historically, British governments had assumed that the three countries would be absorbed into the Union and had been relatively unperturbed by the processes of South African economic penetration. As we have seen, a common customs union was signed with South Africa in 1910 and in 1933 the rand became the currency of the three countries, in effect creating a common currency union. The customs union was renewed in 1969. It was reckoned that because of the absence of any formal agreements with South Africa governing the use of the rand in the BLS countries, private foreign investment suffered considerably.[73] Significantly, the BLS countries wished to have undisputed control over foreign exchange transactions and the long-term liabilities relating to them while still cooperating with South Africa economically.[74] Botswana withdrew from the common currency in 1974 and established its own.

Given the common customs and currency unions, it was not surprising that South Africa provided the bulk of private investment. Britain's attitude to BLS was determined largely by the Republic's economic policy towards Britain. South African membership of the sterling area meant easier investment relations between Britain and the BLS countries. However, when South Africa introduced policies to protect new industries in the Republic, British businessmen operating in BLS were adversely affected.

Of the three countries, Botswana had been more determined to reduce its financial and economic links with South Africa, although it stressed that it was part of southern Africa and must therefore maintain close relations with the countries of that region.[75] Seretse Khama stressed the need to diversify economic relations and recognised the importance of Britain in this process as 'a major contributor to sustaining' the country's independence.[76] Indeed, Britain's decision to grant independence meant a commitment to sustain it through financial assistance. Although not always able to provide the massive capital required, Britain had always accepted the need for greater assistance to these countries.[77]

In terms of investment BLS suffered from the same problem of limited markets as the residual sterling bloc countries.

Despite the mining potential in Botswana and Swaziland, British private capital made little impact. The only substantial economic link has been in aid and technical assistance.

The balance of payments and its constraint on British investment

As we have seen, the twelve Commonwealth African States' policies towards foreign investment varied from total acceptance, through participation, to extensive control. There was a strong sense of economic nationalism in all of them as the State was used in one form or another to regulate economic development and external economic relations. The means varied from outright nationalisation as in Tanzania to the limitation of private capital expansion as in Ghana under Nkrumah, to State partnership with foreign capital as in Acheampong's Ghana, in Zambia, in Obote's Uganda and in Sierra Leone in 1969, to domestic private capital partnership with foreign investors as in Nigeria and Kenya, and finally to attempts to diversify away from an unpleasant regional power, South Africa, in favour of Britain, as in Botswana, Swaziland and Lesotho.

All wished to have greater control over the running of their economies, but all were agreed that however nationalistic and independent they wished to be the scarcity of indigenous capital required them to make room for foreign investment. Thus, although their enthusiasm varied, none declared itself an enemy of foreign capital.

For this reason Britain was optimistic about the role which foreign investment could play in the flow of resources to Commonwealth Africa.[78] She refused to accept the aid targets set by the Pearson Report, which recommended that each industrial country should make available to developing countries the ratio of 0.7 and 0.3 per cent of their gross national product for official aid and private foreign investment respectively. Britain insisted that foreign investment should be accorded a higher percentage than 0.3, although she accepted the principle of the one per cent target of capital flows to developing countries.[79]

In the mid-1960s, however, Britain's foreign investment was constrained by persistent balance of payments troubles. In 1964 the deficit rose to an exceptionally high level and forced on the new Labour government plans to restrict spending and private investment overseas.[80] A change of policy was deemed essential because of the short-term effects on the balance of payments.[81]

To this end the government introduced exchange controls and tax measures, including a corporation tax, to check the outward flow of private capital.[82] The 1965 plan anticipated that companies would be obliged to restrict the growth either of the dividends they paid their shareholders or of the profits they ploughed back abroad, or they could combine both moves. The former would restrict the incentive and the latter the ability to invest abroad. Other measures withdrew the special provisions on overseas trade corporations which encouraged foreign investment; abolished the relief granted by the Income Tax Act of 1952[83] and replaced it by a form of relief applicable only to a British company controlling not less than 25 per cent of the voting power of an overseas company;[84] liberalised the amount of credit allowable to an individual resident in Britain, which had been limited by reference to his effective rate of British tax;[85] and finally removed the entitlement to unilateral relief against income tax charged on the dividend for the 'underlying' tax which shareholders who received dividends from an overseas company had previously enjoyed.[86]

These fiscal measures affected private investment in the developing countries adversely. Between 1965 and 1966 it fell from £157 million to £95 million. In Commonwealth Africa total direct investment by Britain fell from £307 million in 1965 to £252 million in 1966.[87]

The Confederation of British Industry complained bitterly. On corporation tax, it maintained that the total tax paid on foreign income exceeded the total tax paid on domestic income whenever the total foreign taxes paid exceeded the standard corporation tax of 45 per cent.[88] This arose because the foreign tax was credited only against the UK corporation tax and not against the withholding tax, the result being that where foreign tax exceeded 45 per cent no relief was given for the unrelieved foreign tax. This limitation of double taxation relief tended to bear particularly severely on income from investments in developing countries, where tax rates were frequently high.

From the perspective of private investors, relations with Commonwealth Africa suffered from two major problems: economic fiscal controls which tended to make investment there more costly than domestic investment irrespective of the attractive fiscal and financial incentives, and political controls stemming from economic nationalism. The latter was considered a major problem. In a statistical study by the Overseas Development Institute of attitudes to East Africa, investors were reported to have expressed the view that, if profit margins were high, so was political instability, and their reluctance was due mainly to political risk.[89] They felt, however, that Britain's tax policies were at odds with her positive statements on Commonwealth development.[90]

What private investors wanted was a revision of the tax position and the establishment of an insurance scheme for private investment in developing countries, similar to that provided by America and other Western countries, against the risks of nationalisation, revolution, war and delayed compensation.[91]

In the face of its balance of payments problems, the British government refused to review taxes and rejected the insurance scheme suggested by the CBI.[92] At this stage it was interested in a multilateral insurance scheme which Britain would join when her balance of payments improved.[93] In the absence of the multilateral scheme it generally preferred to emphasise the need to encourage developing countries themselves to accept international agreements on the treatment of foreign capital.[94]

One such scheme which did not require insurance cover by the industrial countries was that of the International Centre for the Settlement of Investment Disputes. Its object was to provide a mechanism which the host government and the foreign investor could settle investment disputes direct, without the intervention of the investor's own government.[95] The convention came into force on 14 October 1966, and by 15 June 1972 ten of the twelve Commonwealth African States had signed it.[96]

By the time the Conservative government came to power in Britain in 1970 the balance of payments deficit had turned to surplus and so provided a fitting background for the introduction of radical measures to promote private investment abroad. The Conservatives had always worked closely with the CBI; both supported the free market system and the role of foreign investment in the developing countries. An insurance scheme was felt to be necessary. They also wished to redirect British aid from the Commonwealth to more profitable areas, to channel a high proportion to the Commonwealth Development Corporation, which should begin to operate wherever opportunities offered in developing countries regardless of

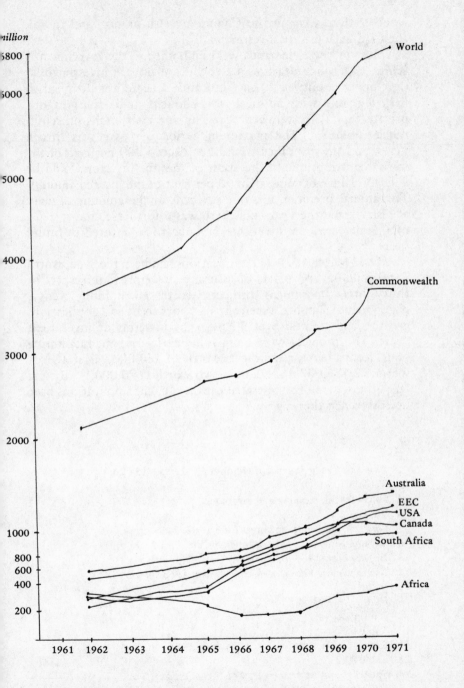

£million

Fig. 8.1   UK overseas investment, by area and country.

whether they were in the Commonwealth or not, and to link the CDC with private investment.[97]

Most of these demands were embodied in the government's White Paper on measures to encourage private investment in developing countries.[98] The insurance scheme was designed to help investors with political risks thought to be too great for private capital:[99] war, expropriation and restrictions on remittances home.[100] The maximum period of cover was fifteen years, and the insurance would not exceed 200 per cent of the initial contribution. In the event of loss the investor would be able to claim not more than 90 per cent of the insured amount. The annual premium was one per cent of the amount actually at risk during the year, and there was a further committee fee of 0.5 per cent on any other amount to be insured in future years.[101]

By 31 March 1974 211 applications had been received, worth £100 million, and offers of insurance were made in respect of thirty-three investment projects worth £8 million. Kenya, Nigeria and Zambia received 44.4 per cent of applications granted and a little over 50 per cent in terms of investment value. The projects were mainly industrial and manufacturing ones. Kenya had three projects worth £1,160,000, Nigeria seven worth £2,476,000 and Zambia two worth £690,000.[102] By and large the scheme has operated cautiously, and applications have been screened thoroughly.

Notes

1 *Board of Trade Journal*, 6 October 1961, pp. 715–20.
2 Table 8.1.
3 Excludes oil, banking and insurance.
4 Table 8.2.
5 *Ghana Today* supplement, 5 June 1963, p. 3.
6 Kwame Nkrumah, *Neo-colonialism: the Last Stage of Imperialism*, 1965, p. x.
7 Ghana, *Seven Year Development Plan, 1963/64–1969/70*, p. xiii.
8 *Ibid.*
9 *Ibid.*, p. x.
10 Table 8.1.
11 *Ghana Today* supplement, 10 August 1966, pp. 3–6.
12 Table 8.1.
13 *Speeches and Interviews by Col. Acheampong*, Vol. I, 1973, p. 31.
14 *Ibid.*, p. 33.

15 Tanzania, *Five Year Plan, 1964–1969.*
16 *Second Five Year Development Plan, 1969–1974* (Dar es Salaam), 1969, p. x.
17 J. K. Nyerere, *Freedom and Socialism: a Selection from Writings and Speeches, 1965–1967*, Part III.
18 *Ibid.*, p. 240.
19 J. K. Nyerere in *Freedom and Socialism*, 1968, pp. 252–3.
20 *Ibid.*, p. 254.
21 *Ibid.*
22 Table 8.1.
23 H.C. Debates, 14 February 1972, col. 1.
24 Kaunda, *Zambia's Economic Revolution*, (Mulungushi), 19 April 1968, p. 5.
25 Kaunda, *Take up the Challange*, (Lusaka), 1970, p. 49.
26 *First National Development Plan, 1966–1970*, (Lusaka), July 1966 p. 36.
27 Kaunda, *Zambia's Economic Revolution* (Lusaka), 1968, p. iii.
28 *Ibid.*, p. 50.
29 Kaunda, *Towards Complete Independence* (Lusaka), 1969 p. 33.
30 *Ibid.*, p. 29.
31 Kaunda, *This Completes Economic Reforms: Now Zambia is Ours* (Lusaka), pp. 1–5.
32 *Ibid.*, p. 9.
33 Table 8.1.
34 H/R Debates, Okotie Eboh, 29 March 1962.
35 *Ibid.*, p. 353.
36 H/R Debates, 29 November 1961, p. 346.
37 *Ibid.*, p. 351.
38 *The National Development Plan, Progress Report* (Lagos), 1965, p. 8.
39 *The Second National Development Plan, 1970–74, First Progress Report* (Lagos), pp. 35–6.
40 *Third National Development Plan, 1975–80,* Vol. I (Lagos), 1975, p. 19.
41 *Ibid.*, p. 19.
42 *Ibid.*, p. 20.
43 *Third National Development Plan, op. cit.*, p. 20.
44 Sessional Paper No. 10 of 1963/65, pp. 16–17.
45 *Ibid.*, p. 8.
46 *Towards a Better Future for our People*, 1966, p. 25.
47 *Kenya Development Plan, 1964–1970*, 1964, pp. 37–8.
48 *Ibid.*, p. 13.
49 *Ibid.*, p. 14.
50 Table 8.1.
51 Uganda, *Plan III, Third Five Year Development Plan 1971/72–1975/76*, p. 20.
52 *Ibid.*, p. 20.

53   *Ibid.*, p. 20.
54   *Ibid.*, p. 21.
55   *Ibid.*
56   *Industry and Trade*, 18 January 1973, p. 106.
57   H.C.Debates, Sir Alec Douglas Home, 30 November 1972, Vol. 847, col. 223.
58   However, other non-sterling investors were allowed to repatriate profits.
59   *Sessional Paper No. 5, 1966*, 1966, p. 2.
60   *New Commonwealth*, No. 9, 1967, p. 401.
61   Caroline McMaster, *Malawi — Foreign Policy and Development*, 1974.
62   *Industrial Development in Malawi: a Guide for Prospective Investors*, 1970, p. 3 and pp. 20—22.
63   *Investment Opportunities* (Ministry of Information and Broadcasting of the Sierra Leone Government), 1962, p. 7.
64   *Ibid.*, pp. 9—12.
65   Sierra Leone, H/R Debates, 8 July 1968, col. 366.
66   *Industrial Development in Malawi, op. cit.*, p. 3.
67   McMaster, *op. cit.*, p. 84.
68   *Sierra Leone Trade Journal*, October/December 1969, Vol. 9, No. 4, p. 93.
69   *West Africa*, 16 April 1973, p. 514.
70   Table 8.1.
71   *Ibid.*
72   *Ibid.*
73   *Report of the Ministry of Overseas Development on the Bechaanaland Economy, op. cit.*, p.11.
74   *Botswana National Development Plan, 1973—1978*, Part I, *Policies and Objectives*, 1973, p. 25.
75   Khama, *Botswana and South Africa*, 13 November 1970, p. 2.
76   *Ibid.*, p. 8.
77   H.C. Debates, 4 April 1967, Vol. 744, col. 13.
78   Cmnd. 4568.
79   *Ibid.*
80   Cmnd 2764, 1965, p. 6.
81   *Ibid.*, p. 71. See also W. B. Reddaway *et al., Effects of UK Direct Investment Overseas*, p. 338 in Final Report, 1968.
82   Cmnd 2646, 1965.
83   *Ibid.*, p. 4.
84   *Ibid.*, p. 5.
85   *Ibid.*, p. 5.
86   *Ibid.*
87   Table 7.1.
88   Memorandum submitted by the CBI to the Select Committee on Overseas Aid, 1969—70, 27 May 1970, Appendix 1.
89   *British Private Investment in East Africa*, Report of a Survey and a Conference, ODI, by D. J. Morgan (UK), 1965, pp. 14—15.

90 *Ibid.*, p. 53.
91 *Ibid.*, pp. 15 and 45.
92 Memorandum submitted by the Treasury to the Select Committee on Overseas Aid, Session 1969–70, *op. cit.*, para. 18.
93 Mr Littler, Assistant Secretary Finance (Exchange Control), *ibid.*, q. 433.
94 *Ibid.*, para. 19, Minister of State at the Treasury's memorandum.
95 *Investment Laws of the World: The Developing Nations*, 1972.
96 *Investing in Developing Countries* (OECD), 1972, p. 103. Only Tanzania and the Gambia remained at the time to sign.
97 Memorandum of the CBI, *op. cit.*, p. 14.
98 Cmnd 4565, 1972.
99 *Ibid.*, para. 5.
100 *Ibid.*, para. 5.
101 *Trade and Industry* (UK), 7th September 1972, p. 403.
102 Overseas Investment and Export Guarantees Act, 1972, Report by the Secretary of State for Industry, 31 March 1974, pp. 1–2.

Conclusion

Two distinct models of co-operation stand out in Britain's economic relations with Commonwealth Africa: the sterling area model which had its heyday in the period of decolonisation, and the development-oriented model which dominated after independence. Each rested on a different set of assumptions and led to different policies and a different pattern of economic relations.

Within the sterling area British power and influence predominated over African nationalist objectives. Relations were conducted against the background of the Commonwealth—sterling area system, whose primary purpose was to resolve sterling's problems and protect Britain's balance of payments. There was much confidence in the Commonwealth as an organisation capable of solving members' liquidity problems, and, although relations with other countries were maintained, the Commonwealth was sufficiently cohesive to resist economic penetration from other centres of power.

What may justifiably be called the monetary syndrome exercised an all-pervading influence over other forms of economic co-operation. For instance, trade policy could not be considered separately from sterling's problems and the balance of payments; similarly a direct relationship was established between the monetary objectives and Britain's aid and investment policies. The latter two forms of co-operation were formally biased towards the Commonwealth—sterling area.

Commonwealth African countries accepted the assumptions and values of this model, which stressed that because the colonial economies were closely intertwined with the sterling area, progress in decolonisation could be made only by supporting dollar discrimination and a high level of reserves. They made no serious attempt to offer an alternative model of economic co-operation, preferring instead to react to the existing one.

This nationalist reformist approach led to two developments. Firstly, it fostered a uniform pattern of economic decolonisation in colonial Africa, with an emphasis on caution in financial management and external economic relations. Thus all the African countries, apart from Botswana, Lesotho and Swaziland, entered statehood with a strong British presence in both their domestic economies and their external economic relations; this made complete disengagement difficult to achieve. For instance, even though the sterling area's usefulness in providing member governments with liquidity was drastically reduced after the end of the dollar pool in 1959, they remained in the sterling area until its dissolution in 1972. Sierra Leone, Gambia and Malawi even continued to peg their currencies to sterling and maintained open payments arrangements with Britain after the pound was allowed to float in 1972. Also, all the African countries continued to hold a sizeable proportion of their reserves in sterling, and there was a considerable time lag before their newly created central banks completed the phasing out of the colonial exchange standard. The pattern was repeated in trade, aid and investment, where, despite diversification, Britain continued to be the single most important partner.

Secondly, African reforms led to periodic conflicts in the relationship. The persistently British-oriented economic structure provoked the view in African circles that there were two stages of decolonisation: the political and the economic. Failure to achieve economic development at independence led to the belief that the old model of economic co-operation should be restructured. African leaders felt that political independence was meaningless without its economic corollary. However, policies aimed at furthering economic decolonisation clashed directly with British interests and often affected Anglo-African relations. Conflicts of interest arose on a whole range of economic relations, in the monetary, trade and investment fields.

In monetary relations, the African countries argued that the sterling area policy that required them to invest substantial balances in Britain thwarted their economic development. The measures they took, at independence, to correct the situation — mobilising their reserves and establishing local financial institutions — challenged sterling's role in Africa and contributed to the currency's difficulties in the foreign exchange markets. In investment relations, various forms of control, from nationalisation through partnership to indigenisation, were instituted to protect the growth of local enterprise. These policies affected British investment in Commonwealth Africa. Also, the African countries pursued diversification in trade not only to increase their foreign exchange earnings but to reduce their dependence on Britain.

Anglo-African relations inevitably suffered as a result of some of these measures. Although the measures were not always directed against her, as the ex-colonial power Britain was always hardest hit. There were times when she was compelled to respond with the only effective form of economic pressure available to her: the aid weapon. Thus following Tanzania's termination of pension payments to ex-British civil servants and the nationalisation of British property without prompt payment, the government responded by cutting off aid. Britain also stopped her aid to Uganda in 1972 following the Asian crisis and the mass nationalisation of British investments. And when Acheampong unilaterally terminated the payment of Ghana's medium-term debts Britain withdrew ECGD cover for British exports to Ghana.

Unlike the sterling area model, the development-oriented model which succeeded it was more diverse and open, and Britain's authority and influence were very much reduced. This model was strengthened by three major developments: African independence, sterling convertibility in 1958, and the end of dollar discrimination in 1959. The last two reduced the effectiveness and cohesiveness of the sterling area, and with the proliferation of developing States in the Commonwealth the priority accorded to sterling in economic relations was superseded by the issue of development. Starting with Ghana's independence, Commonwealth African States projected an independent image and diversified their economic links.

The direct relationship which was established between trade, aid, investment and monetary relations during the decolonisation era became less well defined at independence. Commonwealth African countries pursued different trade and monetary policies without much consideration of sterling's position; Britain's aid and investment policies were no longer aimed at enabling them to play a part in the task of propping up sterling. Each member had much more freedom in determining its own economic policy.

Under this model the Commonwealth itself changed as it became preoccupied with the developing members' problems. As if to symbolise the change, development was accepted as the central concern of the Secretariat when it was established in 1965, a process which was extended with the formation of the first Commonwealth multilateral aid scheme in 1971, the Fund for Technical Co-operation (CFTC). As an admission of the different patterns of economic co-operation the CFTC made an attempt to reflect these changes in its philosophy by making developing members participate as both donors and recipients. Perhaps this was a healthy advance in the process of de-Anglicising the Commonwealth; developing members may well begin to assume responsibility for strengthening Commonwealth co-operation. At the same time the new system is inevitably weaker than the old. The major challenge to the new Commonwealth has been the new forms of extra-Commonwealth co-operation, as witness Britain's membership of the EEC and the Lomé Convention, Third World economic solidarity groupings and regional forms of co-operation in Africa.

The development model of co-operation is likely to continue to govern Anglo-African relations because of the sharp economic divisions between the developed and developing members of the Commonwealth and because of the new climate of opinion in the wider campaign for a new international economic order. Britain will continue to be pressed by Commonwealth Africa to support development-oriented policies. Even were she tempted to revive it there is no likelihood of the sterling area model reasserting itself. It belonged to a period when African countries were still dependent and when most members felt that there was a possibility of sterling recovering its pre-war international position by wide-ranging defensive measures.

This, then, forms our general conclusion. Specific conclusions will now be offered on the four main areas of economic co-operation — monetary, trade, aid and investment relations — which have been reviewed in the preceding chapters.

Monetary relations   Perhaps the saddest note in the history of Anglo-African monetary relations is the unavoidable echo of failure: despite the great efforts of the 1940s and 1950s to sustain sterling, often at the expense of other economic goals, the currency never recovered its pre-war strength. All the major currencies were put on a basis of floating exchange rates in the early 1970s and the sterling area was officially ended in 1972. Although the African nationalists were persuaded to remain in the sterling area during the decolonisation period, they never really identified with sterling's problems. There was always a feeling that it was the currency of the colonial power and that the policies of monetary and commercial discrimination served British interests more than those of the colonies. This feeling was most evident in Ghana and Nigeria — both important holders of sterling — where the leading nationalists in the alliance governments were often embarrassed by the demands of opposition MPs, supported at times by the rank and file of their own parties, for trade liberalisation.

Matters were not helped when Bank of England officials tried to resist nationalist pressures for central banks in Commonwealth Africa. By insisting that central banks had no role to play in developing countries which lacked established capital and money markets the officials completely misjudged the meaning and significance of central banks to African nationalists. The question of whether or not to have a central bank was at bottom political; although nationalist opinion stressed that the role of the central bank was to promote development, its main significance was a mark of independence and a symbol of maturity.

As the Bank of England officials expected, however, too high hopes of their development role in economies that lacked sufficient capital led to the new central banks becoming overstretched as governments turned to them for support; the fiduciary element and their lending powers were increased, which later affected the reserves. By the mid-1960s Commonwealth Africa's significance in the sterling area had declined steeply.

Commonwealth African States no longer looked to the sterling area to solve their monetary problems. With the changes in the fortunes of sterling and new developments in the international monetary system, they joined other developing countries in demanding an expansion of liquidity through the medium of IMF Special Drawing Rights, a higher proportion of which, they argue, should be allotted to the developing countries.[1] Most pegged their currencies to SDRs, which are denominated in terms of a basket of the currencies of all the major trading nations of the world. Sterling's international pretensions were finally buried by the monetary crisis of 1976 and the IMF rescue operation. When the Chancellor of the Exchequer, Denis Healey, announced the IMF measures in the Commons on 11 January 1977 he stressed that the safety net was to enable 'the government to achieve an orderly reduction in the role of sterling as a reserve currency'.[2]

Residual forms of Anglo-African monetary relations will persist, however, because of the continued significance of Britain in Commonwealth Africa's trade, aid and investment. Thus, for example, after the oil boom of 1973 Nigeria greatly increased its holdings of sterling. Such action, however, derives from necessity or convenience rather than from a concerted plan to prop sterling up.

Trade relations   Commonwealth Africa's trade with Britain has declined, and the trends indicate a further decline. Both parties have accepted the principle of diversification. Harold Wilson's ill-fated plan was the last attempt to inject new life into intra-Commonwealth trade. Commonwealth African States have persistently judged trade relations in terms of their development objectives. Their main concern has been to increase their earnings of foreign exchange from exports without jeopardising the advantages they enjoy in the British market. Their attempts to sustain a constant level of imports for development have not been successful, as many have had to resort to medium-term commercial credits.

The debt problem is likely to persist, with continued falls in commodity prices and limited capital flows for development. No binding solution has yet been worked out to check the international credit race between the major exporting countries, and it seems that most of the developing countries are not yet prepared to accept the financial discipline necessary to avoid debt problems arising from medium-term loans.

As a result of the campaign for a new international economic order and the decision by members of the Commonwealth and by the Secretariat to participate, Anglo-African trade relations will no doubt continue to focus on the question of development and the need to restructure the world economy. But it seems likely that the sticking point will continue to be how to marry the demands of the developing countries for 'indexation' and the integrated commodity programme with the more immediate economic preoccupations of the developed countries such as unemployment, inflation and monetary control.[3] Although there has been an agreement on the establishment of a Common Fund to support an integrated programme for commodities, there are still differences over its scale and functions.

Anglo-African trade relations have been integrated into the wider Euro-African trade system, and under the Lomé Convention the Stabex plan has been held up as a model for North—South relations. Its limitations are obvious, however, to both the EEC and the developing associate members. Stabex is a form of international social security system which does not interfere with the market forces which the developing countries want to correct. For this reason it has yet to demonstrate whether it is not a diversion from the main demands of the developing countries.

Aid relations   Commonwealth African countries have diversified their sources of aid. Their greatest problem here has been the problem of tied aid. Although Britain has consistently advocated a general policy of untied aid by all industrialised countries, like the other major donors she has been constrained by balance of payments problems in introducing it.

The Ministry for Overseas Development's demonstration that aid helped the balance of payments cleared the way for an expansion of the British aid programme. But this was done by stressing the commercial aspects. Thus British aid is likely to be redirected to potential markets for British exports. The pressures on the MOD for the acceleration of the process are likely to come from the CBI, as the report of the 1978 Select Committee on Overseas Aid shows. However, the MOD is still opaque in its statements on British aid; it continues to stress the need to strike a balance between trade promotion and meeting real development needs. Because of the persistence of Commonwealth co-operation, British aid seems likely to be concentrated in the Commonwealth as in the past. Other considerations apart, the MOD's knowledge of Commonwealth developing countries and the easier channels of communication between Britain and the Commonwealth facilitate the process.

There is the problem also of the backlog of British aid commitments to Africa: the land transfer scheme, the pensions scheme, the Overseas Service Aid Scheme and budgetary aid; all part of the necessary price of decolonisation. When these schemes were being implemented in the 1960s it was difficult to apply a commercial orientation. Fortunately for British policy some of these programmes have now either ended or

are drawing to a close. Budgetary aid has ceased for all Commonwealth African countries; the pension scheme was settled in 1970,
although Britain took responsibility only for pre-independence
pensions; the land transfer scheme in Kenya has slowed down
and is gradually drawing to a close; the Overseas Service Aid
Scheme is likely to end as the Commonwealth African countries
increase their pool of national technicians and administrators.

These developments should allow Britain more freedom in
redirecting its aid in the future. One thing is certain, aid to the
BLS countries will decline after the termination of these programmes, and they will be in a similar position to Sierra Leone
and Gambia in the British aid league. With her oil revenues
Nigeria is likely to break out of the simple typology of Britain
versus Commonwealth Africa. She has increasingly offered aid
to other Commonwealth African countries and has stopped
receiving capital aid from Britain.

Investment relations   Problems are likely to remain in investment relations. Investment is more vulnerable than the other
forms of economic relations because it represents the only
visible British presence in the economies of Commonwealth
Africa. Problems will no doubt continue to centre particularly on investment in the extractive industries; as these were
a by-product of the colonial system, Britain will inevitably
suffer in any acts of nationalisation. Commonwealth African
States have instituted various forms of control, ranging from
nationalisation through partnership to indigenisation. British
investments have suffered more in the first than in the latter
two categories. Investment relations with the indigenisation
States will depend on whether private enterprise will survive
within the local economy. If it does, then there may come a
time when foreign competitors will demand more open policies
from these States or threaten retaliatory measures, as Japan
has in its relations with Western Europe.

Investment relations are also likely to be affected by the
political problem of white minority governments in southern
Africa. African countries are gradually closing ranks and putting
pressure on Britain and Western countries to use economic
sanctions against South Africa. Britain is far more exposed
than any other country in its investment and trade relations
with the Republic. She has joined other Western powers therefore in resisting African demands. How far this will continue
is difficult to say, for as the former Nigerian Foreign Minister,

Brigadier Garba, warned in 1978, the West will have to choose between 'the hospitality of Nigeria and the imagined economic and strategic advantages of doing business in South Africa.[4] The choice is therefore going to be difficult for Britain to make. So far there has been no serious move to force a confrontation, apart from Nigeria's stand against Barclay's[5] and BP, and Tanzania's decision to nationalise Lonhro's assets because of alleged sanctions-busting in Rhodesia. Investment relations with Commonwealth Africa will continue to be affected by the politics of southern Africa as the political struggle there intensifies.

These specific conclusions form part of the general conclusion. During the period of decolonisation aid, trade and investment relations were inseparable from the monetary situation. At independence, however, they acquired an autonomous existence, symbolising the collapse of British centralised control and the diversification policies of the African States. It seems likely that Anglo-Commonwealth African economic relations will continue to be conducted on this pattern.

Most of the Commonwealth African States have completed the first and second levels of economic decolonisation: domestic economic decolonisation and regional economic decolonisation. Attention has now shifted to the third level, of global economic decolonisation. There is no doubt that African and Third World countries continue to suffer great social and economic depri-vation in the present lopsided international economy. But despite years of campaigning for a new international economic order no tangible reforms, which would guarantee the welfare of the majority of the world's poor, have been implemented, apart from the proliferation of NIEO literature, conferences and institutions (the diplomacy syndrome); indeed, NIEO has become a growth industry without development! Perhaps the Third World countries are on the wrong strategy for the securing of a new order. If history is anything to go by, international systems have been changed not by diplomacy and conferences (although they have played a role after major conflicts) but by the maximisation and utilisation of power. No wonder OPEC has been hailed a success. Certainly few of the poor countries have resources like oil, which enjoys an unprecedented import-ance in the economies of the Western world. But their failure to intervene effectively and collectively in areas where they command strength, their inability to shift resources away from export areas to food crops, and their refusal to introduce radical changes in their domestic political economies, really underline the basic weakness of Third World elites in international relations; their behaviour often leads to a dependency syndrome on NIEO, which is rather ironic, and makes metropole—periphery relations, like the one this study has examined, appear an exercise aimed largely at extracting whatever small crumbs fall from metropolitan tables.

Notes

1 *Essays in International Finance*, 'Less Developed Countries and the Post-1971 International Financial System' by Carlos S. Diaz-Alejandro, No. 108, April 1975 (Princeton University), pp. 25—7.
2 Stephen Fay and Hugo Young, 'The day the pound nearly died', Part three, *The Sunday Times Weekly Review*, 28 May 1978, p. 34.
3 Geoffrey Goodwin and James Mayall, 'The Political Dimensions of the UNCTAD Integrated Commodity Scheme', *Millenium;* Vol. 6, No. 2, autumn 1977, p. 153.
4 *West Africa*, 3 April 1978, p. 636.
5 *West Africa*, 3 April 1978, p. 636. All public bodies in Nigeria were instructed to close their accounts with Barclay's.

Bibliography

Primary sources

Britain

Departmental Committee appointed to inquire into matters affecting the currency of the British West African Colonies and Protectorates, Cmnd 6426, 1912.

The Ottawa Agreements Act, 1932 (Bill 127, 1932), Cmnd 4174.

The Defence (Finance) (Definition of Sterling Area) (No. 5) Order, 1941, 28 November 1941, No. 1890.

Charter of the Congress of Peoples against Imperialism (mimeo), 1948.

The Colonial Development Act, H.C. Bill 9, 1929.

Interim Reports of the Colonial Development Advisory Committee, 1930–39.

Eleventh and Final Report of the Colonial Development Advisory Committee, Cmnd 6298, 1940.

Colonial Loans Acts, 1949–52.

Colonial Development and Welfare Act Reports, 1940–59.

The Colonial Development Corporation Act, 1948.

The Colonial Development Corporation Act, Annual Report and Statement of Accounts, April 1958, Bill 64.

An Economic Survey of the Colonies, 1951. Colonial No. 281 (1) (2) (3), Vols. I–III.

Some Notes on Bulk Purchase of Colonial Commodities, Memo. No. 3 (Colonial Office), Reference and Information Section, 12 March 1948.

The West Indian Royal Commission, 1938–39, Recommendations (HMSO), Cmnd 6174.

Colonial Office, Colonial Primary Products Committee, Interim Report, January 1948 (United Kingdom), Col. No. 214.

The Conservative Party, Reports of the Annual Conference of the Conservative Party, 1945—55.

— Reference Pamphlet on the Colonies, No. 141, March 1955.

— The Expanding Commonwealth, 1956: Conservative Policy on Colonies (London), 1956.

The Labour Party, Reports of the Annual Conference of the Labour Party (London), 1945—51.

— The Colonies. The Labour Party's Postwar Policy (London), March 1943.

— Labour's Colonial Policy: II, Economic Aid (London), 1957.

Memorandum on the Sterling Assets of the British Colonies, HMSO (London), Col. No. 298.

The Chancellor of the Exchequer, addressing the African Governor's Conference in November 1947, Cabinet Office press release No. 12, 1947, No. 3.

Report of the Commission of Enquiry into disturbances in the Gold Coast, 1948, Col. No. 231.

The Radcliffe Report on the Working of the Monetary System, CMND 827 (1959).

The Basle Facility and the Sterling Area, Cmnd 3787, October 1968.

The National Plan, Cmnd 2764, September 1965.

World Economic Interdependence and Trade in Commodities, Cmnd 6061, May 1975.

Exchange of Letters between the Government of the United Kingdom and the Government of Botswana concerning the guarantee by the United Kingdom and the maintence of the Minimum Sterling Proportion by Botswana, Cmnd 4224, 1 September 1969.

Assistance from the United Kingdom for Overseas Development, March 1960, Cmnd 974.

United Kingdom's role in Commonwealth Development, Cmnd 237, July 1957.

The Overseas Civil Service, Col. No. 306, 1954.

Service with Overseas Governments, October 1961, Cmnd 1193.

The Overseas Service Act, Bill 43, 1960/61.

The Department of Technical Co-operation Act, 1961.

Public Officers Agreement between the government of the United Kingdom and the government of Ghana, April 1957, Cmnd 158.

Public Officers Agreement between the government of Britain and the government of Sierra Leone, October 1961, Cmnd 1529.

Aid to Developing Countries, Cmnd 2147, September 1963.

Ministry for Overseas Development, The Work of the new Ministry, August 1965, Cmnd 2736.

— Overseas Development: the Work in Hand, January 1967, Cmnd 3180.

— The Development of the Bechuanaland Economy, Economic Survey Mission, (November) 1965.

— The Future of the Overseas Service Aid Schemes and other Supplementation arrangements, April 1969, Cmnd 3994.

— Aid Policy in One Country: Britain's Aid to Kenya 1964, 1968 (London), 1970.

Report of an Economic Survey Mission: Basutoland, Bechuanaland and Swaziland (HMSO) 1960.

Fourth Report from the Select Committee on the Estimates, Session 1959—1960, H.C. 260 (Bill 260), July 1960.

Select Committee on Overseas Aid, Session 1968—1969, H.C. 285.

Seventh Special Report from the Select Committee on Overseas Aid, 22 July 1969, No. 394.

Seventh Report from the Estimates Committee, Session 1967—1968, 23 October, 1968.

Tenth Report from the Estimates Committee, Session 1963—1964, 28 July 1964.

Office of Population Censuses and Surveys (Social Survey Division), Aid and Overseas Development: a survey of public attitudes, opinions and knowledge (London), 1971, compiled by I. Rauta.

The West African Currency Board Annual Reports, 1954—1963 (London).

The Corporation Tax, Cmnd 2646, April 1965.

Overseas Investment and Export Guarantees Act, 1972, Cmnd 4656.

Overseas Investment and Export Guarantees Act, 1972, Report by the Secretary of State for Industry, 31 March 1974 (HMSO).

Britain and the Developing Countries: Africa, COI Reference pamphlet 94, HMSO (London), 1970.

Report of the Commission on Representational Service Overseas, appointed by the Prime Minister under the Chairmanship of Lord Plowden, 1962—1963, Cmnd 2276 (February 1974).

Export Credits Guarantee Department: Review of Export Credits Guarantee Department, March 1972 (London), 1972.

Agreements between Britain and Ghana on medium-term commercial debts owed by the government of Ghana, Treaty Series No. 31 (1967), Cmnd 3247, (1969) Cmnd 3944, (1971) Cmnd 4763, (1974) Cmnd 6039.

Progress Report of the Brussels negotiations, Miscellaneous No. 25 (1962), Cmnd 1805.

The United Kindom and the European Communities, July 1971, Cmnd 4715.

Britain and the European Communities: an Economic Assessment, February 1970, Cmnd 4289.

Britain and the European Communities, COI, Reference pamphlet 99 (HMSO), 1971.

House of Commons Parliamentary Debates, 1945–1975.

Commonwealth Africa

Financial Devolution, The Gold Coast (Accra), 1948, No. IV.

The Gold Coast, Report on Industrialization and the Gold Coast, by W. A. Lewis, 1953 (Accra), Government Printer, 1953.

The Gold Coast, The Development Plan (Accra), 1951.

The Gold Coast, Handbook of Trade and Commerce, Ministry of Trade and Labour (Accra), May 1955, Fourth Issue.

Ghana, Second Five Year Development Plan (Accra), 1959.

Ghana, Seven Year Development Plan, 1963/64–1969/70, (Accra), 1964.

Republic of Ghana, Third Year in Office of Col. I. K. Acheampong, 13th January 1972–12th January 1975 (Accra), 1975.

The Convention Peoples' Party, Programme for Work and Happiness (Accra).

Nigeria: Handbook of Commerce and Industry (Lagos, 1954).

Report of the Committee to advise the Federal Government on the stimulation of Industrial Development by affording relief from Import Duties and Protection to Nigerian Industry (Lagos), 1956.

Nigeria, National Development Plan, Progress Report (Federal Ministry of Economic Development (Lagos), March 1965.

Building the new Nigeria: Industry, Second National Development Plan, 1970–1974 (Lagos), 1970.

Nigeria, The Second National Development Plan, 1970–1974, First Progress Report (Central Planning Office, Lagos), 1970.

Nigeria, Third National Development Plan, 1975–1980 (Central Planning Office, Lagos), 1975.

Sierra Leone, Peace for Progress: a progress report on Economic and Social Development, 27 April 1961—March 1965 (Government Printer, 1965).

Sierra Leone, Investment Opportunities (Minstry of Information and Broadcasting), 1962.

Sierra Leone, National Development Plan, 1975—1978 (Freetown), 1974.

The Gambian Currency Board, Annual Report, 1965—1970.

Sessional Paper No. 7 (1967), British Financial Aid to the Gambia 1967/68—1970/71, and a study of the economy of Gambia (Bathurst), 1967.

Report on Banking Conditions in the Gold Coast and the desirability of setting up a National Bank (Accra), Government Printer, 1951, by Sir Cecil Trevor.

Report on the desirability and practicability of a Central Bank in Nigeria (Government Printer), Nigeria, 1953, by J. L. Fisher.

Report on the establishment of a Nigerian Central Bank, the introduction of a Nigerian Currency and other associated matters (Lagos), 1957, by J. B. Loynes.

Report on the Problems of the Future Currencies of Sierra Leone and the Gambia (Bathurst), Government Printer, 1961.

The East African Currency Board Reports, 1954—1965 (London and Nairobi).

Investment Opportunities in Tanganyika, by the Economist Intelligence Unit for the United Republic of Tanzania.

Tanzania, Five Year Plan for Economic and Social Development, 1 July 1964—30 June 1969 (Dar es Salaam), 1964.

Tanzania, Second Five Year Development Plan for Economic and Social Development, 1969—1974, Vol. I, General Analysis (Government Printer), 1969.

Republic of Kenya, Sessional Paper No. 10 of 1963/65, African Socialism and its application to planning in Kenya (1965).

Kenya, Towards a better future for our people, 1966 (Ministry of Economic Planning and Development), 1966.

Kenya, Development Plan, 1964—1970 (Ministry of Economic Planning and Development), 1964.

Kenya Development Plan, 1974—1978, Part I (Government Printer), Nairobi, 1974.

Uganda's Plan III, Third Five Year Development Plan, 1971/72—1975/76.

Northern Rhodesia, Ministry of Finance (Lusaka), Economic Report, 1964 (Government Printer), 1964.

Republic of Zambia, Ministry of Finance (Lusaka), Economic Report, 1965.

Zambia, First National Development Plan, 1966—1970 (July 1966, Lusaka).

Industrial Development in Malawi: a Guide for prospective investors (Government Printer), January 1970.

Lesotho, First Five Year Development Plan, 1970/71—1974/ 75 (Maseru), 1970.

Botswana, National Development Plan, 1973—1978, Part I, Policy Objectives (1973).

Botswana, National Development Plan, 1970—1975, September 1970 (Government Printer, Gaberone).

Ministry of Finance and Development Planning, Department of Customs and Excise: Report on the Establishment and organization of the Department of Customs and Excise, 1970—1974 (Government Printer, Gaberone).

The Gold Coast Debates, 1951—56.

Ghana Debates, 1957—65.

Nigeria, House of Representatives Debates, 1951—65.

Sierra Leone, House of Representatives Debates, 1960—66 and 1968—70.

Tanzania, Parliamentary Debates, 1961—65.

Kenya, Parliamentary Debates, 1963—65.

Uganda, Parliamentary Debates, 1962—70.

Zambia, Parliamentary Debates 1965—70.

Malawi, Parliamentary Debates, 1965—70.

General

Proceedings of the United Nations Conference on Trade and Development (Geneva), 23 March—16 June 1964, Vol. I, Final Act and Report, Econ/conf. 46/141.

Proceedings of UNCTAD, 23 March—16 June 1964, Vol. II, Policy Statements, Econ/Conf. 46/141.

Theses

McMaster, Carolyn Kilburn, 'Malawi's Foreign Policy' (M.Phil., London University, 1971).

Millar, T. B., 'The Image of the British Commonwealth of Nations' (Ph.D., University of London, 1960).

Ojedokun, O. A., 'Nigeria's Relations with the Commonwealth, with Special Reference to her Relations with Britain, 1960—1966' (Ph.D., University of London, 1968).

Pettman Jeanette, 'Zambia: the Search for Security, 1964—1970' (Ph.D., University of London, 1971).

Nordman, Curtis, 'Prelude to Decolonization, 1964–1970' (D.Phil., Oxford, 1979).

Speeches and writings of the political actors
The Diaries of Hugh Dalton (London School of Economics).
Butler, R. A., *The Art of the Possible: the Memoirs of Lord Butler*, 1971.
Lyttleton, Oliver (Viscount Chandos), *The Memoirs of Lord Chandos*, 1962.
Macmillan, Harold, *Britain, the Commonwealth and Europe*, 1962.
– *Riding the Storm, 1945–1955*, 1971.
– *Pointing the Way, 1959–1961*, 1972.
– *Mr. Macmillan and Africa* (Conservative Political Centre, London), 1960.
Wilson, Harold, *The Record of the Labour Government, 1964–1970*, 1971.
Jones, Arthur Creech, *The Future of the African Colonies*, Cast Foundation Lecture, University of Nottingham, 1951.
– 'The Labour Party and Colonial Policy', in A. C. Jones (ed.), *New Fabian Colonial Essays*, 1959.
Azikiwe, Nnamdi, *Selected Speeches*, 1961.
– *The Future of Pan-Africanism*, 1961.
Awolowo, Obafemi, *Path to Nigerian Freedom*, 1947.
– *Towards Independence: Speeches and Statements*, 1958.
Nkrumah, Kwame, *Towards Colonial Freedom*, 1962.
– An Autobiography, 1957.
– *Neo-colonialism: the last Stage of Imperialism*, 1965.
Nkrumah, Kwame, *Consciencism: Philosophy and Ideology for Decolonization*, 1964.
– 'A Broadcast to the Nation, 7th March 1959', in *Hands off Africa*, by K. Owusu-Akyem (Accra), 1960.
– 'United we Stand', *Ghana Today Supplement*, 5 June 1963.
Balewa, Alhaji Abubakar Tafewa, *Mr. Prime Minister: a Selection of Speeches* (Lagos), 1964.
Nyerere, J. K., *Freedom and Unity: a Selection from Writings and Speeches, 1952–65*, 1967.
– *Freedom and Socialism: a Selection from Writings and Speeches, 1965–67* (Dar es Salaam), 1968.
– *South Africa and the Commonwealth* (Dar es Salaam), 1971.
– 'A United States of Africa', *Journal of Modern African Studies*, 1.1 (1963).
– 'For Commonwealth and/or African Unity', *Commonwealth*

Journal of the Royal Commonwealth Society, November—December 1961, Vol. IV, No. 6.

Acheampong, Col. Ignatius, *Speeches and Interviews* (Ghana), Vols. I and II.

Mboya, Tom, 'Pan-Africanism and the Commonwealth: are they in Conflict?' Lecture delivered on 10 August 1964 at Makerere University College, Kampala. Slightly condensed speech in Ali Mazrui, *The Anglo-African Commonwealth: Political Friction and Cultural Fusion*, 1967, Appendix V.

Juxon-Smith, A. T. (National Reformation Council, Sierra Leone), 'Focus on Sierra Leone: stabilizing the economy ... to pave the way for future prosperity', *New Commonwealth*, 9 November, 1967.

Stevens, Dr Siaka, Speech to the Commonwealth Heads of Government Meeting, Ottawa, 7 August 1973, 'Trade Tariffs and Monetary Affairs'.

Gowon, General Yakubu, Speech to the Commonwealth Heads of Government Meeting, Ottawa, Agenda 3, 'The Changing Pattern of the Commonwealth: Independence and Co-operation', Commonwealth Heads of Government Meeting (Jamaica), 1975.

— 'Four Steps to National Stability', Broadcast on the 1968—69 Budget, 29 April 1968.

Agiyi-Ironsi, Major General J. T. U., Broadcast to the nation (Nigeria), 24 May 1966.

Margai, A. M., *Budget Speech, 12 July 1962* (Sierra Leone), 1962.

Fornah, Dr M. S., *Budget Speech, 9 July 1968* (Sierra Leone), 1968.

King, R. G. O., *Budget Speech, 31 March 1965* (Sierra Leone), 1965.

Speech on the Development Programme, 30 July 1962, 1962.

Juxon-Smith, Col. A. T., *Statement on the Budget for 1967—68, 30 June 1967*, 1967.

Ankrah, General J. A. (National Liberation Council), 'Budget Statement for 1966/67', *Ghana Today Supplement*, 10 August 1966.

Kaunda, Dr K. D., *Zambia's Economic Revolution* (Mulungushi), 19 April 1968 (Lusaka).

— *A Path for the Future* (Lusaka), 1971.

— *Take up the Challenge*, Mulungushi Hall (Lusaka), 1970.

— *The Rich and Poor Nations* (Lusaka), 1968.

— *Towards Complete Independence* (Lusaka), 1969.

— *This Completes Economic Reforms: Now Zambia is Ours* (Lusaka), 1970.

Khama, Seretse, 'Botswana and South Africa', Address to the Foreign Policy Society, Denmark, November 1970.

— *A Decade of Achievements* (Botswana), 1971.

The Commonwealth

The Commonwealth Finance Ministers' Meetings, Final Communiqués, 1949, 1966, 1967, 1968.

Commonwealth Prime Ministers' Conferences, Final Communiqués, 1960, 1961, 1962, 1964, 1965, 1966, 1969.

Commonwealth Heads of Government Meeting, Ottawa 1973, 2–10 August 1973, Final Communiqué (Commonwealth Secretariat).

Commonwealth Heads of Government Meeting, Kingston, Communiqué, June 1975 (Commonwealth Secretariat).

Commonwealth Trade Ministers' Conference, Final Communiqué, 1966.

Commonwealth Economic Conference 1952, Final Communiqué (London), 1952.

The Commonwealth Economic Conference at Montreal, 1958, Final Communiqué.

Report of the Commonwealth Trade and Economic Conference held in Montreal, 15–26 September 1958, Cmnd 539.

The Montreal Conference (London), 1958.

The Montreal Conference, 1958: an Expanding Commonwealth in an Expanding World (London), 1958.

Annual Report of the Commonwealth Economic Consultative Committee (London), 1949–57.

The Commonwealth Economic Consultative Council, 1–2 September 1964, Final Communiqué.

The Commonwealth Economic Consultative Council, Final Communiqué, 22–23 September, 1966.

Commonwealth Secretariat, Reports of Commonwealth Secretary General: *First Report*, 1966; *Second Report*, 1966–68; *Third Report*, 1968–70; *Sixth Report*, 1975–77.

— *Flow of Future Commonwealth Aid*, 1966.

The Special Commonwealth African Assistance Plan, *Reports*, 1962, 1963, 1964, 1965.

The Commonwealth Fund for Technical Co-operation, *Commonwealth Skills for Commonwealth Needs* (Commonwealth Secretariat).

Anthony Tasker (Managing Director of CFTC), *An Address to*

the Commonwealth Section of the Royal Society of Arts, London, 10 November 1977: The Commonwealth Fund for Technical Co-operation (Commonwealth Secretariat Publication).

Shridath Ramphal, 'The Role of the Commonwealth in the context of the New International Economic Order', *The Commonwealth and Development* (ODI), Report of the Conference jointly sponsored by ODI and St Catherine's Cumberland Lodge) at Cumberland Lodge, 13—15 February 1976.

Commonwealth Trade with the United States, 1948—57: memorandum prepared in the Intelligence Branch of the Commonwealth Economic Committee (London, 1959).

Commonwealth Development and its Financing, 5. *Nigeria,* Commonwealth Economic Committee (1963).

'Towards a New International Economic Order', Report by a Commonwealth Experts Group, *Final Report* (Commonwealth Secretariat, 14 March 1977).

Commonwealth Development Corporation, *Annual Report.*

Commonwealth Development Corporation, *Partners in Development*, 1973, *Finance Plus Management.*

Books and articles

Ady, P., *The Future of the Sterling Area*, Oxford University Institute of Commonwealth Studies, Reprint Series, No. 26.

Ahmad, Naseem, *Deficit Financing, Inflation and Capital Formation: the Ghanaian Experience, 1960—65* (Germany), 1970.

Amin, Samir, *Neocolonialism in West Africa*, 1973.

Austin, Dennis, *Politics in Ghana, 1946—1960*, 1964.

— *West Africa and the Commonwealth*, 1957.

— *Britain and South Africa*, 1966.

Ayida, A. A., 'Contractor Finance and Suppliers' Credit in Economic Development', *Nigerian Journal or Economic and Social Studies*, Vol. 7, No. 2, July 1965.

Bell, P. W., *The Sterling Area in the Postwar Period, 1946—52*, 1956.

Beloff, Max, *The Future of British Foreign Policy, 1964—1966*, 1966.

Beloff, Nora, *The General says No: Britain's Exclusion from Europe*, 1963.

Birmingham, W., Neustadt, I., and Omaboe, E. N., *A Study of Contemporary Ghana*, 1967, Vol. I, *The Economy of Ghana.*

Boersner, D., *The Bolsheviks and the National and Colonial Questions* (Geneva), 1957.

Brown, C. V., *The Nigerian Banking System*, 1966.

Brett, E. A., *Colonialism and Underdevelopment in East Africa*, 1973.

Camps, Miriam, *Britain and the European Community, 1955–63*, 1964.

Carrington, C. E., *The Commonwealth in Africa: Report of an unofficial Study Conference held at Lagos, Nigeria, 8–16 January 1962* (London), 1962.

Caves, R. E., and associates, *Britain's Economic Prospects* (Brookings Report), Washington, D.C., 1968.

Cohen, Sir Andrew, *British Foreign Policy in Changing Africa*, 1959.

Conan, A. R., *The Rationale of the Sterling Area*, 1961.

Cohen, B., *The Future of Sterling as an International Currency*, 1971.

Cox-George, N. A., *Finance and Development in West Africa: the Sierra Leone Experience*, 1961.

Crick, W. F., *Commonwealth Banking Systems*, 1965.

Davidson, Basil, *Black Star: a View of the Life and Times of Kwame Nkrumah*, 1973.

Davies, P. N., *The Trade Makers*, 1973.

Day, Alan, *The Future of Sterling*, 1956.

Diaz-Alejandro, C. F., 'Less Developed Countries and the Post-1971 International Financial System', *Essays in International Financial*, No. 108, April 1975 (Princeton).

Ekimfare, R. O., *An Economic History of Nigeria, 1860–1960*, 1973.

Faber, M. L. C., and Potter, J. G., *Towards Complete Independence: Papers on the Nationalization of the Copper Industry in Zambia*, 1971.

Fieldhouse, D. K., *Unilever Overseas*, 1978.

Fitch, B., and Oppenheimer, M., *Ghana: End of an Illusion*, 1966.

Frankel, J., *British Foreign Policy, 1945–73*, 1975.

Galton, J., *The European Community: a Super-power in the Making*, 1973.

Gardner, Richard, *Sterling–Dollar Diplomacy*, 1956.

Genoud, R., *Nationalism and Economic Development in Ghana*, 1969.

Goldsworth, D., *Colonial Issues in British Politics, 1945–61*, 1971.

Goodwin, G. L., and Mayall, James, 'The Political Dimensions of the UNCTAD Integrated Commondity Scheme', *Millenium Journal of International Studies* (London School of Economics), autumn 1977, Vol. 6, No. 2.

Greaves, Ida, *Colonial Monetary Conditions*, 1953.

— 'The Colonial Sterling Balances', *Essays in International Finance*, No. 20, September 1954.

Green, R. W., 'Commonwealth Preferences', *Board of Trade Journal*, 11 June and 31.December 1965.

Gupta, G. A., *Imperialism and the British Labour Movement, 1914–64*, 1975.

Hall, Richard, *The High Price of Principles: Kaunda and the White South*, 1969.

Hancock, K., and Gowing, M. M., *Britain's War Economy*, 1959.

Hayes, J. P., and Maynard, G. W., 'Aid and the Balance of Payments', *Economic Journal*, March 1970.

Hazlewood, A. D. (ed.), *African Integration and Disintegration: Case Studies in Economic and Political Union*, 1967.

— *Economic Integration: the East African Experience*, 1975.

Holthorn, G., and Hazlewood, A., *Aid and Inequality in Kenya*, 1976.

Hopkins, A. G., *An Economic History of West Africa*, 1973.

Ingram, Derek, *The Imperfect Commonwealth*, 1977.

Jackson, N. W., 'Free Africa and the Common Market', *Foreign Affairs*, No. 40, 1961–62.

Johnson, Harry, 'Commonwealth Preferences: a system in need of analysis', *Round Table*, October 1966.

Jones, David, *Aid and Inequality in Southern Africa: British Aid to Botswana, Lesotho and Swaziland*, 1977.

Kalin, George MacTurnan, *The Afro-Asian Conference*, 1956.

Kay, R. B., *The Political Economy of Colonialism in Ghana: a Collection of Documents and Statistics, 1900–60*, 1962.

Kirkham, W. P., *Unscrambling an Empire: a Critique of British Colonial Policy, 1955–60*, 1966.

Kirkwood, Kenneth, *Britain and Africa*, 1965.

Krassowski, A., *Development and the Debt Trap: Economic Planning and External borrowing in Ghana*, 1974.

Krassowski, A., 'Aid and the British Balance of Payments', *Wall Street and Moorgate Review*, spring 1965.

Kratz, Joachim, W., 'The East African Currency Board', *IMF Staff Papers*, July 1966.

Landell-MIlls, P. M., 'The 1969 Southern African Customs

Union Agreement', *Journal of Modern African Studies*, 1971.

Leifer, M. (ed.), *Constraints and Adjustments in Britain's Foreign Policy*, 1972.

Leith, J. C., *Foreign Trade Regimes and Economic Development*, Ghana, Vol. II, 1974.

Lenin, V. I., *On the National and Colonial Questions* (Peking), 1970.

— *Imperialism: the Highest Stage of Capitalism* (Peking), 1970.

Leubuscher, C., *The West African Shipping Trade, 1909—59* 1963.

Leys, Colin, *Underdevelopment in Kenya: the Political Economy of Neocolonialism*, 1974.

Little, I. M. D., *Aid to Africa: an Appraisal of United Kingdom Policy for Aid to Africa South of the Sahara*, 1964.

Livingstone, J. M., *Britain and the World Economy*, 1966.

London University, Institute of Commonwealth Studies, 'The Changing role of Commonwealth Economic Connections' (London), 1971, mimeo.

Manderson-Jones, R. B., *The Special Relationship: Anglo-American Relations and West European Unity, 1947—56*, 1972.

Mansergh, Nicholas, *Documents and Speeches on British Commonwealth Affairs*, Vol. I, *1931—52*; Vol. 2, *1952—62*. 1953 and 1963.

May, R. S., 'Direct Overseas Investment in Nigeria, 1953—63', *Scottish Journal of Political Economy*, Vol. XII, No. 3, November 1965.

Mayall, James, 'Africa and the enlarged EEC', *Millenium Journal of International Studies* (London School of Economics), Vol. 3, No. 2, autumn 1974.

Mazrui, A. A., *The Anglo-African Commonwealth: Political Friction and Commonwealth Fusion*, 1967.

— *Towards Pax Africana: a Study of Ideology and Ambition*, 1967.

— 'African Attitudes on the European Economic Community', *International Affairs*, January 1963.

McMaster, Carolyne, Malawi, *Foreign Policy and Development*, 1974.

Metcalfe, G. E., *Great Britain and Ghana: Documents of Ghana, History 1807—1951*, 1964.

Miles, C., 'British Aid: an Assessment', *The World Today*, April 1967.

Miller, J. D. B., *Survey of Commonwealth Affairs: Problems of Expansion and Attrition, 1953—69*, 1974.

Morgan, D. J., *British Private Investment in East Africa*, 1965.

Nolutshungu, S. C., *South Africa in Africa: a Study in Ideology and Foreign Policy*, 1975.

Northedge, F. S., *British Foreign Policy, 1945—73: Descent from Power*, 1974.

Nottidge, C. P. R., and Goldsack, The Department of Settlement of Nairobi, *The Million Acre Scheme, 1962—66*.

Nye, J., *Pan-Africanism and East African Integration*, 1965.

Okigbo, P. N. C., *Africa and the Common Market*, 1967.

Olankampo, O., 'The Loynes Report and Banking in Sierra Leone', *Bankers Magazine*, No. 1420, July 1962.

Payer, Cheryl, *The Debt Trap: the IMF and the Third World*, 1974.

Pedler, F. J., 'Foreign Investment in West Africa', *International Affairs*, Vol. 31, No. 4, 1955.

Pearson, Lester, *Partners in Development: Report of the Commission on International Development*, 1969.

Pettmen, Jan, *Zambia: Security and Conflict*, 1974.

Polk, Judd, *Sterling: its Meaning in World Finance*, 1956.

Pratt, Cranford, *The Critical Phase in Tanzania, 1945—68*, 1976.

Ranis, G., *Government and Economic Development*, 1971.

Reddaway, W. B., *et al.*, *Effect of United Kingdom Direct Investment Overseas, Interim Report* (1967), *Final Report* (1968).

Rendell, William, *The Commonwealth Development Corporation, 1948—72*, 1976.

Saylor, R. F., *The Economic System of Sierra Leone*, 1967.

Seidman, A., and Green, R. H., *Unity or Poverty? The Economics of Pan-Africanism*, 1968.

Shannon, H. A., 'The Evolution of the Colonial Sterling Exchange Standard', *IMF Staff Papers*, Vol. I, No. 3, April 1951.

Shonfield, Andrew, *British Economy Policy since the War*, 1959.

— (ed.), *International Economic Relations of the Western World, 1959—71*, 1976.

Smith, Hadley, *Readings on Economic Development and Administration in Tanzania* (Tanzania), 1966.

Soper, T. (ed.), *Europe and the Commonwealth*, 1962.

— 'European Trade with Africa', *African Affairs*, June 1967.

— 'Africa: the Economics of Independence; External Aid', *African Affairs*, April 1966.

Sowelen, R. A., *Towards Financial Independence in a Developing Country: an Analysis of the Monetary Experience of the Federation of Rhodesia and Nyasaland, 1952–63*, 1967.

Spence, J. E., 'British Policy towards the High Commission Territories', *Journal of Modern African Studies*, 11/2, 1964.

Strange, Susan, *Sterling and British Policy*, 1971.

— *The Sterling Problem and the Six*, 1967.

Streeton, Paul, and Corbet, Hugh (eds.), *Commonwealth Policy in a Global Context*, 1971.

Tandon, Yashpal, *Readings in African International Relations*, Vol. I (East Africa Literature Bureau), 1972.

Thompson, W. Scott, *Ghana's Foreign Policy, 1957–66*, 1969.

Turner, B., 'A fresh start for the Southern African Customs Union', *African Affairs*, 1970.

Uri, Pierre (ed.), *From Commonwealth to Common Market*, 1968.

Wallace, William, *The Foreign Policy Process in Britain*, 1975.

Wasserman, Garry, *Politics of Decolonization: Kenya Europeans and the Land Issue, 1960–1965*, 1976.

Wells, Sidney, *British Export Performance: a Comparative Study*, 1964.

Williams, Peter, *Aid in the Commonwealth*, 1965.

— *British Aid: Technical Assistance*, 1964.

Wright, Q., 'Colonialism: an attempt at understanding imperial colonial and neocolonial relationships', *Political Studies*, Vol. XIII, No. 3, 1965.

Younger, Kenneth, *Changing Perspectives in British Foreign Policy*, 1964.

Zartman, W., *The Politics of Trade Negotiations*, 1971.

— 'Europe and Africa: Decolonization or Dependence?' *Foreign Affairs*, January 1976.

Newspapers and periodicals

Standard Bank Annual Economic Review: Malawi, 1967–72; East and Central Africa, July 1966; Uganda, 1968–72; Kenya, 1973–74; Sierra Leone and the Gambia, 1967–73; Nigeria, 1967–73; Zambia, 1967–73; Ghana, 1967–72 and 1974.

Reserve Bank of Malawi, *Economic and Financial Review.*

Bank of Uganda, *Quarterly Bulletin.*

Bank of Sierra Leone, *Economic Review.*

— *Annual Reports.*

Central Bank of Nigeria, *Annual Reports* (Lagos).

Bank of Zambia, *Report and Statement of Accounts.*
Bank of Ghana, *Quarterly Economic Bulletin.*
– *Reports of the Board.*
Bank of Tanzania, *Economic Bulletin.*
Central Bank of Kenya, *Annual Reports.*
The Economic Bulletin of Ghana, 1960–1970.
United Nations (Economic Commission for Africa), *Survey of Economic Conditions in Africa.*
– *Annual Reports.*
African development (London).
New African Development (London).
Africa (London).
Africa Confidential (London).
West Africa (London).
The Financial Times (London).
The Times (London).
The Guardian (London).
The Daily Telegraph (London).
The Daily Express (London).
The Banker (London).
The Banker's Magazine (London).

Index

G